A Culture of Teaching

ALSO BY REBECCA W. BUSHNELL

Prophesying Tragedy: Sign and Voice in Sophocles' Theban Plays

Tragedies of Tyrants: Political Thought and Theater in the English Renaissance

REBECCA W. BUSHNELL

A Culture of
Teaching

Early Modern Humanism in Theory and Practice

CORNELL UNIVERSITY PRESS   ITHACA AND LONDON

First published 1996 by Cornell University Press.

Printed in the United States of America

Library of Congress Cataloging-in-Publication Data
Bushnell, Rebecca W., 1952–
   A culture of teaching : early modern humanism in theory and practice / Rebecca W. Bushnell.
      p.   cm.
   Includes bibliographical references and index.
   ISBN 0-8014-3235-9 (alk. paper). —ISBN 0-8014-8356-5 (pbk: alk. paper)
   1. Education, Humanistic—England—History—16th century.
   2. Teaching—England—History—16th century.   I. Title.
   LC1011.B837   1996
   370.11'2'094209031—dc20   95-43035

⊚ The paper in this book meets the minimum requirements of the American National Standard for Information Sciences— Permanence of Paper for Printed Library Materials, ANSI Z39.48-1984.

Dedicated to John David Toner,
Ruth Bushnell Toner,
and Emily Bushnell Toner

CONTENTS

ILLUSTRATIONS

ACKNOWLEDGMENTS

This book belongs partly to David Boyd, who read every word in manuscript, several times over. Because he cares deeply about teaching and scholarship he was an ideal reader, but he is also an inspiring friend. Phyllis Rackin also kept her sharp eye on the text; as always, I am grateful for her friendship and unflagging support. Other good friends and colleagues read or edited parts of this book as it grew, and they nurtured it with a bracing mixture of encouragement and criticism: Gregory Bredbeck, Peter Conn, Alan Filreis, Beverly Haviland, Constance Jordan, Victoria Kahn, Donald Kelley, Roger Mason, Robert Nelsen, Elisa New, Jeffrey Perl, Maureen Quilligan, Barbara Riebling, David Sacks, Julie Solomon, Peter Stallybrass, Max Thomas, Gary Tomlinson, and Robert Turner. The students in my graduate seminars on English humanism and Renaissance languages also helped me germinate many of my ideas. When I started the book, Catherine Michaud was a valuable research assistant; for most of it, the incomparable Suzanne Daly scrolled through endless microfilms, decoded black letter, and lent her intelligence and good humor to the enterprise. The staff at the University of Pennsylvania libraries and, in particular, Daniel Traister and Hilda Pring were understanding and helpful. Georgianna Ziegler of the Folger Shakespeare Library lent her expertise to the task of tracking down the illustrations. William Kennedy and Anthony Grafton served as sympathetic and rigorous readers for Cornell University Press, and Bernhard Kendler once again proved a stalwart editor. I also thank Raphael Seligmann and Kay Scheuer for their scrupulous and thoughtful editing of the manuscript. The research was aided by a Research Grant from the University of Pennsylvania. I thank John Richetti for his generous help in securing the computer hardware and support I needed, and I also appreciate his friendship.

The Folger Shakespeare Library gave permission to reproduce Figures 3–6; Special Collections of the Van Pelt Library of the University of Pennsylvania, permission for Figure 2; and Roger-Viollet, Paris, permission for Figure 1. Oxford University Press granted permission to use material from my essay "From Books to Languages" published in *Common Knowledge* 3.1 (1994): 16–28, in Chapter 4. Chapter 5 includes material first published in "George Buchanan, James VI, and Neo-Classicism," in *Scots and Britons: Scottish Political Thought and the Union of 1603*, ed. Roger Mason (Cambridge: Cambridge University Press, 1994), pp. 91–111, copyright © Cambridge University Press, 1994, reprinted by permission of Cambridge University Press. A few paragraphs of Chapter 5 also appeared in an earlier version in my essay "Time and History in Early English Classical Drama," in *Law, Literature, and the Settlement of Regimes: Proceedings of the Folger Institute Center for the History of British Political Thought*, ed. Gordon J. Schochet (Washington, D.C.: The Folger Shakespeare Library, 1990), vol. 2, pp. 73–86.

The dedication reflects my love and respect for my husband and daughters, from whom I have learned much about teaching and growing.

R. W. B.

Doylestown, Pennsylvania

A NOTE ON TEXT AND TRANSLATIONS

In the interest of readability, I have modernized the spelling, but not the punctuation, in citations from early modern English works. Throughout, however, I have reproduced the original spelling of these works' titles to assist those readers who would like to use my citations as bibliographical references (Shakespearean titles are the only exceptions). I have translated materials from foreign languages (including James VI's "Scottish"), but I have cited the original texts where I thought it relevant, either in the body of the text or in the notes. Translations are my own except where I have indicated otherwise. Dates of texts included in parentheses after a title refer to the accepted date of the first publication of a work.

My use of masculine pronouns to refer to early modern teachers and students in general is intentional, insofar as the pedagogical culture I discuss assumed that teachers and students would be male, except when specifically noted to be otherwise in discussions of the education of women.

The Trials of Humanism

T he decade of the 1980s was a hard time for humanist education in the United States, from the elementary schools to the
universities. In the most notorious series of conflicts, the religious right waged a battle against the public schools' promulgation
of what the right called "secular humanism." Their declaration of war
gained national attention in 1986–1987, when fundamentalist Christian
parents raised legal objections to the public school textbooks used in
Mobile, Alabama, on the grounds that those books taught the "religion" of secular humanism. The plaintiffs argued that such "religious"
teaching was unconstitutional, but evidently their real concern was that
humanism threatened traditional American values. On March 4, 1987,
U.S. District Judge W. Brevard Hand indeed banned forty-five textbooks because they promoted secular humanism, a faith that he
claimed puts man before God and teaches the "sweeping fundamental
belief" that "moral choices are purely personal and can only be based
on some autonomous as yet undiscovered and unfulfilled inner self."[1]
The order was overturned on August 26, 1987, when the Federal Appeals court ruled that the schoolbooks conveyed, in "an entirely appropriate secular effort . . . a governmental attempt to instill in Alabama
public school children such values as independent thought, tolerance
of diverse views, self-respect, maturity, self-reliance and logical decision
making."[2]

1. Ruling cited by Stuart Taylor, Jr., in *New York Times*, March 7, 1987, I:7.
2. *New York Times*, August 27, 1987, I:22.

This conflict, and the public debate it generated, showed that Americans meant very different things when they talked about "humanism" and "humanist education": a system of values, a pedagogical program, or a constellation of academic fields. How you defined "humanism" as a value system depended on whether you thought it was a good thing. For one side it could signify "a godless, atheistic, evolutionary, amoral, collectivist, socialistic communist religion," while for its admirers humanism could mean "joyous service for the greater good of all humanity in this natural world and advocating the methods of reason, science and democracy."[3] For both sides humanist education was teaching that fostered such values. More narrowly defined, and principally within higher education, humanist education also served as a synonym for the institutional study of the humanities—art, literature, language study, music, history, and philosophy. (It is worth noting that during this time, while the religious right accused humanists of conspiring to undermine American private and public life, humanities teachers felt demeaned by the contemporary business culture, which they thought dismissed humanistic studies as irrelevant to the "real life" of getting and spending.)[4]

While the religious right attacked secular humanism in the public schools, the traditional practitioners of humanist education, who saw themselves as promulgating the values that the Federal Appeals Court called "humanist," also felt besieged within their own institutions. Allan Bloom's *Closing of the American Mind* (1987) brought the American public's attention to this perceived crisis, but William J. Bennett had

3. See Howard B. Radest, *The Devil and Secular Humanism: The Children of the Enlightenment* (New York: Praeger, 1990). On the differing definitions of secular humanism at the height of the quarrel, see William Safire, "On Language," *New York Times Magazine*, January 26, 1986, pp. 6–7. See also David Bollier, "The Witch-Hunt against Secular Humanism," *The Humanist* 44. 5 (1984): 11–19, 50.

4. See, for example, Robert E. Proctor, *Education's Great Amnesia: Reconsidering the Humanities from Petrarch to Freud, with a Curriculum for Today's Students* (Bloomington: Indiana University Press, 1988), chap. 6, in which he describes the climate of America in the 1980s as dominated by "the drive to amass capital, the constant metamorphosis of money into commodities and commodities into more money, [which] not only creates a world of constant change and transformation; it knows no past. . . . The past can have little or no meaning in a society ruled by the bottom line" (p. 139).

already drawn the battle lines in 1984 in his NEH pamphlet *To Reclaim a Legacy*. These books were followed by Roger Kimball's *Tenured Radicals* (1990) and Dinesh D'Souza's *Illiberal Education* (1991), among others. Such texts depicted a beleaguered band of teachers struggling to transmit humanist culture to the next generation, but impeded by a feminist, "multicultural," and leftist opposition. The traditional humanists accused their antagonists of declaring all meaning relative and of using the humanities, in William Bennett's words, "as if they were the handmaiden of ideology."[5] Traditional humanists believed that they alone defended the principles of equality, rationality, and truth against a phalanx of amoral relativists, who were dismantling the curriculum, changing admissions policies, and politicizing all teaching and campus life.

The violence of this threat and its influence on academic tradition have been greatly exaggerated. As Stanley Fish has put it, with characteristic forthrightness, "There is no evidence that either Shakespeare or those who teach him have been run out of the academy by an intolerant coalition of Marxists, rabid feminists, godless deconstructionists, and diseased gays."[6] But clearly the two camps within the humanities did disagree considerably about the purpose of humanist education. Most teachers describing themselves as traditional humanists believed their goal was to fashion the free individual for a modern democracy. O. B. Hardison, Jr., writing in 1985, typifies an academic "pro-humanist" view:

> Liberal education is an ideal that has dominated Western thought about the aims of education for almost three millennia. The term "liberal" (from Latin *liberus*, meaning "free man") is apt because it emphasizes the fact that the individual and political concerns of liberal education are two sides of the same coin. According to Socrates in Plato's *Republic*, education is the process of learning truth. It frees the individual from bondage to illusions—from

5. William Bennett, *To Reclaim a Legacy: A Report on the Humanities in Higher Education* (Washington, D.C.: National Endowment for the Humanities, 1984), p. 16.

6. Stanley Fish, *There's No Such Thing as Free Speech and It's a Good Thing, Too* (New York: Oxford University Press, 1994), p. 53.

the myriad superstitions, mythologies, and prejudices that imprison the ignorant. The result is wisdom, which is a combination of self-confidence and humility.[7]

The terms of this description encapsulate what the defenders of liberal humanist education saw as the end of their efforts. The most important words here are "free," "individual," and "truth." To be an individual is to be free and truly "human"; the discovery of truth through learning makes the student free. The product of such an education resembles the paradoxical image of the Renaissance humanist prince: the successful student is self-confident and recognizes no limits, yet he or she is constrained by humility.

Such a passage exposes itself on every front to the critique of the academic postmodern and antihumanist theorists of the 1980s, who replaced the individual with the subject, confined freedom in discourse, and historicized what is human and what is true. Postmodern theory identifies each of Hardison's concepts with a specific historical or philosophical discourse, and the analysis of these discourses is *the* topic of postmodern education. According to Mas'ud Zavarzadeh and Donald Morton, two of the many advocates of a postmodern pedagogy:

> The teacher makes it possible for the student to become aware of his position, of his own relations to power/knowledge formations. Such a teacher often has an adversarial role in relation to the student: the teacher is a deconstructor, not a mere supporter in the traditional sense of the word. She helps reveal the student to himself by showing him how his ideas and positions are the effects of larger discourses (of class, race and gender, for example) rather than simple, natural manifestations of his consciousness or mind.[8]

7. O. B. Hardison, Jr., "The Future of Liberal Arts: A Humanist's View," *Georgia Review* 39 (1985): 576.

8. Mas'ud Zavarzadeh and Donald Morton, "Theory Pedagogy Politics: The Crisis of 'The Subject' in the Humanities," in Morton and Zavarzadeh, eds., *Theory/Pedagogy/Politics: Texts for Change* (Urbana: University of Illinois Press, 1991), pp. 11–12. For a critique of this position, see Gregory Jay and Gerald Graff, "A Critique of Critical Ped-

Paradoxically, this teacher will free the students by suggesting that their "ideas and positions" are "effects of larger discourses" and thus not really their own. The knowledge given is not of truth itself, but how "truth" is fashioned by material conditions and thus may change. Stanley Aronowitz and Henry Giroux have defined the key principles of this "liberation": "its refusing forms of knowledge and pedagogy wrapped in the legitimizing discourse of the sacred and the priestly, its rejection of universal reason as a foundation of human affairs, its claim that all narratives are partial, and its call to perform critical readings on all scientific, cultural and social texts as historical and political constructions."[9] The "freedom" that is the goal of such pedagogy, perhaps characteristically American, is simultaneously defined by refusal and self-assertion.

As is evident in these patches of rhetoric, traditional humanist and antihumanist or postmodern teachers do share certain notions. Both understand that education is inseparable from political life, and both focus on demystification—the teacher's releasing the student from "bondage to illusions" in the name of freedom. For Hardison's side learning offers the freedom to participate in liberal democracy; for Zavarzadeh and Morton education develops in a student "a critical oppositional position in relation to the dominant order"[10]; for Aronowitz and Giroux the student is to be "emancipated" for "critical citizenship."[11] As the traditional humanist sees it, one throws off the shackles of illusion to become free to join democratic society; in postmodern theory, demystification itself is a form of resistance because it gives the

---

agogy" in Michael Berubé and Cary Nelson, eds., *Higher Education under Fire: Politics, Economics, and the Crisis of the Humanities* (New York: Routledge, 1995), pp. 202–4.

9. Stanley Aronowitz and Henry A. Giroux, *Postmodern Education: Politics, Culture, and Social Criticism* (Minneapolis: University of Minnesota Press, 1991), p. 82.

10. Zavarzadeh and Morton, "Theory Pedagogy Politics," p. 12. See also James Donald, *Sentimental Education: Schooling, Popular Culture, and the Regulation of Liberty* (London: Verso, 1992): "As Foucault suggests, the exercise of freedom consists not in the enlightenment promised by universal Humanity, Reason or Society, but in unpicking the particularity and contingency of the discourses, knowledges and practices that define and form us as subjects" (pp. 134–35).

11. Aronowitz and Giroux, *Postmodern Education*, p. 82: in their view, postmodern theory provides "the pedagogical grounds for radicalizing the emancipatory possibilities of teaching and learning as part of a wider struggle for democratic public life and critical citizenship."

student power to combat social and political repression. Postmodern pedagogues see the humanists' "freedom" as permission to obey authority and police one's own behavior or as an atomistic individualism that serves a market economy; the humanists see postmodern "freedom" as nihilistic, destroying our world without leaving tools with which to rebuild it, and encouraging conflict over race, class, and gender.[12]

The religious right and the postmodern left might agree thus on a few things about their enemy, broadly defined as "secular humanism." Both see it as the official ideology of the modern democratic state, which interferes in people's lives and attempts to shape their beliefs, ironically by promulgating individualism. Individualism is indeed a tricky issue for both. For the religious right, individualism may undermine the values of religious community and promote disobedience to God's word; however, its members also believe that the "immoral" and "violent" books central to humanist education, in the words of John Conlan, "biased toward increasing the centralized power of a secular humanist state, will ultimately destroy the family, decent social standards, and basic principles of decentralized government that safeguard every American's individual freedom."[13] The left regards individualism as a capitalist fiction that blocks collective action by those excluded from mainstream society. While these antihumanists would fiercely defend each person's right to resist oppression, they also link individualism with "essentialism," the positing of a universal, ahistorical human nature (which thereby excludes everyone different from the mainstream European type). For example, in his *Radical Tragedy*, published in 1984, Jonathan Dollimore characterized humanism, including

12. For a discussion of these differing viewpoints, which also posits an alternative to an "atomistic" humanist construction of the individual, see Alan Sinfield, *Faultlines: Cultural Materialism and the Politics of Dissident Reading* (Berkeley: University of California Press, 1992), chap. 2; for a parallel discussion of the "atomistic" self, see Wayne C. Booth, "Individualism and the Mystery of the Social Self; or, Does Amnesty Have a Leg to Stand On?" in Barbara Johnson, ed., *Freedom and Interpretation: The Oxford Amnesty Lectures, 1992* (New York: Basic Books, 1993), pp. 69–101. For Zavarzadeh and Morton's construction of the opposition, see "Theory Pedagogy Politics," p. 3.

13. John Conlan, foreword to James C. Hefley, ed., *Textbooks on Trial* (Wheaton, Ill.: Victor Books, 1976), cited in James E. Davis, ed., *Dealing with Censorship* (Urbana, Ill.: NCTE, 1979), p. 9.

"essentialism," as a "residual metaphysic within secularist thought," which has "made possible the classic ideological effect: a specific cultural identity is universalized or naturalized . . . [and] activated in defence of one cultural formation, one conception of what it is to be truly human, to the corresponding exclusion of others."[14]

As these comments suggest, both left and right also persistently point out that "secular humanism" would deny its own status as a religion or an ideology but instead presents itself as transcendent truth or mere common sense, the lingua franca of all modern democracies. The religious right saw the triumph (however brief) of the Hand ruling in its establishment of humanism as just one belief system among many, albeit one that had taken over the government. After the Alabama book banning Robert Skolrood was gratified to see that "humanism is out of the closet for the first time."[15] Such is the focus of postmodern antihumanism as well, which objects to the humanists' hypocrisy in rejecting "ideology" while denying their own biases and their continual recourse to the "human" as a category that transcends history and politics. Both sides are thus devoted to exposing humanism's "hidden agenda."

My point here is certainly not to suggest any essential resemblance between these opponents of humanism (to the horror of either side).[16]

---

14. Jonathan Dollimore, *Radical Tragedy: Religion, Ideology, and Power in the Drama of Shakespeare and his Contemporaries* (Chicago: University of Chicago Press, 1984), p. 258. Cf. what Fish says about the humanist "ethicist": "In short, the ethicists are not *the* ethicists, in the sense of being the sole proprietors of a moral vision in a world of shameless relativists; rather, they are the purveyors of a *particular* moral vision that must make its way in the face of competition from other moral visions" (*There's No Such Thing as Free Speech*, pp. 41–42). For a vigorous critique of Dollimore and others in Shakespeare studies who attack "essentialist humanism," see Graham Bradshaw, *Misrepresentations: Shakespeare and the Materialists* (Ithaca: Cornell University Press, 1993).

15. *New York Times*, March 5, 1987, I: 12.

16. Paulo Freire, in *Pedagogy of the Oppressed*, trans. Myra Bergman Ramos (1970; reprint, New York: Continuum, 1986), argued many years ago against what he calls both rightist and leftist sectarianism: "For the rightist sectarian, 'today,' linked to the past, is something given and immutable; for the leftist sectarian, 'tomorrow' is decreed beforehand, is inexorably pre-ordained. This rightist and this leftist are both reactionary because, starting from their respectively false views of history, both develop forms of action which negate freedom" (p. 23). For the reaction that Freire himself is a kind of "sectarian," acknowledging only the truth of Marxism, see Jay and Graff, "A Critique of Critical Pedagogy," pp. 202–4. For a later view of the authoritarianism of both the right and

Nonetheless, both stimulated a general climate of "antihumanism" that, I believe, framed how many scholars then interpreted another "humanism" and "humanist education" much more narrowly defined: a historical, early modern humanist pedagogy. That humanism may be described as the new ways of teaching, reading, and thinking about classical texts that began in Italy in the fourteenth century and spread to northern Europe through the fifteenth and sixteenth centuries. And that humanism is the subject of this book.

Definitions of Renaissance or early modern humanism are as varied as modern ones, of course, to the extent that, as Quentin Skinner has noted, "several authorities have recently proposed that in order to avoid further confusion, the word 'humanism' ought to be excised from all future accounts of early-modern thought."[17] Some define early modern "humanism" as a secularist philosophy focusing on the cultivation of virtue; others prefer, as Skinner does, to confine the term *humanist* "to refer to the students and protagonists of a particular group of disciplines centered around the study of grammar, rhetoric, history and moral philosophy."[18] Beneath that dry definition, however, lies the recognition of a set of shared practices associated with early modern humanism: a shift from scholasticism's emphasis on logic to the study of "grammar" and rhetoric (the arts of writing and speaking); a renewed interest in reading and teaching classical Greek and Latin texts; and a habit of reading texts in the context of history, that is, as a philologist rather than as a logician. The influence of these practices goes far beyond antiquated disputes waged in the early modern colleges and studies. Though scholarly accounts of this historical humanism typically treat it as a separate phenomenon, they also implicitly link it to the telos of modern humanist education.

This book aims to reconsider the relationship between the past and present practices of humanist education. It centers on the complicated

---

left, see David Bromwich, *Politics by Other Means: Higher Education and Group Thinking* (New Haven: Yale University Press, 1992), pp. 100–1.

17. Quentin Skinner, *The Foundations of Modern Political Thought*, vol. 1: *The Renaissance* (Cambridge: Cambridge University Press, 1978), p. xxiii. Skinner himself provides an excellent overview of humanism's emergence and diffusion and its role in European political thought.

18. Ibid., p. xxiii–xxiv. Skinner here follows the influential example of Paul Kristeller.

and often contradictory texts (mostly from the sixteenth century) that were essential to the humanist educational movement in Britain. I have tried to remain open to the multiple resonances of these texts rather than merely tuning in those themes repeated in our own time, and I have looked for what terms, tropes, and theories were generated and exchanged in the past rather than laying a grid of modern theory over those texts. Yet imitating the early humanists' own vacillation between the philologist's historicism and the moralist's search for relevance, I also insist that more is at stake than a scholarly quarrel about what really happened in early modern schoolrooms in Britain, or what the early humanists *really* meant. The early debates over teaching form this book's center, but that center is framed by my effort to understand the contemporary dilemmas of humanist education. In looking back at the early modern humanist educational reform, I have tried to understand how we came to our present situation and how that story might have been different. Thus, the book ends with an epilogue considering some current educational dilemmas that touch on the questions I examine in early modern pedagogy: in particular, the authority of teachers, the freedom and identity of students, and the formation of the canon. I do not mean to draw a direct line between the early modern and post-modern periods or to give a comprehensive history of Anglo-American education; nor, indeed, would I want to imply that nothing has changed from the past to the present. Partly, the comparison is heuristic; I use the configurations of the past to discover new dimensions of the present conflict. I cannot offer solutions here, but I do hope to reframe the questions that have almost paralyzed the discussion of humanist education in our own time.

CHAPTER 1

Introduction:
Humanism Reconsidered

I t is easy to forget that any canon maker must be first a canon breaker. Even Desiderius Erasmus, that notorious humanist defender of "good letters," once saw himself in the avant-garde. In his dialogue *The Antibarbarians* (1520) Erasmus's fictional spokesman Jacob Batt mocked the fear of the new humanist learning felt by the old scholastic "barbarians." He describes how these men spoke out against him (and thus Erasmus) "in public, in taverns, in workshops, at barbers, in brothels, . . . drunk and sober, saying that some unknown outsider was sowing a new heresy, that the best authors, Alexander, Ebrardus Graecista, Modista, *Breviloquus, Mammetrectus, Catholicon,* . . . were now to be shamefully driven out." Instead, "some unheard-of and dreadful absurdities of the pagans (*ethnicorum*) were being introduced: Horace, Virgil and Ovid." From these writers, Batt's — and Erasmus's — antagonists complained, children would learn only of love, and things that not even adults should know, and they proclaimed that "if plans were not made as soon as possible, it would mean the end of the Christian religion; and the age of the Antichrist would be here, or at least about to begin. For teachers had come, who would soothe those whose ears itch to hear something new (*nouarum rerum*)."[1]

---

1. *Antibarbarorum liber,* in Desiderius Erasmus, *Opera Omnia,* vol. 1, bk. 1, ed. Kazimierz Kumaniecki (Amsterdam: North-Holland, 1969), p. 61. The translation is my own, but I have consulted *The Antibarbarians,* trans. Margaret Mann Philips, in *Collected Works of Erasmus,* vol. 23: *Literary and Educational Writings,* vol. 1, ed. Craig R. Thompson (Toronto: University of Toronto Press, 1978). See also Joan Simon, *Education and Society in Tudor England* (Cambridge: Cambridge University Press, 1966), who recounts the

While this view of the sixteenth-century canon conflict may seem amusingly archaic, several elements of the current canon debate are traceable in it, particularly in the accusation that "new wave" scholars have abandoned tradition and are pushing unknown and indecent texts on their students. Each of the two groups of antagonists also distorts the other's position, as much as in the present debate: the old guard fears the new's dedication to, as George Will put it, "delegitimizing Western civilization by discrediting the books and ideas that gave birth to it,"[2] and the new sees the old as the embittered defenders of an oppressive, antiquated order.

Although surely different in content, elements of the early modern canon debate thus foreshadow the present because in both debates an argument concerning the literary canon overlies a deeper conflict about the goals of education. In our time we quarrel about whether learning should transmit tradition or develop cultural awareness and critical judgment. As John Guillory points out, the advocates of the early humanist revolt, too, wanted more than a mere "revaluation of authors or texts"; they sought to replace the scholastic teaching of logic with instruction in grammar and rhetoric for a new generation of civic-minded men (and sometimes women).[3] Even though this change evoked a return to the twelfth-century classroom — where teachers publicly lectured on authors such as Virgil, Juvenal and Lucan, as well as the Christian fathers — we cannot underestimate the influence of the early humanists' self-image as educational radicals determined to transform the intellectual landscape of Europe.[4]

---

violent reaction against the introduction of a humanities course at Corpus Christi College, Oxford, in 1517 (pp. 82–85).

2. George F. Will, "Literary Politics," *Newsweek*, April 22, 1991, p. 72.

3. John Guillory, "Canonical and Non-Canonical: A Critique of the Current Debate," *ELH* 54 (1987): 509. See Emile Durkheim, *L'évolution pédagogique en France*, (1938; 2d ed., Paris: Presses Universitaires de France, 1969); trans. by Peter Collins as *The Evolution of Educational Thought: Lectures on the Formation and Development of Secondary Education in France* (London: Routledge and Kegan Paul, 1977), p. 141; see also L. D. Reynolds and N. G. Wilson, *Scribes and Scholars: A Guide to the Transmission of Greek and Latin Literature* (Oxford: Oxford University Press, 1968), pp. 96–97.

4. On the curriculum authors of the medieval schools, see Ernst Robert Curtius, *Europäische Literatur und lateinisches Mittelalter* (Bern: A. Francke, 1948), trans. by Willard R. Trask as *European Literature and the Latin Middle Ages* (Princeton: Princeton University Press, 1953), pp. 36–54.

In recent decades, however, many scholars have been concerned to remind us that this self-image was also self-promotion. In their 1986 book *From Humanism to the Humanities*, Anthony Grafton and Lisa Jardine attacked early modern humanist education on two fronts, criticizing widely accepted views of its historical function and significance and linking its inadequacies to the failures of the modern humanities. Astute scholars of Renaissance culture, Grafton and Jardine argued against previous historians of humanist education who, despite the evidence of their own archival research,

> have treated the rise of the classical curriculum and the downfall of scholasticism as the natural triumph of virtue over vice. Like the humanists they study, whose words they often echo faithfully, they assume the barbarity and obsolescence of medieval education and the freshness and liberality of humanism. The new system, they hold, offered such vistas of intellectual and spiritual freedom as to make it irresistible.[5]

Instead, what Grafton and Jardine saw in the historical evidence was a wide gap between the theory and practice of humanist education. While the theory may have been admirable, the practice "stamped the more prominent members of the new élite with an indelible cultural seal of superiority, it equipped lesser members of the new élite with fluency and the learned habit of attention to textual detail, and it offered everyone a model of true culture as something given, absolute, to be mastered, not questioned—and thus fostered in its initiates a properly docile attitude towards authority."[6]

Of course, Grafton and Jardine were not the first scholars to castigate early modern humanist teachers for falsely claiming to liberate Europe from "barbarism." Nor were they the first to argue that the humanists

5. Anthony Grafton and Lisa Jardine, *From Humanism to the Humanities: Education and the Liberal Arts in Fifteenth- and Sixteenth-Century Europe* (Cambridge: Harvard University Press, 1986), p. xii.

6. Ibid., p. xiv. For an interesting and sympathetic view of the extraordinary scholarship of Anthony Grafton, and the resemblance of his method to those "humanists he studies," see Robert DeMaria, Jr., "Latter-Day Humanists and the Pastness of the Past," *Common Knowledge* 3.1 (1994): 67–76. See also Lisa Jardine, *Erasmus, Man of Letters: The Construction of Charisma in Print* (Princeton: Princeton University Press, 1993), on techniques of self-promotion.

served the needs of the emerging European state system "with its closed governing élites, hereditary offices and strenuous efforts to close off debate on vital political and social questions."[7] The earlier part of this century saw both pessimistic and Christian reactions against Jacob Burckhardt's celebration of the Renaissance's "emancipation" of the human mind from (in Douglas Bush's words) "the shackles of superstition." As Bush saw it on the eve of World War II, when

> we look around our world and consider where the emancipated mind has landed us, we may think that liberal historians might be a little less complacent about progress. And, in spite of our long subservience to secular liberalism, the climate of opinion in some quarters has changed a good deal. Voices can be heard declaring that the Renaissance, so far as it involved a secular revolt, was more of a calamity than a triumph.[8]

In his 1954 introduction to *English Literature in the Sixteenth Century, Excluding Drama* (from the multi-volume *Oxford History of English Literature*), C. S. Lewis blasted the early modern humanists for rejecting medieval "barbarism" while their own work was "stillborn." He accused them of "killing the medieval Latin" but not replacing it with anything living.[9] All the humanists had to offer was empty copying, burdened by an excessive admiration of "order and discipline, weight, and decorum." Interested only in their own advancement, they were driven by a "vulgar" distaste for anything *they* called vulgar.[10] For Lewis, in short, their New Learning was the "New Ignorance."[11]

While Lewis was less concerned with the politics of the humanist

7. Grafton and Jardine, *From Humanism*, p. xiv.

8. Douglas Bush, *The Renaissance and English Humanism* (Toronto: University of Toronto Press, 1939), p. 32.

9. C. S. Lewis, *English Literature in the Sixteenth Century, Excluding Drama* (Oxford: Oxford University Press, 1954), pp. 20–21.

10. Ibid., p. 24.

11. Ibid., p. 31. These statements must be set in context of the general turn against humanism at the time: see Wallace K. Ferguson, *The Renaissance in Historical Thought: Five Centuries of Interpretation* (Cambridge: Riverside Press, Houghton Mifflin, 1948), chap. 11, who recounts the "revolt of the medievalists" after Burckhardt; this revolt took the various forms of denying originality to the humanists, of blurring any line of demarcation between the Middle Ages and Renaissance, and of seeing the Renaissance as the decline or even decadence of the Middle Ages (p. 372).

movement, his rhetoric implies a reaction to the humanists' class consciousness when he damns them as social climbers eager to insert themselves into the established hierarchy. For Lewis, the humanists' very distaste for vulgarity marked their inherent lack of *noblesse*. Also in 1954, in *Humanism and the Social Order in Tudor England*, Fritz Caspari took up a complementary argument in the field of political thought by calling the humanists politically conservative. Even though they may have seen themselves as part of a scholarly "new wave," they were traditionalists insofar as they "evolved a social doctrine with which they tried to defend and improve the existing order of society. They used their knowledge of Plato and Aristotle, of Cicero and Quintilian, to justify the aristocratic structure of English society, the hierarchy of 'order and degree' in the state. Their particular concern was to devise means whereby, in the social and political framework of Tudor England, its ruling members would be its 'best' men."[12] According to Caspari, the sixteenth-century English humanists accepted the old order and merely tried to secure their own place in it.[13] Ten years later, James McConica argued that the English humanists were instrumental to the Henrician and Edwardian governments' programs of religious reform:[14] that is, they may have been "reformist" but only in support of the growing bureaucracy of the Tudor state. The common theme of all these texts is the English humanists' self-interest, their service to the state's interests, and their failure to effect the kind of cultural and political "emancipation" that some historians, literary and otherwise, had claimed for them.[15]

12. Fritz Caspari, *Humanism and the Social Order in Tudor England* (Chicago: University of Chicago Press, 1954), p. 1.

13. In his epilogue, however, Caspari also notes that while humanist political thought may have "stressed the right of monarchs and gentlemen to rule, humanism also emerged on the other side as 'classical republicanism' " (*Humanism*, p. 207).

14. James Kelsey McConica, *English Humanists and Reformation Politics Under Henry VIII and Edward VI* (Oxford: Clarendon, 1965).

15. For an account of the competing versions of the politics of English humanism, see Alistair Fox, "Facts and Fallacies: Interpreting English Humanism," in Fox and John Guy, eds., *Reassessing the Henrician Age: Humanism, Politics and Reform 1500–1550* (Oxford: Basil Blackwell, 1986), pp. 9–34. For a stronger view of humanism as "reformist," see Arthur B. Ferguson, *The Articulate Citizen and the English Renaissance* (Durham, N.C.: Duke University Press, 1965), chap. 11. On humanism and political thought in Northern

Focusing more narrowly on humanist education, Grafton and Jardine differed from their predecessors not only in their politics but also in their emphasis on the practices and institutions of humanist pedagogy. For these later scholars, humanist pedagogic discipline, and not just humanist ideology, served the burgeoning early modern bureaucracies. To ground their analysis, Grafton and Jardine turned to social historians without making any explicit theoretical alliances. Even more recent interpreters of early modern pedagogy, coming from the discipline of literary history, have used quite different analytical tools, their strategies heavily influenced by Michel Foucault's *Discipline and Punish* (1975) and its account of the classical techniques of discipline. Typical is Richard Halpern's *Poetics of Primitive Accumulation* (1991), which argues that "the ideological function of Tudor schooling must . . . be understood to include not only the transmission of doctrine or governing representations, but also the imposition of certain productive or disciplinary practices. The schools hammered in ideological content and also laid down economies of recreation and labor, punishment and reward. They thus participated in the disciplinary 'accumulation of men' which, according to Foucault, complemented, and reinforced the accumulation of capital."[16] In such critiques Foucault's archaeology often finds its complement in the sociology of Pierre Bourdieu and Jean-Claude Passeron's *Reproduction in Education, Society, and Culture* (1970). Bourdieu and Passeron state that "all pedagogic action is, objectively, symbolic violence insofar as it is the imposition of a cultural arbitrary by an arbitrary power" and as such "contributes by reproducing the cultural arbitrary which it inculcates, toward reproducing the power relations which are the basis of its power of arbitrary imposition (the social reproduction function of cultural reproduction)."[17]

Europe, see Quentin Skinner, *The Foundations of Modern Political Thought*, vol. 1, *The Renaissance* (Cambridge: Cambridge University Press, 1978), chaps. 7–9.

16. Richard Halpern, *The Poetics of Primitive Accumulation: English Renaissance Culture and the Genealogy of Capital* (Ithaca: Cornell University Press, 1991), p. 26.

17. See Pierre Bourdieu and Jean-Claude Passeron, *La reproduction: elements pour une theorie du systeme d'enseignement* (Paris: Minuit, 1970), trans. Richard Nice, *Reproduction in Education, Society, and Culture* (London: Sage, 1977), pp. 5, 10. For a summary and critique of Bourdieu, see Richard Jenkins, *Pierre Bourdieu* (London: Routledge, 1992). As Jenkins explains "symbolic violence," it "is the imposition of systems of symbolism

These theoretical models are powerful, although they have not been uncontested within the fields of history, sociology and literary criticism.[18] We have seen almost two decades of criticism, as well as encomium, of Foucault's picture of a disciplinary power "both absolutely indiscreet, since it is everywhere and always alert, since by its very principle it leaves no zone of shade and constantly supervises the very individuals who are entrusted with the task of supervising; and absolutely 'discreet,' for it functions permanently, and largely in silence."[19] Yet *Discipline and Punish* continues to influence the field of the history of education: for example, in an essay collection, *Foucault and Education: Discipline and Knowledge*, published in 1991, the editor proposes that "the application of Foucauldian analysis to education will unmask the politics that underlie some of the apparent neutrality of educational reform."[20] *A Culture of Teaching*, like Mary Thomas Crane's recent *Framing Authority*,[21] intervenes against the tendency to read early mod-

---

and meaning (i.e., culture) upon groups or classes in such a way that they are experienced as legitimate" (p. 104). For an example of such an approach, see Jonathan Goldberg, who in his *Writing Matter: From the Hands of the English Renaissance* (Stanford: Stanford University Press, 1990) suspends his reading of early modern English education in the web of a Derridean construction of writing, Antonio Gramsci's view of the traditional intellectual, Norbert Elias's account of the civilizing process, and Bourdieu and Passeron's notion of cultural capital. See Norbert Elias, *The History of Manners*, trans. Edmund Jephcott (Oxford: Basil Blackwell, 1978); also Antonio Gramsci, *Selections from the Prison Notebooks*, ed. and trans. Quintin Hoare and Geoffrey Nowell Smith (New York: International, 1971), pp. 1–23.

18. The critiques of Foucault are too numerous to list: influential ones focusing on *Discipline and Punish* include Edward Said, "Criticism between Culture and System," in *The World, The Text, and the Critic* (Cambridge: Harvard University Press, 1983), pp. 178–225; Frank Lentricchia, *Ariel and the Police: Michel Foucault, William James, Wallace Stevens* (Madison: University of Wisconsin Press, 1988), chap. 1; Charles Taylor, "Foucault on Freedom and Truth," *Political Theory* 12 (1984): 152–83; and Richard Rorty, "Moral Identity and Private Autonomy," in his *Essays on Heidegger and Others: Philosophical Papers* (New York: Cambridge University Press, 1991), vol. 2, pp. 193–98. For a summary of critiques of Bourdieu, see Jenkins, chap. 5.

19. Michel Foucault, *Surveiller et punir: Naissance de la prison* (Paris: Gallimard, 1975), trans. by Alan Sheridan as *Discipline and Punish: The Birth of the Prison* (New York: Pantheon, 1977), p. 177.

20. Stephen Ball, ed., *Foucault and Education: Discipline and Knowledge* (London: Routledge, 1991), introduction, pp. 5, 7.

21. Mary Thomas Crane, *Framing Authority: Sayings, Self, and Society in Sixteenth-Century England* (Princeton: Princeton University Press, 1993), argues that English hu-

ern humanist—and all successive—pedagogies in terms of a Foucauldian saturation of disciplinary power. My own impulse to resist may be called "humanist," even though under the current circumstances the term may be, in Edward Said's words, "a description for which I have contradictory feelings of affection and revulsion."[22] Yet my humanism is less tied to Allan Bloom's or William Bennett's than looking back to the best instincts of the early humanist pedagogy that this book examines. This is a humanism based on the belief that people are largely responsible for what happens on this earth; committed to tolerance, attention to the differences among people and the need to treat them with equal respect; shaped by a cheerful acceptance of ambivalence and contradiction; and informed by an almost painful historical consciousness, which sees the past as estranged yet able to illuminate present concerns. These are the values I learned from and brought to my reading of primarily English humanist pedagogical writings of the sixteenth and early seventeenth centuries. As I read, I encountered the remarkable contradictions and paradoxes often noted as characteristic of Tudor rhetoric: before my eyes, the pedagogical texts oscillated between play and work, freedom and control, submission and mastery.[23] In reading the histories of education in the period, I also found that humanist teachers themselves constituted a paradox in their social and political roles: at once high and low, marginal and at the center of political life.

---

manism "possessed greater theoretical sophistication, manifested a more complex and problematized ideological stance, and exerted a more pronounced (but different kind of) influence than has generally been recognized" (p. 7). Crane's book appeared late in my own writing of this book. While her focus on commonplace books differs from mine, we cover some of the same territory and agree on several issues.

22. Edward W. Said, "Opponents, Audiences, Constituencies, and Community," *Critical Inquiry* 9 (1982): 1.

23. In this perception of humanist rhetoric, I have been particularly influenced by Victoria Kahn, *Rhetoric, Prudence, and Skepticism in the Renaissance* (Ithaca: Cornell University Press, 1985), and Terence Cave, *The Cornucopian Text: Problems of Writing in the French Renaissance* (Oxford: Clarendon, 1979). For a comprehensive account of how this ambivalence functioned rhetorically in Tudor drama, see Joel B. Altman, *The Tudor Play of Mind: Rhetorical Inquiry and The Development of Elizabethan Drama* (Berkeley: University of California Press, 1978); also see Marion Trousdale, *Shakespeare and the Rhetoricians* (London: Scolar Press, 1982) and Crane, *Framing Authority*.

Playful contradiction was the hallmark of Erasmus, who in many ways is the linchpin of this book,[24] but, beyond him, what Joel Altman has called "the moral culture of ambivalence" shaped the rhetoric and politics of Tudor humanism.[25] When one combines social and political instability with the paradoxes of pedagogical rhetoric and theory, a situation and attitude emerge that differ from the uniformly repressive (however "loving or gentle") regime often depicted. I would never deny that the early modern humanist teacher could be boring, brutal, or a fatal combination of both, whether in the town grammar school or the royal nursery. But I have tried to see the other side of humanist pedagogical theory and practice: an insistence on play, pleasure, and kindness, a respect for the child's nature, and an admiration of variety and range in reading struggling against a will to control, a love of purity, and a belief in hierarchy and exclusivity. I have also tried to understand the humanists' failures sympathetically. One can always argue, from Foucault's point of view (as Halpern does), that "gentleness" in discipline, far from opposing the disciplinary regime, made control more effective. But my reading raises questions about whether Foucault's model of the school, derived primarily from French examples of the classical age, can be applied universally to the early English humanist schoolroom, given the latter schoolroom's persistently unstable political, social, and emotional dynamics.[26]

My primary theoretical category is "ambivalence," or contradiction set into motion—a fluctuation between opposites. This principle of ambivalence differs from a poststructuralist or Derridean textual inde-

24. On Erasmus's influence on educational theory and institutions in northern Europe and England in particular, see: Grafton and Jardine, *From Humanism*, chap. 6; R. R. Bolgar, "From Humanism to the Humanities," *Twentieth Century Studies* 9 (1973): 8–21; and T. W. Baldwin, *William Shakspere's Small Latine and Lesse Greeke*, 2 vols., (Urbana: University of Illinois Press, 1944). See also McConica, *English Humanists*, chaps. 2, 5, 6 and 8, for Erasmus's political influence; but cf. Fox, "English Humanism and the Body Politic," in *Reassessing the Henrician Age*, pp. 35–51, for the view that Erasmian humanism had little influence on English politics.

25. Altman, *Tudor Play of Mind*, chap. 2.

26. See Alan Sinfield's criticism of Grafton and Jardine and Goldberg for being "in danger of making the case too total—as if the effect were unitary, coherent and purposeful, not embedded in conflict and contradiction and subject to negotiation," in *Faultlines: Cultural Materialism and the Politics of Dissident Reading* (Berkeley: University of California Press, 1992), pp. 146–47, 185–86.

terminacy in which the play of "différance" cancels out the value of opposed terms. Nor does it work like the Foucauldian paradox, in which one gesture or move is subsumed by its apparent opposite; that is, what appears to be a negative gesture is really a productive one.[27] Rather, I read for *functional* ambivalence: to see where one tendency of early modern humanist pedagogy always allowed for the realization of an opposite one, without undermining or effacing itself in turn.[28] Implicit in my method is the belief, shared by many scholars, that "humanism" was never a coherent ideology, whether construed in the most general terms as a value system or in the narrower sense of an intellectual and pedagogical practice. As Lauro Martines has described it, "humanism in itself had no strict or narrow political ideology. But it did not exist in itself. Consequently, it spoke up for princely rule or for republican government; and it could plump for absolute power under kingship, or instead, favor republican states based upon an educated urban nobility and *haute bourgeoisie*."[29] As a historicist philological method, a divided attitude toward national and classical traditions, and a "liberal" pedagogy, it functioned, in James Tracy's words, as "an optical glass for seeing the world, whose uses were as diverse as the intentions of those who thought and wrote within its framework."[30] This book will suggest that in both theory and practice early English humanist pedagogy—with its fluctuations between the extremes of liberation and control, variety and limits, play and discipline—matched the heterogeneity of early modern society and politics. Its own ambiv-

27. See, for example, Foucault's question, "By what spiral did we come to affirm that sex is negative? What led us to show, ostentatiously, that sex is something we hide, to say it is something we silence?" in *La volonté de savoir* (Paris: Gallimard, 1976), trans. by Robert Hurley as *The History of Sexuality*, vol. 1, *An Introduction* (New York: Random House, 1980), p. 9.

28. See Kahn, *Rhetoric, Prudence, and Skepticism*, for a discussion of the humanists' "insistence on argument *in utramque partem*" as "conducive to action or as a substitute for action" (p. 22); Kahn adds that "the pragmatism of humanist rhetoric rejects the validity of universal truth claims and insists on the principle of decorum. Truth is not correspondence to a theoretical standard; rather, truth itself changes according to the situations in which one finds oneself" (p. 25).

29. Lauro Martines, "The Protean Face of Renaissance Humanism," *Modern Language Quarterly* 51 (1990): 107.

30. James Tracy, "From Humanism to the Humanities: A Critique of Grafton and Jardine," *Modern Language Quarterly* 51 (1990): 139.

alence was a symptom of a world of uncertain hierarchies, shifting relations, conflicting authorities, and contradictory values.

This project's historical focus is quite specific: it centers on a relatively small constellation of texts, events, and social data, circumscribed by time and space and a set of common interests, all of which indicate the complexity of humanist pedagogy in England — and in one case, Scotland — in the sixteenth and early seventeenth centuries. By humanist pedagogy, I mean programs that represent themselves as dedicated to educational reform (which might or might not include restrictions on corporal punishment) and to a curriculum based on grammar and rhetoric, through the study of mostly — but not exclusively — classical literature. This book does not offer a broad account of European humanist pedagogy (although it includes those Continental writers who influenced English pedagogical theory) or a detailed history of education in Tudor and Stuart England, accounts ably presented by other scholars.[31]

Reflecting my training as a literary historian, *A Culture of Teaching* is concerned more with the rhetoric and ideas of educational treatises and commentaries than with the raw material of textbooks, surviving student notebooks, and school archives.[32] Much will escape my consideration, and some names (such as Richard Mulcaster or George Bu-

31. This book draws on the wide body of work on the social history of education in Renaissance England; see, for example: Joan Simon, *Education and Society in Tudor England* (Cambridge: Cambridge University Press, 1966); Michael Van Cleave Alexander, *The Growth of English Education, 1348–1648: A Social and Cultural History* (University Park, Pa.: Pennsylvania State University Press, 1990); Lawrence Stone, ed., *Schooling and Society: Studies in the History of Education*, pts. 1 and 2 (Baltimore: Johns Hopkins University Press, 1976); Hugh Kearney, *Scholars and Gentlemen: Universities and Society in Preindustrial Britain 1500–1700* (Ithaca: Cornell University Press, 1970); Kenneth Charlton, *Education in Renaissance England* (Toronto: University of Toronto Press, 1965), and Baldwin, *William Shakspere's Small Latine and Lesse Greeke*. On humanist pedagogy, more broadly considered, I found particularly useful R. R. Bolgar, *The Classical Heritage and Its Beneficiaries* (Cambridge: Cambridge University Press, 1954), as well as (despite my disagreements with it) Grafton and Jardine's *From Humanism to the Humanities*.

32. This kind of illuminating historical work using the "raw data" of educational history is exemplified by the scholarship of Grafton and Jardine in *From Humanism to the Humanities* and, more recently, their history of humanist reading, " 'Studied for Action': How Gabriel Harvey Read His Livy," *Past and Present* 129 (1990): 30–78. See also William H. Sherman, *John Dee: The Politics of Reading and Writing in the Renaissance* (Amherst: University of Massachusetts Press, 1995).

chanan) will come forward while others (such as Thomas More) recede. This is a necessary distortion of my focus. Chapter 2 explores the ambivalence in the early humanist construction of pedagogic authority, focusing on the debate over corporal punishment, from the petty school to the royal nursery: it suggests that in both social practice and theory the humanist teacher's authority was at once ineffectual and absolute, outside and at the center of the political sphere when the teacher was a master and a servant, a father, prince, tyrant, and lover. This instability leads to Chapter 3's consideration of the humanists' fashioning of the student and his or her "nature," centering on how the analogy between teaching and gardening represents the student as completely malleable yet with a natural resistance to manipulation. Chapter 4 takes up the issues of freedom and control, variety and uniformity, central to the pedagogic relationship and extends them to the humanists' attitudes toward texts and reading and to the institutional pressures that influenced their choice of books to be read in schools. Only Chapter 5 moves outside the schoolroom walls, to compare different uses of tradition—both literary and political—by humanists of diverse political stripes, to see how variously an appeal to cultural tradition could function in a political context.

With this focus, this book resuscitates the original New Historicist attention of "local knowledge," a term and a method taken from Clifford Geertz signifying a description of cultural events that uses the events' own particular language and structure rather than abstract theories or teleologies.[33] At the same time, I have tried to remain aware of the limitations of such an approach. Geertz himself noted that "to turn from trying to explain social phenomena by weaving them into

33. For a different application of the notion of local reading within Renaissance studies see Leah Marcus, *Puzzling Shakespeare: Local Reading and Its Discontents* (Berkeley: University of California Press, 1988). Marcus uses the term "local reading" to describe her suggestive version of topical reading: the investigation of a historically specific constellation of tropes, idioms, and thoughts. I seek the same goal as Marcus insofar as I want, in her words, "to interrogate and expand cultural *explication de texte* by coming to terms with the materials that appear to resist systematic modeling" (p. 37). Similarly, I would agree with her that "in the Renaissance, a preference for the 'local' place and local meaning tended to correlate with resistance to various forms of political and cultural totalization. If that correlation holds, then local reading will almost inevitably gravitate towards antitotalizing interpretations" (p. 217).

grand textures of cause and effect to trying to explain them by placing them in local frames of awareness is to exchange a set of well-charted difficulties for a set of largely uncharted ones."[34] Among those difficulties now charted are the acknowledged impossibility of ever completely escaping one's own frame of awareness and the inability of such analysis to explain the process of social change.[35] It seems to me that the New Historicists' problems in using "local knowledge" have resulted from their trying to fit the local within a Foucauldian frame, so that the saturation of power obliterates the disruptive effects of "decentering" things.[36] Ideally, a focus on the "local," whether in the complex rhetoric of a text or the shifting dynamics of a single relationship, allows us to appreciate the multiple and contradictory *possibilities* of a historical moment. No one story or text should ever be taken to exemplify general historical conditions. On the contrary, the specific or the local can undermine any grand narrative, always allowing for the opposite or the exception, for what goes against the grain. In my examination of the texts and practices of early English humanist educational reform, I have tried always to remain open to all the possibilities latent in them, no matter how the stories end.

34. Clifford Geertz, *Local Knowledge: Further Essays in Interpretive Anthropology* (New York: Basic Books, 1983), p. 6.

35. See Vincent P. Pecora, "The Limits of Local Knowledge" in H. Aram Veeser, ed., *The New Historicism* (London: Routledge, 1989); this political critique of Geertz and his appropriation by New Historicists offers the view that "the entire rubric of 'local knowledge' . . . actually produces a kind of 'understanding' whose cultivated abstraction effectively conceals the 'essences and dichotomies' with which it juggles under the cloak of thickly described semiotic systems" (p. 264).

36. On the differences between Geertz and Foucault, see Pecora, ibid., pp. 247–48; for a polemical analysis of the New Historicist appropriation of Foucault, see Lentricchia, *Ariel and the Police*, pp. 86–102. For a contrasting model of historicist method that can read particularity and dispersion as a counter-politics, see Richard Helgerson, *Forms of Nationhood: The Elizabethan Writing of England* (Chicago: University of Chicago Press, 1992).

CHAPTER 2

The Sovereign Master
and the Scholar Prince

In the woodcuts and paintings that depict early modern school-rooms one item is rarely missing, although it may lie in an ob-scure corner. Somewhere you will always find a slender stick or a bundle of birch switches, the symbol of the master's authority. In G. F. Cipper's 1715 painting "The Village Schoolteacher," the master drapes one affectionate arm over the student's shoulders, while holding in the other hand the instrument of discipline, intimidating when merely shown but unforgettable when used (Figure 1).[1] Accounts of fifteenth- and sixteenth-century schooling echo the children's cries of pain: the recalcitrant son of Thomas Ingelend's play *The Disobedient Child* (1570?) refuses to go where scholars' "tender bodies both night and day / Are whipped and scourged, and beat like a stone / That from top to toe the skin is away."[2]

What was corporal punishment meant to accomplish? Some peda-gogues warned of the consequences of sparing the rod, while others deplored the ill effects of beating, yet few could explain clearly why beating itself should produce a model citizen. For the most part, its

1. On corporal punishment, see also Philippe Ariès, *L'enfant et la vie familiale sous l'Ancien Régime* (Paris: Plon, 1960), trans. by Robert Baldick as *Centuries of Childhood: A Social History of Family Life* (New York: Random House, 1962), p. 258; and Walter J. Ong, "Latin Language Study as a Renaissance Puberty Rite," *Studies in Philology* 56 (1959): 111–12.

2. Thomas Ingelend, *The Disobedient Child* (London, 1570?), in *The Dramatic Writings of Richard Wever and Thomas Ingelend*, ed. John S. Farmer (1905; reprint, New York: Barnes and Noble, 1966), p. 48.

Figure 1. The master's love and the student's fear. "The Village Schoolmaster," by G. F. Cipper, known as Todeschini (1715). In a private collection. Reproduced by permission of Roger-Viollet, Paris.

advocates thought it was enough that the Bible says and precedent shows that if you spare the rod the results will be disastrous. In *Centuries of Childhood*, Philippe Ariès argues that after the fifteenth century corporal punishment was meant to humiliate the child and render him or her submissive; institutional beating thus supported an "authoritarian, hierarchical—in a word, absolutist—concept of society."[3] In this view, as Richard Halpern puts it, "the pedagogue both assumed and reinforced the sovereign authority of the monarch or magistrate."[4] In inculcating obedience through the fear of pain, beating should have fashioned the model subject.

However, the real life of the early modern classroom complicated this process. Although the master might have imagined himself as a monarch, it was unlikely that his students, their parents, or the larger community recognized his absolute rule. In the sixteenth century, schoolmasters were only beginning to regain the stature they had achieved in the twelfth century. Teachers' complaints offer ample evidence of their low social status, misrule was common in the classroom, and masters were still mocked in poems and plays.[5] This situation was exacerbated when the student was a gentleman or lady, or in extreme cases, a prince or monarch in his or her minority, while the teacher was a mere commoner. In general, schoolroom society blurred the status distinctions that would be reinstated in maturity.[6] In *The Disobedient Child*, when the son refuses to go to school for fear of being

3. Ariès, *Centuries*, p. 261.

4. Richard Halpern, *The Poetics of Primitive Accumulation: English Renaissance Culture and the Genealogy of Capital* (Ithaca: Cornell University Press, 1991), p. 26. Halpern's reading of the transition from corporal punishment to a "loving" mastery is influenced by Foucault's *Discipline and Punish*; according to Halpern, the transition paralleled the movement from public torture to "punishment," a change in which a "coercive, corporal, solitary, secret model of the power to punish replac[ed] the representative, scenic, signifying, public collective model" (Michel Foucault, *Surveiller et punir: Naissance de la prison* [Paris: Gallimard, 1975], trans. by Alan Sheridan as *Discipline and Punish* [New York: Pantheon, 1977], p. 131).

5. See Keith Thomas, *Rule and Misrule in the Schools of Early Modern England* (Reading: University of Reading, 1976), pp. 13–14.

6. Ariès, in *Centuries*, p. 261, contends that class distinctions were blurred in a disciplinary system under which all children could be birched. Cf. Nicholas Orme, *From Childhood to Chivalry: The Education of the English Kings and Aristocracy, 1066–1530* (London: Methuen, 1984), who argues instead that corporal punishment in medieval society was widespread not as a special punishment for children, but as a mark of "their inclusion in the world of adult values and practices" (p. 33). See also a line from one of the fifteenth-century *vulgaria*, or Latin translation exercises, which complains of a change, whereby "some think themself too old and too great to be beat with the rod, and I hold well with them, if their conditions were according to their stature. Howbeit, when I came first to this university, there was no difference in correction between great and

beaten, the father insists that "this kind of fashion / Is not showed to children of honest [respectable] condition," but the son replies, "Of truth, with these masters is no difference, / For alike towards all is their wrath and violence."[7] Correspondingly, to beat anyone with a rod was to treat him or her as a child and a slave: when Puck teases Demetrius in *A Midsummer Night's Dream*, calling him a low coward and "child," he threatens to "whip thee with a rod. He is defiled / That draws a sword on thee."[8] Writers on education worried about the "gentle" or noble child's enslavement to the rod, especially when wielded by a master of inferior status. While such discipline may have provided a model of authority to imitate, in the act of chastisement a social inferior might be seen to overcome his betters.

SCHOOLS OF PLAY AND PAIN

In his now obscure play *The Disobedient Child* Thomas Ingelend meant to display the horrifying consequences of the failure to beat children. This play argues that if "correction" is not administered in youth, the adult will be incurably corrupted. In *The Disobedient Child*, the young boy who avoids the schoolmaster's rod gets his punishment later from his wife; another Tudor interlude, *Nice Wanton* (1560) depicts the disasters that befall a boy and girl who were not beaten and the success of their brother who was. *Nice Wanton* begins conventionally by citing Solomon as to the positive effects of correction, which will keep youth "in awe" and teach children "to fear God, and their parents obey, / To get learning and qualities, thereby to maintain / An honest quiet life, correspondent always / To God's law and the king's."[9] Other texts advocating corporal punishment frequently repeat this point, often joining it with Ecclesiastes 20, which warns that the parent disciplining the child should "bow down his neck while he is young, hit him on

---

small. As all things in process of time decayeth, so good rule goeth backward" (*A Fifteenth-Century School Book*, ed. William Nelson [Oxford: Clarendon, 1956], p. 31).

7. Ingelend, *Disobedient Child*, p. 49.

8. William Shakespeare, *A Midsommer Nights Dreame*, in *Mr. William Shakespeares Comedies, Histories, and Tragedies* (London, 1623), facsimile ed. prepared by Helge Kökeritz and Charles T. Prouty (New Haven: Yale University Press, 1954), pt. 1, p. 156 (act 3, sc. 2).

9. *Nice Wanton* (London, 1560), in Farmer edition, *Dramatic Writings*, p. 95. See also pp. 106, 113–14.

the sides, while he is but a child, lest he wax stubborn, and give no more force of thee."[10]

More important than the prevention of mischief was the bending of the child's will. In his *Positions Concerning the Training Up of Children* (1581), the Merchant Taylor's School's head Richard Mulcaster praised the rod as the "mean which in a multitude may work obedience."[11] For him, beating brought about the child's humiliation, out of which should come the habit of patient obedience. In his treatise "On the Early Education of Children" (1529) Erasmus condemned such schoolmasters who justified flogging with the argument that *"nihil commeruit . . . sed erat humiliandus"* (the child didn't deserve it but should be humiliated).[12] Above all, Mulcaster and other disciplinarians believed that they would thus fashion a child appropriate for a monarchy, one who "in his tender age showeth himself obedient to schoolorders, and either will not lightly offend, or if he do, will take his punishment gently: without either much repining, or great stomaching."[13] Such a child is not ambitious and at home is "so obsequious to parents, so courteous among servants, so dutiful toward all, with whom he hath to deal."[14]

The plot of *The Disobedient Child* purports to demonstrate this

10. W. Averell, *A Dyall for Dainty Darlings, rockt in the cradle of securitie. A Glass for all disobedient sonnes to look in, A myrrour for vertuous maydes* (London, 1584), sig. D2v.

11. Richard Mulcaster, *Positions wherin those primitive circumstances be examined, which are necessarie for the training up of children, either for skill in their booke, or health in their bodie* (London, 1581), reprint, ed. Robert Hebert Quick (London: Longmans, Green, 1888), p. 274. As this book went to press, I consulted a new edition of the *Positions*, ed. William Barker (Toronto: University of Toronto Press, 1994), which lists textual variants and offers a valuable introduction.

12. Erasmus, *De pueris statim ac liberaliter instituendis* (1529), ed. Jean-Claude Margolin, in Desiderius Erasmus, *Opera Omnia*, vol. 1, bk. 2 (Amsterdam: North-Holland, 1971), p. 57. In most cases the translations of this text are my own, but I have also used the translation by Beert C. Verstraete, "A Declamation on the Subject of Early Liberal Education for Children," in *Collected Works of Erasmus*, vol. 26: *Literary and Educational Writings*, vol. 4, ed. J. K. Sowards (Toronto: University of Toronto Press, 1985), as noted in the text.

13. Mulcaster, *Positions*, p. 150.

14. Ibid., p. 151. Halpern comments upon this passage: "For Mulcaster, the ability to endure punishment 'gently' signifies a global disposition that will manifest itself in all social and political relations: with parents, companions, servants, and monarchs. . . . Schooling imbues all such relations with a style of restraint . . . which bears a specific class character but attempts to extend itself throughout the social body" (*Poetics*, pp. 27–28).

theme. The child's position resembles a subject's resistance to a despot, when he defiantly claims: "Nay, by the mass, I hold ye a groat, / Those cruel tyrants cut not my throat: / Better it were myself did slay, / Than they with the rod my flesh should flay."[15] In later life, however, the son is ultimately punished for avoiding pain and mastery by marriage to a violent shrew. The last episodes of the play display his wife's brutality: when the now grown-up son fails to do the laundry correctly, she pummels him and confines him to the house.[16] The Perorator interprets the play's "witty lesson" as signifying that here a father may learn "betimes to correct his son being tender, / And not let him be lost and undone / With wantonness, of mischief the mother; / For as long as the twig is gentle and pliant. . . . With small force and strength it may be bent . . . / This twig to a child may well be applied, / Which, in his childhood and age of infancy, / With small correction may be amended, / Embracing the school with heart and body."[17] That is, the child may be easily molded while young: the bending of his body, like the gardener's tying up the young vine, is both a metaphor for and a cause of regulated behavior.

The Disobedient Child also tells us that corporal punishment makes you a man. Without it, a boy will be misled by mischief's "mother" and later be subject to the tyranny of women, a trope for the tyranny of desire and will.[18] Enrollment in school, whether under a tutor at home or in a town or church, should mark a boy's separation from the world of women (traditionally at the age of seven). If a boy does not bow to the socially accepted violence of the schoolmaster, the play tells us, he will be crushed by illegitimate and tyrannical feminine violence, which imitates that of the tyrannical schoolmaster. The play signals this fear with a curious episode preceding the son's marriage, in which a female cook herself tries to act the grammar master, claiming that "in times past I went to school, / And of my Latin primer I took assay."

15. Ingelend, *Disobedient Child*, pp. 50–51.
16. Ibid., pp. 78–79.
17. Ibid., pp. 88–89.
18. See Rebecca W. Bushnell, *Tragedies of Tyrants: Political Thought and Theater in the English Renaissance* (Ithaca: Cornell University Press, 1990), chaps. 1 and 2, on the association of the tyranny of women with the tyranny of desire and lack of self-control.

Her efforts are mockingly misunderstood, when translated into vulgar English by the man to whom she displays her learning.[19]

The Disobedient Child thus offers two potentially contradictory justifications for the beating of male children. The most obvious message is that the boy should be punished to teach him to submit. *The Disobedient Child* also suggests, however, that if a boy is not punished early, his later punishment will be the worse kind of submission: to a woman. Rather than becoming rebellious or proud, the child will become overly submissive and thus unmanly. One can resolve this contradiction by arguing that corporal punishment produces fear of the authority that exercises social control and thus leads to self-control; without that fear the child lacks self-control, a disorder symbolized by his domination by a woman. However, this logic is not worked out in the play text. Instead, the simple message is that lacking a schoolmaster's beating a man will be beaten by his wife.[20] In presenting them as opposed alternatives, the play also suggests an uncomfortable analogy between the schoolmaster's and the shrew's tyranny, both forms of uncontrolled passion.

Early humanist arguments against pedagogical flogging address such slippages in the defense of corporal punishment. First, they shift the focus from the school's function of social training to its role in teaching letters. Most often, they argue that, rather than encouraging children to learn through pleasure and love, flogging turns them away from books, creating the kind of hatred that Will Summer expresses in Thomas Nashe's *Summer's Last Will and Testament*: "Here, before all this company, I profess my self an open enemy to ink and paper. I'll make it good upon the accidence's body, that in speech is the devil's Pater Noster: Nouns and Pronouns, I pronounce you as traitors to boys' buttocks: Syntaxis and Prosodia, you are tormentors of wit, and good for nothing but to get a schoolmaster two pence a week."[21] The humanists moved explicit attention from the mastery of the mind and

19. Ingelend, *Disobedient Child*, pp. 59–60.

20. Ariès argues that in England the linking of self-control with corporal punishment began only in the nineteenth century (*Centuries*, p. 265).

21. Thomas Nashe, *Summers Last Will and Testament*, in *The Works of Thomas Nashe*, ed. Ronald B. McKerrow (Oxford: Basil Blackwell, 1958), vol. 3, pp. 279–80.

body to the "allurement" to learning.[22] In structuring the relationship of student and teacher as one of love, Erasmus understood flogging itself as a form of perverse eroticism. He tells of a master who loved him (*praeceptor cui prae caeteris eram charus*) yet decided to demonstrate that great love by the test of the rod, accusing Erasmus unjustly of a crime and beating him. As Erasmus wrote, this abuse drove out all "love of study" (*studiorum amorem*) from him and dejected his spirit so that he nearly wasted away with sorrow.[23] Like Roger Ascham and Thomas Elyot, Erasmus advocated a controlled eros in teaching (evident in the amorous vocabulary of this passage),[24] the opposite of the sadism of teachers "swollen with pride of their learning, capricious, alcoholic and savage, satisfying their base nature . . . while gaining pleasure from torture of others (*ex alieno cruciatu capiant voluptatem*)."[25] Because the humanists idealized the schoolroom, in Roger Ascham's words, as the "house of play and pleasure, and not of fear and bondage,"[26] they saw the flogging master's infliction of pain as demonstrating his own lack of erotic self-control.[27]

22. *The Scholemaster* begins precisely on this note when Ascham's interlocutors discuss the ways in which "young children, were sooner allured by love, than driven by beating, to attain good learning" (Roger Ascham, *The Scholemaster* [London, 1570; reprint, ed., Edward Arber, Boston: Willard Small, 1888], p. 48).

23. Erasmus, *De pueris*, p. 56. On the function of eros or seduction in teaching, see two essays in a special edition of *Yale French Studies*, edited by Barbara Johnson, called *The Pedagogical Imperative: Teaching as a Literary Genre* (*Yale French Studies* 63 [1982]): Joan De Jean, "*La Nouvelle Héloïse*, or the Case for Pedagogical Deviation" (pp. 98–116); and Jane Gallop, "The Immoral Teachers" (pp. 117–28).

24. See also Thomas Elyot, *The Boke named The Governour* (London, 1531), ed. H. H. S. Croft (1883; reprint, New York: Burt Franklin, 1967), vol. 1, p. 32: "Not withstanding, I would not have them enforced by violence to learn, but according to the counsel of Quintilian, to be sweetly allured thereto with praises and such pretty gifts as children delight in."

25. Erasmus, *De pueris*, p. 56. See Quintilian's condemnation of corporal punishment in the *Institutio oratoria*, bk. 1.3.15–17, where he alludes darkly to shameful abuses in corporal punishment, of which modesty forbids him to speak, but which clearly have erotic significance.

26. Ascham, *Scholemaster*, p. 47.

27. See Elizabeth Wirth Marvick's discussion of pedagogic sadomasochism in *Louis XIII: The Making of a King* (New Haven: Yale University Press, 1986). In the case of Louis XIII, whose father insisted that his governors " 'whip him every time he is stubborn or does something bad . . . there is nothing in the world that will do him more good' " (p. 30), she recounts how Louis himself "sometimes submitted to whipping with

While they condemned flogging as the expression of unrestrained passion, the humanist theorists also feared its cruelty would bring forth a generation of slaves rather than Mulcaster's obedient subjects. The humanist argument assumed that a productive subject would be a "free-born" gentleman, whether by birth or training. For example, because Henry Peacham was concerned with the education of "the compleat gentleman," he censured those teachers who practiced "indiscretion in correction, in using all natures alike, and that with immoderation, or rather plain cruelty." Unlike base natures, "the noble, generous and best natures, are won by commendation, enkindled by glory; . . . to whom conquest and shame are a thousand tortures."[28] Writers like Peacham believed that flogging was an inappropriate way to train one inherently "gentle"; worse, beating might turn one who was noble into a slave. As Erasmus puts it, it is slavish (*servile*) to change only from fear of punishment; but "by consensus 'our' sons are called free (*liberos*), and should thus have a 'liberal education' (*liberalis educatio*), not a servile one (*seruili multum dissimilis*)."[29]

For the humanist who sought to establish an absolute mastery of love, "a slavish disposition" implied servility, but also, paradoxically, a propensity to violent resistance. In his treatise *De tradendis disciplinis* (1531), the Spanish humanist and educational theorist Juan Luis Vives described how in town or church schools, severe discipline might have a particularly bad effect on children already inclined to vice: faced with severe teachers, they become "hardened against both the word and the wound [or blow] (*obdurant ad verba, et verbera*)." "Egged on by their comrades, or driven by the sweetness of pleasure (*dulcedine voluptatis*)," they continue to suffer punishment. Only fear can keep such a child to his duty, but "fear makes him into a slave (*mancipium*)."[30] Vives thus

---

apparent enjoyment. . . . The bundle of switches that was applied to his bare or covered buttocks was called the *verges*—a word that also means penis" (p. 31). Halpern argues that the humanist rejection of flogging fashioned the teacher into "the edifying spectacle of the pedagogue who restrains himself from violence" (*Poetics*, pp. 28–29).

28. Henry Peacham, *The Compleat Gentleman* (London, 1622), p. 23.

29. Erasmus, *De pueris*, p. 57.

30. Juan Luis Vives, *De tradendis disciplinis* (1531), bk. 2, chap. 1, p. 282, in *Opera Omnia*, vol. 6 (1745; reprint London: Gregg Press, 1964). The translations are my own, but I consulted *On Education. A Translation of the "De Tradendis Disciplinis" of Juan Luis Vives*, ed. and trans. Foster Watson (Cambridge: Cambridge University Press, 1913), p.

acutely observes two important points about corporal punishment. First, schoolchildren resist as a community and will push a companion to disobey rather than obey. This community defines itself in opposition to the master's authority and is more powerful, just as the desire for pleasure overcomes the fear of pain.[31] The violent schoolmaster hinders desire and community, with the result that the child becomes even more unruly. Second, under this law of violence when the child does obey it is false obedience based on fear, and such obedience, Vives argues, is not the freeman's willing service but the craven bowing of the slave.

Before we are tempted to praise Vives's insight, however, we should remember that he thought the rod useful at home, where the child is alone under the daily influence of parents, and love comes first—then fear. If love is not enough, writes Vives, "awe and fear will help (*reverentia et metus*), which should be instilled in infancy and confirmed with usage; thus the child could neither hope nor desire to be freed from them (*et a quo spes non sit solvi ut possint, saepe ne voluntas quidem*)." The *virga*, or rod of discipline, "should always be in sight and at his back (*disciplinae virga perpetuo ante oculos pueri, et circum dorsum versabitur*)," as Solomon recommended.[32] Vives may have confirmed the notion of a "free service" in love, but in fact he reverses it by giving the child no choice at all to want freedom when paternal love becomes a bond far stronger than the schoolmaster's tyranny.

Erasmus also compared the education of free children to that of slaves in a way that seems quite "liberal" while also making an implicit analogy between children and slaves. He reminded his reader of masters who would have never gained the loyalty of their slaves if they ruled by the lash. If corrigible (*sanabilis*), a slave is better corrected by warnings and a sense of shame and duty than by beatings. On the contrary, if incorrigible (*insanibilis*), a slave will be hardened into ex-

---

67. Vives would be including here the various types of "public" (i.e., outside of the home) schools, e.g., "petty" schools for the education of younger children, grammar schools for older ones, and church schools including the cathedral schools and chantries.

31. See Thomas, *Rule and Misrule*, pp. 20–35, on the expression of student solidarity in early modern schools and, in particular, the practice of "barring-out," a form of strike which the class would use to bargain for holidays.

32. Vives, *De tradendis*, bk. 2, chap. 2, p. 285.

treme evil by beating. By analogy, then, Erasmus argued, if a wise man prefers "slaves who serve 'freely' (*seruos ita habeant ut seruiant liberaliter*), or free men (*libertos*) before slaves as servants, then how absurd it is to render someone naturally free a slave through the process of education (*quam absurdum est e natura liberis educatione reddere seruos*)."[33] While distinguishing between "free children" and "slaves," the analogy places them in exactly the same position, where, like the slave, the child enveloped in kindness does not know he or she is being ruled. Conversely, as in Vives, violence is understood to produce resistance. Teachers should abjure violence, thus, because it makes children, like slaves, at once too servile and not servile enough.

The conflict between wanting "free" children and needing to control them is part of a more general incoherence in the humanist version of a teacher's authority. This instability stands out when Erasmus's text tries to differentiate between a schoolmaster and a father: "A master can exert his authority only through compulsion, but a father who appeals to his son's sense of decency and liberality (*pater pudore ac liberalitate consuefacit filium*) can gradually build up in him a spontaneous capacity for moral conduct that is untainted by any motive of fear; and whether or not his father is with him, the son will remain steadfast in this principle."[34] As Vives did, Erasmus contrasted the master's authority with that of the father, insofar as the master has no natural authority over the child, but rather rules him "by compulsion." The pedagogic relationship is artificial, instituted too late, whereas from the beginning the father can train the child into "spontaneous" moral conduct.[35] Erasmus's rhetoric hints at a persistent anxiety that the teacher's authority is, in fact, illegitimate. Any teacher who cannot rule humanely shows that "he know[s] not how rule free men (*nescire imperare liberis*)." The difference between a father and master resembles that "between a king and tyrant (*regem ac tyrannum*)," for a king rules by nature and a tyrant by force.

When Erasmus compared the schoolmaster's lack of natural author-

---

33. Erasmus, *De pueris*, pp. 57–58.

34. Ibid., p. 58; here the translation is from Verstraete's translation of Erasmus, *"Early Liberal Education,"* p. 328.

35. Note, however, that nothing is said here about the father's rule being "natural": what Erasmus dwells on is the fact that fatherly rule is practiced over the long term.

ity to that of a tyrant, he also affirmed the right to resist both, noting the irony that "we remove a tyrant from a republic (*tyrannum sub-mouemus a republica*), but as parents we subject our sons to tyrant-schoolmasters (*filiis vel tyrannos asciscimus*) or set ourselves up as tyrants over them (*vel ipsi in eos tyrannidem exercemus*)." Finally, this ever-slippery text suggests that we might not be able to distinguish between the king and tyrant, father and master at all, for if the father beats the child he becomes like the tyrannical schoolmaster. In order to support the restriction of the schoolmaster's power, equivalent to the king's containment by the law, Erasmus later cited examples of parental brutality, reminding the reader that "human and humane laws restrain paternal power (*humanae leges patriam potestatem temperant*)" and allow servants legal recourse against their master's abuse.[36] Thus, even while he set up a model for a "natural" and absolute system for controlling children, Erasmus justified resistance to that control by comparing it to legitimate political resistance.

At the core of arguments about flogging we thus find the early modern discourse of political authority, monarchy, tyranny and resistance, with the schoolroom a highly charged site for defining and acting out different poses of authority and resistance. Schoolmasters themselves were fond of calling the schoolmaster a prince, just as their critics liked to compare them to tyrants. Richard Mulcaster defended the flogging master in explicitly political language:

Is not obedience the best sacrifice, that [the student-subject] can offer up to his prince and governor, being directed and ruled by his country laws? And in the principles of government, is not his master his *monarchy*? and the school-laws his country laws? Whereunto if he submit himself both orderly in *performance* and patiently in *penance*, doth he not show a mind already armed, not to start from his duty? and so much the more, because his obedience to his master is more voluntary, than that to his prince, which is mere necessary.[37]

36. Erasmus, *De pueris*, p. 58.
37. Mulcaster, *Positions*, pp. 151–52.

For Mulcaster, as opposed to Erasmus, the student's submission to the teacher's rule was "voluntary" as opposed to compulsory, unlike the "necessary" service to the monarch, but the teacher's rod was still the monarch's sword and scepter. Mulcaster proclaimed his belief that "the rod may no more be spared in schools, than the sword may in the Prince's hand. By the rod I mean correction, and awe: if that scepter be thought too fearful for boys, which our time devised not, but received it from anciently, I will not strive with any man for it, so he leave us some mean which in a multitude may work obedience."[38] As a "scepter" the rod symbolized male authority and the right to speak: as a "sword" it expressed that power through the threat of violence.[39]

As we have seen, however, the obverse of comparing ruler and master is naming the master as the tyrant, at once recognizing his power and undermining it. (See Figure 2, for Hans Holbein's marginal drawing illustrating the "tyranny of school masters.") Several writers used the curious anecdote about the deposed tyrant Dionysus of Syracuse's putative interlude as a schoolmaster to this double effect. Peacham made the comparison to denigrate the flogging master, who handles the boys as roughly as "Dionysus himself taking revenge upon the buttocks of poor boys for the loss of his kingdom."[40] In his *Boke Named the Governour* (1531), Thomas Elyot used the example of Dionysus oddly in comparing a schoolmaster's authority to a monarch's:

38. Ibid., pp. 273–74. See also Ascham, *Scholemaster*, p. 47: "M. Peter, as one somewhat severe of nature, said plainly, that the rod only, was the sword, that must keep, the school in obedience, and the scholar in good order."

39. Not everyone would have assented to this comparison. In the scene from *A Midsommer nights Dreame* cited above, a sword is something to be used by someone of dignity against an equal, unlike the schoolmaster's rod. In *The Second Part of King Henry the Fourth*, in 1623 folio facs., pt. 2, p. 92, (4.1) Hastings compares Bolingbroke's exhaustion of his own power to that of a schoolmaster who has worn down all his switches: "Besides, the King hath wasted all his rods/On late offenders, that he now doth lack/ The very instruments of chastisement:/So that his power, like to a fangless lion,/May offer, but not hold." This passage has a double meaning: it would appear to elevate the schoolmaster in the analogy, but the context draws attention to Henry's lack of power and authority, which undercuts the master's image. As Phyllis Rackin has pointed out to me, it would be interesting to pursue the implications of the schoolmistress's wielding of the clearly phallic rod (in analogy to Elizabeth I's own possession of the scepter).

40. Peacham, *Compleat Gentleman*, p. 24.

Figure 2. The tyranny of schoolmasters. Marginal drawing by Hans Holbein, in Holbein's copy of Erasmus's *The Praise of Folly* (Basel: 1515). Reproduced from this copy of Desiderius Erasmus, *Encomium moriae* (Basel: 1515), in facsimile ed. Heinrich Alfred Schmid (Basel: Henning Oppermann Verlag, 1931), by permission of the Department of Special Collections, Van Pelt-Dietrich Library, University of Pennsylvania.

Moreover teaching representeth the authority [*auctoritie*] of a prince: wherefore Dionysus, king of Sicily, when he was for tyranny expelled by his people, he came into Italy, and there in a common school taught grammar, where with, when he was of his enemies embraided, and called a school master, he answered them, that although the Sicilians had exiled him, yet in despite of them all he had reigned, noting thereby the authority that he had over his scholars. And when it was of him demanded what availed him Plato or philosophy, wherein he had been studious: he answered that they caused him to sustain adversity patiently, and made his exile to be to him more facile and easy: which courage and wisdom considered of his people, they eftsoon restored him unto his realm and estate royal, where, if he had procured against them hostility or wars, or had returned into Sicily with any violence, I suppose the people would have always resisted him, and have kept him in perpetual exile: as the Romans did the proud king Tarquin, whose son ravished Lucrece.[41]

At first, the comparison between the schoolmaster and the tyrant seems inapt to illustrate Elyot's point about teaching representing the prince's authority, especially given Dionysus's defiant reply to his enemies and the marginal identification of him as "Dionysus the tyrant." But then we see that, while a schoolmaster, Dionysus was morally reformed, demonstrating courage and wisdom and, most pertinently, patient suffering. The people restored Dionysus to "natural" authority or "estate royal" for having learned self-restraint as a teacher. Even more remarkably, given the monarchical bias of Elyot's text, the comparison ends by insisting on the people's ability to resist Dionysus should he offer violence. In comparing the tyrant and schoolmaster, the passage betrays the suspicion that the teacher's rule was "compulsive" and unnatural, yet the narrative then shows the tyrant changed into a proper king by the experience of being a schoolmaster. At the same time, this authority was contingent on his virtue and subject to the will of the governed. The teacher, in this comparison, is thus figured as both morally authoritative and politically constrained.

Such anxieties about the teacher's authority reflect the uneven history of the social status of both private tutors and public schoolmasters. Accounts of this subject establish a pattern of rise and fall in the reputation of teachers from the twelfth through the fifteenth centuries. From his study of the municipal and legal records of late medieval England, Nicholas Orme concludes that in the twelfth century school-

41. Elyot, *Governour*, p. 34.

masters garnered a fair amount of respect, evident in their relatively high salaries, the size of their estates, and the frequency of their appointment to high office.[42] Orme detects a gradual decline after this time, which began to reverse only in the fifteenth century.[43] This revival was particularly evident in royal education, where the grammar master (as opposed to the knightly tutor) gained increasing importance. Orme reports that "the fifteenth century also provides us with the first clear cases of professional schoolmasters being employed to teach the prince his grammar."[44] Outside of the royal household, patrons endowed more grammar schools, which for teachers marked an improvement on the chantries, cathedral, and petty schools, because the endowed school provided the master a consistent salary and some job security. Some contemporaries cited Cardinal Wolsey as an emblem of the changing status of schoolmasters. Erasmus described "the fallen Cardinal as fortune's plaything, who had risen from a schoolmaster to be master of a kingdom ('*Hic est fortunae ludus, ex ludimagistro subvectus est ad regnum.*')."[45] A few writers showed real concern about the schoolmasters' ambitions: in his ideal commonwealth (1559), Ferrarius Montanus warned that schoolmasters must be "men of a good zeal, and such as stand not too much in their own conceit, challenging themselves a glorious name of profound learning."[46]

42. Nicholas Orme, *Education and Society in Medieval and Renaissance England* (London: Hambledon Press, 1989), p. 7. Orme observes that "a twelfth-century schoolmaster could be as learned as anyone, and consequently well qualified for appointment to high office" (p. 51).

43. Ibid., pp. 52–53.

44. Orme, *From Childhood*, p. 22.

45. Letter to Juan Vergara, ca. January 13, 1530 (no. 2253), in *Opus Epistolarum Desideri Erasmi Roterdami*, ed. P. S. Allen, H. M. Allen, and H. W. Garrod (Oxford: Oxford University Press, 1906–47), cited by Maria Dowling, *Humanism in the Age of Henry VIII* (London: Croom Helm, 1986), p. 122.

46. *A woorke of Joannes Ferrarius Montanus, touchynge the good orderynge of a common weale*, trans. William Bavande (London, 1559), fol. 77r–v. Ferrarius continues "but they must be learned indeed . . . and such as can take their scholars as their children, whom the scholars must so much the more reverence, because they receive the beginning of their living of their parents, but of living well, of their schoolmasters." See also Kenneth Charlton, *Education in Renaissance England* (London: Routledge and Kegan Paul, 1965), p. 72, on the careful negotiation between the scholar's ambition and service to the commonweal in Thomas Starkey's *Dialogue between Reginald Pole and Thomas Lupset* (1535).

However, despite these gains and, as Maria Dowling contends, "despite the propaganda of the humanist theorists the status of tutors remained low."[47] Such was the experience of John Palsgrave and Richard Croke, tutors of Henry Fitzroy, duke of Richmond and a bastard son of Henry VIII who once had expectations for the succession. When Palsgrave taught Fitzroy in 1525–26, he wrote to Thomas More complaining of his poverty and his effort to have some sway in a household that did not respect learning and encouraged his charge to hawk and hunt instead.[48] When Richard Croke replaced Palsgrave, he too had little success in setting the day's schedule or choosing the child's schoolroom companions. This kind of unstable situation surely stimulated the increasingly vehement defenses in pedagogical texts of the grammar master's professional status.

Literary representations of teachers similarly suggest their professional insecurity and social unpopularity. Shakespeare's teacher characters, for example, seem to have difficulty mastering anything or anyone. In *The Second Part of Henry the Sixth*, Jack Cade condemns the Clerk of Chartam, a hapless petty-school teacher, to hanging as a villain, conjurer, and traitor because he can write.[49] In *Antony and Cleopatra*, Octavius is offended that Antony sends his schoolmaster as an ambassador: the tutor describes himself as "of late as petty to his ends / As is the morn-dew on the myrtle leaf / To his grand sea."[50] In *Love's Labor's Lost*, Holofernes has a larger role—but only to be mocked for his pedantry, ignorance, and pretension to play three of the Worthies.[51] The King's "academy" itself avoids the problem of the royal tutor's status by having no teachers at all; only noble students who will study, as the king puts it, "to know which else we should not know," a phrase

---

47. Dowling, *Humanism*, p. 196, recounts several other examples.

48. *The Correspondence of Sir Thomas More*, ed. Elizabeth Frances Rogers (Princeton: Princeton University Press, 1947), pp. 403–5. (This letter is misdated 1529.) See Dowling, *Humanism*, on this controversy, pp. 210–11.

49. *The Second Part of Henry the Sixth*, in 1623 folio facs., pt. 2, pp. 138–39 (4.2).

50. *Anthony and Cleopatra*, in 1623 folio facs., pt. 3, p. 356 (3.13).

51. Scholars have speculated that the depiction of Holofernes alludes to a variety of real-life schoolteachers or pedants including Richard Mulcaster, George Chapman, and John Florio. See Richard L. DeMolen, "Richard Mulcaster and the Elizabethan Theatre," *Theatre Survey* 13 (1972): 28–41.

that Berowne takes as, "To know the thing I am forbid to know," or to know "things hid and barred . . . from common sense."[52] Armado and Moth's relationship complements this suppression of teachers, for, as G. R. Hibbard remarks, in their "little academe" the "relationship of teacher to the taught is inverted" when the boy addresses his master as "negligent student."[53]

In the household and outside of it the child's parents offered the clearest challenge to the master's rule. Some schoolmasters depicted the home as a place of freedom and indulgence.[54] Mothers, in particular, were blamed, just as any female role in the child's education was suspect. One passage set for the boys to imitate (in Latin) in an early Tudor schoolbook ventriloquizes the master's disdain for the mother, warning that "though thou have been brought up here afore with thy mother wantonly, yet I counsel thee to put out of thy mind that wantonness here, for and if thou do not, thou shall say hereafter that thou hast a great cause to complain."[55] Elsewhere, the mother is blamed for letting the child sleep late, cursing in his presence, and playing with him like a doll.[56] The schoolmaster's relationship to the child's father was more complex because, as we have seen, in humanist pedagogic theory, the ideal teacher's authority was often compared to the father's at the same time that the real master competed with him. A common trope casts the schoolmaster as the "father" of the mind,

---

52. *Loves Labour's Lost*, in 1623 folio facs., pt. 1, p. 122 (1.1).

53. See G. R. Hibbard, introduction to *Love's Labours' Lost* (Oxford: Clarendon Press, 1990), p. 34 : "It is Moth who instructs and provides the examples and definitions — 'Define, define, well-educated infant,' says Armado to him at one point (1.2.90); . . . Moth's most telling way of going to work is by repeating, and in the process, reversing whatever Armado says." Note the similarity here to the structure of the catechism, where the student who is questioned holds the floor far longer and appears to instruct the questioner.

54. This gesture may have its rhetorical origins in Quintilian, *Institutio oratoria*, bk. 1.2.5–9, where Quintilian blames parents for spoiling their children.

55. Orme, *Education*, p. 145, reproduced from an exercise in a manuscript, British Library Royal MS 12.B.XX. fols. 35–49.

56. Nelson, ed., *Fifteenth-Century School Book*, p. 13: "The mothers must have them to play withal instead of puppets, as children were born to japes and trifles. They bold them both in word and deed to do what they list, and with wantonness and sufferance shamefully they run on [a]head." See also schoolbook exercises in Orme, *Education*, p. 139, which castigate mothers for letting scholars sleep late.

in contrast to the father (and the mother) of the body. In Thomas Becon's catechism, the son (who voices all the arguments in favor of corporal punishment) asks that the scholars revere the master "even as another father. . . . For if that father which only begetteth the gross body, in this point not much differing from the brute beasts, be worthy of honor; how much more is he to be honored and reverenced, which tilleth, trimmeth, decketh, and garnisheth both body and mind with honest virtues and godly qualities!"[57] Both parents were thus contaminated (the mother unambiguously) with the corruption of the flesh.[58] In his *De tradendis disciplinis*, Vives carried the argument even further, calling the teacher the parent of the child's *animus* or rational soul: "the teacher is the truer parent, insofar as the *animus* is the truer part of man, than the body *(tanto scilicet praeceptor est parens verior, quanto verius ex homine est animus, quam corpus)*."[59] Just as in early modern historical literature the father often usurps the mother's place,[60] here the schoolmaster's spiritual parentage supersedes that of the father, who merely begets the body.

The confusion implicit in this analogy with parental authority permeates humanist pedagogical discourse. Just as later defenses of monarchy set up the king as a patriarch, the teacher's identification with the father naturalized the former's position and removed the element of compulsion.[61] In humanist educational theory the natural quality of the relationship between teacher and pupil is evident in their mutual affection rather than the threatening of the rod. Peacham cited Vives

57. *A New Catechisme sette forth Dialogue-Wise in Familiare talke between the father and the son*, first printed in *The Works of Thomas Becon* (London, 1564), reprinted in *The Catechism of Thomas Becon*, ed. John Ayre (1844; reprint, New York: Johnson Reprint Co., 1968), pp. 385–86.

58. See the qualification of this statement in the exercises reproduced in Orme, *Education*, p. 142.

59. Vives, *De tradendis*, bk. 2, chap. 4, p. 295.

60. See Phyllis Rackin, *Stages of History: Shakespeare's English Chronicles* (Ithaca: Cornell University Press, 1990), chap. 4, pp. 146–202.

61. On "natural" arguments for patriarchalism, see Gordon J. Schochet, *The Authoritarian Family and Political Attitudes in Seventeenth-Century England: Patriarchalism in Political Thought* (New Brunswick: Transaction, 1988). Schochet argues that the full political use of patriarchalism entered England with the theory of absolutism: not even James himself depended completely on patriarchal theory, though he used patriarchal analogies.

on this subject when he wrote that, instead of beating, "there ought to be a reciprocal and a mutual affection betwixt the master and scholar, which judicious Erasmus and Lodovicus Vives . . . do principally require, *Patris in illum induendo affectum*, by putting on a Father's affection toward him: and, as Pliny saith, *Amore, non artifice docente, qui optimus Magister est*, to win his heart and affection by love, which is the best Master."[62] The naming of the teacher as a better "father" relied on a distinction between master and parent: the master's authority was superior precisely because it was not fleshly. This distinction marks the competition between parental and pedagogic authority, usually mentionable only when one is speaking of the mother.

Among the humanist teachers, Roger Ascham went furthest in separating parental and pedagogic authority when he tried to grope his way out of such contradictions. In a well-known passage of *The Scholemaster*, Ascham wrote of a conversation he had with Lady Jane Grey when he found her reading while others were delighting in sport. She attributed her love of reading to her affection for her master and fear of her parents:

> One of the greatest benefits, that ever God gave me, is, that he sent me so sharp and severe parents, and so gentle a schoolmaster. For when I am in presence either of father or mother, whether I speak, keep silence, sit, stand, or go, eat, drink, be merry, or sad, be sewing, playing, dancing, or doing any thing else, I must do it, as it were, in such weight, measure, and number, even so perfectly, as God made the world, or else I am so sharply taunted, so cruelly threatened, yea presently some times, with pinches, nips, and bobs, and other ways, which I will not name, for the honor I bear them, so without measure misordered, that I think my self in hell, till time come, that I must go to Mr. Aylmer, who teacheth me so gently, so pleasantly, with such fair allurements to learning, that I think all the time nothing, while I am with him. And when I am called from him, I fall on weeping, because, whatsoever I do else, but learning, is full of grief, trouble, fear, and whole misliking unto me.[63]

---

62. Peacham, *Compleat Gentleman*, pp. 24–25. Peacham conveniently assumed for the moment that natural fathers do not beat their children.

63. Ascham, *Scholemaster*, pp. 101–2.

Whereas in other humanist texts the teacher is asked to imitate the parent-child relationship of love and dignity, here the parents are the tyrannical tormentors; the teacher Aylmer, however, offers gentle pleasure, much as mothers were accused of doing. The passage thus reverses the convention whereby the parents are seen to indulge the child while the master attempts to enforce some discipline. The teacher's approach to the pupil is vaguely eroticized as "allurement," or motherly affection (more acceptable when the pupil is a girl), but not sadomasochism. In this passage, Ascham is reaching toward a pedagogical practice that did not reproduce the law of the father (ironically appropriate in the case of this particular student, whose own claims to sovereignty were so problematic and who fell victim to men who would claim power through her).

In a subsequent passage, Ascham generalizes this anecdotal separation of parental, political, and pedagogic authority into a matter of principle. He maintains the importance of strict discipline, but reserves it for "fatherly correction, than masterly beating, rather for manners, than for learning: for other places, than for schools." The text recalls the discipline used by the Romans, "where we see that children were under the rule of three persons: *Praeceptore, Paedagogo, Parente*." The schoolmaster taught learning, the governor manners, and the parent obedience. Ascham recommends that the schoolmaster not "confound" the teaching of learning and manners (and thus their correction), but "he shall well do both, if wisely he do appoint diversity of time, and separate place, for either purpose: using always such discreet moderation, as the schoolhouse should be counted a sanctuary against fear."[64] Whereas other teachers such as Mulcaster more closely connected education in "manners" with "learning," Ascham envisioned dividing them, either as the functions of two persons or practiced in two different places: one for severe correction and one that remained a safe space, free from fear, where reading and writing could be detached from the violent imposition of obedience. This image of the schoolhouse as a "sanctuary against fear" recalls the visualization of the "space" of the conscience, which political authority may not violate, or conversely the emerging private space of the home, imagined as a ref-

64. Ibid., pp. 102–4.

uge from political oppression and the pressures of public life. In effect, Ascham attempted to shape the place of learning as one which, rather than imitating and maintaining political institutions, offered an escape from them.[65]

We thus see two divided, if connected, impulses in humanist pedagogy's opposition to corporal punishment in schools. Humanism offers to form a free citizen, who learns in a free space of love, pleasure, and play, marked off from the political sphere and even from the family.[66] At the same time, since humanist thinking defines freedom in familial and political terms, and especially in terms of self-rule, the schoolroom is inevitably structured in analogy to the family and state. The teacher becomes the father and the monarch—or the tyrant. If he is the tyrant, the student will fight for freedom against him; conversely, the child only becomes "free" in becoming like the teacher/monarch/father. The teacher's own freedom and sovereignty, in turn, are constantly compromised: he is authoritative but constrained because his authority is moral rather than inherited, and his power is circumscribed by the schoolroom walls. The humanist teacher is thus caught in a web of contradictions: like a father and opposed to the father's rule, a monarch in the classroom yet feared as a tyrant, a lover who holds the instrument of pain, a master who is also, in many cases, a servant of the family and the state.

EDUCATING THE PRINCE

Although I have highlighted Ascham's picture of the schoolroom as a "sanctuary from fear," I would not claim that Ascham was any great lover of freedom or that he had no interest in politics. On the contrary, the text just cited is followed by an extended complaint that the "youth of England [are] brought up with much liberty."[67] Further, this complaint modulates into a criticism of "great men" whose neglect of the

65. On Ascham's attempt "to negotiate the position of the pedagogic class within the reformed courtly/gentle society which the pedagogue claimed to form," see Jonathan Goldberg, *Writing Matter: From the Hands of the English Renaissance* (Stanford: Stanford University Press, 1990), pp. 43–44.

66. For a common humanist source of the notion of early study as play (*lusus*), see Quintilian, *Institutio oratoria*, bk. 1.1.20 and 26.

67. Ascham, *Scholemaster*, p. 104.

education and discipline of their own children allows "mean men's sons [to] come to great authority."[68] From here *The Scholemaster* launches into a general attack against the court and the nobility's lack of wisdom, demanding, "take heed therefore, ye great ones in the Court, yea though ye be the greatest of all, take heed, what ye do, take heed how ye live."[69] Ascham's awkward position thus subtly shifts from that of a schoolmaster giving advice to parents on child-rearing to that of a common man giving advice to his betters. In the midst of the argument, Ascham writes humbly of his being "one poor minister," who, as Elizabeth I's teacher, is thus blessed "in setting forward these excellent gifts of learning in this most excellent Prince." Given his status, at once low and elevated, he wonders about his right to criticize:[70]

> But perchance, some will say, I have stepped too far, out of my school, into the common wealth, from teaching a young scholar, to admonish great and noble men: yet I trust good and wise men will think and judge of me, that my mind was, not so much, to be busy and bold with them, that be great now, as to give true advice to them, that may be great hereafter. . . . Yet, if some will needs press me, that I am too bold with great men, and stray too far from my matter, I will answer them with *St. Paul, sive per contentionem, sive quocumque modo, modo Christus praedicetur, etc..* Even so, whether in place, or out of place, with my matter, or beside my matter, if I can hereby either provoke the good, or stay the ill, I shall think my writing herein well employed.

The schoolhouse that was depicted before as the scholar's "sanctuary from fear" becomes the hoped-for safe place for the *master* to speak out against social and political corruption. Ascham, clearly aware he might be seen to be stepping out of that place to speak of men at court, insists at first that he is staying in the schoolhouse, speaking only of children who might become great. But the second half of the passage becomes more defiant, answering those who think that he "strays" from his matter and his place by comparing Ascham with Paul,

68. Ibid., p. 109.
69. Ibid., p. 141.
70. Ibid., p. 140; see also pp. 131 and 144.

who preached of Jesus, however contentiously. While Ascham authorizes himself in this comparison, his text leaves him "out of order," whether in the schoolroom or outside it, just as his advice to the great ones marks itself clearly as a form of rhetorical disorderliness. Only at the end does Ascham return to his original position in his "sanctuary" and come back to his main theme of schooling: "But, to come down, from great men, and higher matters, to my little children, and poor schoolhouse again, I will, God willing, go forward orderly, as I purposed, to instruct children and young men."[71] His freedom to criticize seems at once attached to the schoolhouse and unfitting to it, for in the schoolroom he is both in place and out of place.

This problem of situating the schoolmaster in the social order pervades the rhetoric of all the literature of instruction to the gentleman and the prince. The schoolmaster strives to maintain his moral authority while acknowledging that he may be socially inferior to those he wishes to instruct. In one of Vives' own school exercises, stereotypical bad and good counselors quiz a boy prince about his submission to his schoolmasters. The bad counselor, Morobulus, wants the young prince Philip to go out for a walk. When Philip replies that he may not because of "Stunica and Sileceus," Morobulus protests, "Who are these Stunica and Sileceus? Are they not your subjects, over whom you have the command, not they over you? (*An non subditi tui, in quos tu habes imperium, non illi in te*)." Philip explains, "Stunica is my educator (*educator*), while Sileceus is my literary tutor (*institutor literarius*). Subjects of mine indeed they are, or to speak more exactly, of my father; but my father, to whom I am subject, placed them over me and subjected me to them (*praefecit illos mihi, et me illis subjecit*)." Morobolus cries in outrage, "What then! Did your father give your highness unto servitude to these men?" to which Philip weakly answers "I don't know." At this point, the good counselor, Sophobolus, interjects with humanist fervor:

> Certainly he made them thy servants (*servos tuos*): he wished them to stick close to thee, as eyes, ears, soul and mind, to be always engaged on thy behalf, each of them to put aside his own affairs, and to make thy affairs his

71. Ibid., pp. 144–45.

sole business, not so as to vex these by imperiousness; but that good and wise men should transform thy uncultivated manners into the virtue, glory and excellence of a man; not so as to make thee a slave, but truly a free man and truly a prince (*non quo te reddant mancipium, sed ut vere liberum*). If thou dost not obey them, then thou wilt be a slave of the lowest order (*tum demum servus eris extremae conditionis*), worst than those here among us who are employed, bought and sold from Ethiopia or Africa.

"Whose slave?" asks Morobulus, and Sophobolus retorts, "Not of men, certainly, but of vices, which are more importunate masters, and more intolerable than a dishonest and wicked man."[72] The analogy pedagogical theory made between the schoolroom and the state, and between schoolroom and home, suggests that teaching should inculcate a lifetime habit of obedience; however, in the royal classroom this model was complicated by the teacher's status as his scholar-prince's subject. Only the promise of eventual self-mastery offered an escape from political indecorum.

Though he himself was not a schoolmaster, Thomas Elyot knew that he might appear arrogant in giving advice on the education of the governing classes. In his "proem" to Henry VIII in *The Boke named the Governour*, Elyot exaggerates his deference to his king, describing his work as "not of presumption to teach any person, I myself having most need of teaching: but only to the intent that men which will be studious about the weal public may find the thing thereto expedient compendiously written."[73] Similarly, after a laborious attempt to establish a connection between wealth and virtue (which turns on the ability to pay for an education), Elyot protests that he has written this work "without arrogance or any spark of vain glory: but only to declare the fervent zeal that I have to my country" and to share his learning with "all the readers that be of any noble or gentle (*gentill*) courage" who will take "no little commodity" from it.[74] In the proem Elyot is thus careful to insist that he has none of the ambition associated with the

---

72. Vives, *Linguae latinae exercitatio* (1539), in *Opera Omnia*: vol. 1, p. 372; translated by Foster Watson in *Tudor School-Boy Life: The Dialogues of Juan Luis Vives* (London: J. M. Dent, 1908), pp. 173–74.

73. Elyot, *Governour*, p. cxcii.

74. Ibid., pp. 27–28.

rise of Wolsey (with whom Elyot was closely associated) or the scholar's arrogance of which Ferrarius was wary: rather, he is merely a public servant, a provider of "commodity" to his social superiors.[75]

However, in the body of his work, Elyot amplifies rather than diminishes the authority of teachers. We have already seen his peculiar use of the tale of Dionysus of Syracuse, claiming that "teaching representeth the authority [*auctoritie*] of a prince" yet reminding us that people have exiled princes when they turned into tyrants. In this "book called *The Governor*," the tutor's function is called "governance": Elyot offers as examples Phoenix's "rule" over Achilles; Epaminondas' mastery of Philip of Maecedon; and the case of Leonidas, tutor to Alexander the Great, who was given "rule and preeminence over all the masters and servants of Alexander."[76] The tutor or "governor" is directed to search for a grammar master "of sober and virtuous disposition," suitable for a young scholar characterized by "shamefastness" and a desire for praise.[77] Elyot points to grammar masters who were granted political status by the princes whom they taught: for example Mark Antony, who made his grammar master Proculus proconsul, and Alexander, who made his teacher consul, "which was the highest office, and in estate next the emperor."[78] The message here is hardly subtle: classical precedent not only demands subjecting princes to a greater

75. On the complexities of *The Governour*'s political stance—a cross between an educational treatise and a book meant "to impress Henry VIII with Elyot's merit as a potential counselor" (p. 56)—see Alistair Fox, "Sir Thomas Elyot and the Humanist Dilemma," in Fox and John Guy, eds., *Reassessing the Henrician Age: Humanism, Politics, and Reform, 1500–1550* (Oxford: Basil Blackwell, 1986), pp. 52–73.

76. Elyot writes that such a tutor should be "an ancient and worshipful man, in whom is approved to be much gentleness [*gentilnes*], mixed with gravity, and, as nigh as can be, such one as the child by imitation following may grow to be excellent. And if he be also learned, he is the more commendable" (*Governour*, pp. 36–37). See Halpern, *Poetics*, pp. 28–31, on imitation in pedagogy.

77. Elyot, *Governour*, pp. 50–51.

78. Ibid., p. 52. Compare here Erasmus, *Institutio principis christiani* (1516), ed. O. Herding, in Desiderius Erasmus, *Opera Omnia*, vol. 4, bk. 1 (Amsterdam: North-Holland, 1974), pp. 137–38, on the importance of honoring the teachers of the prince for their service to the state: while a country is indebted to a good prince, it owes more to the teacher who made him so through good counsel. Translations are my own, but I have consulted the translation by Neil M. Cheshire and Michael J. Heath, "On the Education of a Christian Prince," in *Collected Works of Erasmus*, vol. 27: *Literary and Educational Writings*, vol. 5, ed. A. H. T. Levi (Toronto: University of Toronto Press, 1986).

moral authority, but it also recommends elevating teachers to positions of real political power. Correspondingly, the sign of the modern age's decline is the lack of respect shown to masters: Elyot notes the small esteem and pay given schoolmasters despite their professional status.[79] He attributes the perceived decline in learning of "noble men" to "the pride, avarice, and negligence of parents, and the lack of fewness of sufficient masters or teachers," not to the inadequacy of schoolmasters themselves.[80]

The contradiction between the "teacher" Elyot's professions of humility and his examples of high-placed masters correcting princes evokes the paradoxes of that most rarefied form of teaching, the education of the prince. Much has been written about this topic as a popular genre of political writing, which offered the prince his ideal mirror and advised a teacher how to steer him that way.[81] I will focus, however, on a question buried deep in the discussions of the education of princes: if the prince refuses to obey his teacher, how should the master chastise his royal charge? How far was he allowed to go in the exercise of discipline? After all, the rod was meant to enforce the habit of bending, but this was the opposite of the monarch's stance. Indeed, in Shakespeare's *Richard II*, the Queen, chastising Richard for acting like a child when he gives in to Bolingbroke, asks incredulously if he will "Pupil-like, / Take thy correction mildly, kiss the rod, / And fawn on rage with base humility, / Which art a lion and a king of beasts?"[82] The question parallels the contemporary debate over resistance to tyranny, which asked what recourse the people had when the prince refused to conform to moral and positive law. Given such a charged climate, how would violent punishment shape the prince's authority, both as a child and when he came to be king?

Much of the literature on education tactfully avoided this issue, as-

79. Elyot, *Governour*, p. 115.

80. Ibid., p. 98.

81. On the *institutio principis* tradition, see Lester K. Born's introduction to Erasmus, *The Education of a Christian Prince* (New York: W. W. Norton, 1968); see also Quentin Skinner, *The Foundations of Modern Political Thought*: vol. 1, *The Renaissance* (Cambridge: Cambridge University Press, 1978), chaps. 5 and 8.

82. William Shakespeare, *The life and death of Richard II*, in folio facs., pt. 2, p. 41 (5.1).

suming that the royal scholar would be naturally good, and thus the master could easily lead him to virtue. In turn, the master's grace would make the scholar virtuous because the child would wish to imitate his teacher. In *The Education of a Christian Prince* (offered to the future Charles V in 1516), Erasmus advised that "the prince's tutor should severely check the licentiousness of youth (*vt praeceptoris seueritas aetatis premat lasciuiam*)," but in a moderate and friendly fashion. The tutor should be able "to scold without injury (*contumeliam*, which can mean both verbal and physical abuse)," while the prince should respect his tutor for "his severe life (*vitae seueritatem*) and love him for his pleasant ways."[83] The passage's opening veers to touch on the problem of imposing discipline, but what form that "check" and "severity" might take is left unsaid. The rest of the passage moves smoothly into the subject of the teacher's self-discipline. In his 1529 treatise, "On the Education of Children," Erasmus seems to assume that the master would be forbidden to touch the children of a king or emperor when he asks what a flogging master would do if assigned to teach such children "whom it would not be proper to strike (*quos caedere fas non est*)." But Erasmus asks this question while pointing out that though it is said that a noble child is exempt from corporal punishment, the children of citizens are as much human beings as the children of kings and are owed as much love (*carus*) as those born royal.[84] One might conclude from this statement that either all children must be beaten or all of them loved.

Richard Mulcaster addressed the consequences of educating a prince with characteristic directness. He was acutely aware that "the greatest prince in that he is a child, is, as other children be, for soul sometimes fine, sometimes gross: for body, sometimes strong, sometimes weak: of mold sometimes fair, sometimes mean." For Mulcaster, childhood leveled social difference, so, "for the time to begin to learn, and the matter which to learn, and all other circumstances, wherein [the young prince] communicateth with his subjects, he is no less subject, then his subjects be." In the experience of learning the prince becomes himself a "subject," although in this passage, which elides the schoolmaster's agency, he is not subject to someone but to something. The text then

83. Erasmus, *Institutio*, pp. 138–39.
84. Erasmus, *De pueris*, p. 64.

retreats to commonplaces about passive resistance and obedience, sighing a bit that "we must take him as God sends him, because we cannot choose, as we could wish." But the master, unlike the ordinary subject, is seen as capable of more than prayer, for he can both encourage the prince's good traits and "restrain" the bad ones:

> If the prince his natural constitution be but feeble, and weak, yet good train[ing] as it helpeth forwardness, so it strengtheneth infirmity: and is some restraint even to the worst given, if it be well applied, and against the liberty of high calling oppose the infamy of ill doing. Which made even Nero stay the five first years of his government, and to seem incomparable good. When the young prince's elementary is past, and greater reading comes on, such matter must be picked, as may plant humility in such height.[85]

If the example of Nero seems ill-chosen here, it is in the typical manner of the humanists, who frequently chose classical examples for inappropriate purposes as if to undercut high ideals with a recognition of historical necessity. By citing Nero, Mulcaster wistfully opines that the good effects of education may last for a little while in princes, if not for long. Most importantly, Mulcaster seeks to produce in his prince what he would fashion in the obedient subject: humility, no matter how much "liberty" may be due to "high calling."

The preceding passage does not mention corporal punishment, although it speaks of subjection, humility, and restraint. In the example that follows, however, the text makes it clear that Mulcaster could conceive of beating the sovereign prince. To make his point about restraint, he cites an incident from Xenophon's *Cyropaedia*, the story of the education of the model Persian king, Cyrus:

> Xenophon maketh Cyrus be beaten of his master, even where he makes him the pattern of the best prince, as Tully sayeth, and minds not the truth of the story, but the perfectness of his device, being him self very mild as it appeareth still in his journey from Assyria after the death of Cyrus the younger. For a soul there could not be one less servile then he, which was

---

85. Mulcaster, *Positions*, p. 220.

pictured out beyond exception: for impunity, there could not be more hope, than in a prince inheritor, and that is more, set forth for a pattern to princes. And yet this prince's child in the absoluteness of device, was beaten by his device, which could not devise any good train exempt from beating being yet the second ornament of Socrates his school. The case was thus, and a matter of the Persian learning. A long boy had a short coat, and a short boy had a long one: The long boy took away the short boy's coat, and gave him his: both were fit: But yet there arose a question about it. Cyrus was made judge, as justice was the Persian grammar. He gave sentence, that either should have that which fitted him. His master beat him for his sentence: because the question was not of fitness, but of right, wherein each should have his own. His not learning, and error by ignorance, was the fault, wherefore he was punished.[86]

While suggesting that this tale is a fiction, Mulcaster draws the reader's attention to its artificiality, which supports the "perfectness" and "absoluteness" of the "device." When "absoluteness" is read as rigor, the "device" of the story may be identified with the rod with which Cyrus was beaten. In turn, the "absoluteness" that made Cyrus a victim of punishment was not any king's sovereignty but rather the justice that was the "Persian grammar" (and implicitly the grammar master's). In the *Cyropaedia*, no joke is made about the "Persian grammar" when the question is explicitly one of property law. Mulcaster's playful addition thus highlights the master's absolute authority—identified with the law—over the prince. The rest of Mulcaster's telling then returns to the story, where at first the boy Cyrus's answer would seem to be just by the standard of common sense; however, the boy was declared wrong because the rights of property ownership were at stake. Cyrus's ignorance of this law brought him to be soundly beaten and rendered humble before it.[87] Thus, Mulcaster sets the absolute master and his "grammar" over the prince to punish royal ignorance just as he would any schoolboy's, yet Mulcaster's subtext suggests that any prince must be punished for misjudging the law that renders each his own, regard-

86. Ibid., pp. 277–78.

87. Xenophon, *Cyropaedia*, bk. 1.3.17–18; trans. Walter Miller (New York: Putnam, 1925), p. 43.

less of what is "fitting" or suits his own "common sense." In contrast to his earlier, simple equation between the rod and the scepter, the teacher and the monarch, Mulcaster here pits the teacher and the law against the prince's instinct and will.

Far from being simply a fanciful anecdote of the classical past, this scenario was played out in two separate British courts of the sixteenth century, where humanist masters endeavored to train their royal charges: the households of England's Edward VI and of Scotland's James VI.[88] Both boys lacked parents from an early age—James VI from infancy—and endured turbulent boyhoods in which they were dominated by a series of father-protectors who were themselves sometimes violently supplanted. Both princes were relentlessly schooled in elaborate, seemingly endless humanist programs of study. While Edward's training seems to have been more humane than James's, evidently both suffered corporal punishment at the hands of their tutors. The surviving stories of their education illustrate the power struggles embedded in the relationship of teacher and royal scholar and illuminate the role of these struggles in shaping the kings these boys would become.

The question of whether a prince should be beaten has surfaced in scholarly debate over whether Edward VI was indeed whipped. Although Erasmus suggested such a practice was conventionally considered unacceptable, much evidence attests to the corporal punishment of royal children in Europe up through the sixteenth century. Orme claims that such whippings were not uncommon until the fifteenth century: Jean Héroard's journal from 1601–10 reports the frequent beating of the French Dauphin, later Louis XIII; and, as we shall see, several stories recount the chastisement of young James VI.[89] Anec-

88. One could also include here the case of Louis XIII, whose beatings are detailed in Héroard's journals and whose situation was in many ways parallel; but the political systems were quite different, and what concerns me here is the British manifestation of that phenomenon. See Marvick, *Louis XIII*.

89. Orme, *Childhood*, p. 33: "It was possible for medieval people to imagine the beating even of a royal prince. In the thirteenth-century chanson de geste *The Story of Fulk Fitz-Warin*, King John is portrayed as a child attacking a friend with a chessboard in a fit of temper, upon which his father Henry II orders him to be beaten by his master—an amusing but apocryphal story. Henry VI may really have been beaten in his childhood. In 1424 his lady mistress Alice Butler was commissioned to chastise him reasonably

dotes of Edward VI's upbringing, however, mention the use of a whipping boy (though this was not incompatible with the beating of the prince's person, as can be seen in the use of both in the raising of Louis XIII). In his prefatory materials to *The Literary Remains of Edward VI*, the antiquarian J. G. Nichols maintains (not without doubt) that Edward himself was never whipped: he cites Fuller, who claims that Barnaby Fitzgerald, Edward's boyhood confidant, was a "proxy for correction."[90] Nichols also relates an anecdote told by Conrad Heresbach, in *De Educandis Erudiendisque Principium Liberis*, "which he heard while ambassador in England (1547) from the Duke of Cleves" to the effect that

> King Edward, by the bad advice of one of his juvenile companions, was once induced to adopt the use of such thundering oaths as he was told were appropriate to his sovereign dignity. On this being observed, an inquiry was made as to the origin of such a change in his behavior; whereupon he ingenuously confessed that one of his playfellows has given him instructions in this right-royal accomplishment. When this has been ascertained, his masters took care to give the guilty boy a sharp whipping in the King's view, and to admonish the latter that he witnessed the appropriate recompense of such presumption, bidding him to remember that he also had deserved the same punishment, and must therefore abstain from that excess for the future.[91]

While the truth of this story is unconfirmed, it is revealing of contemporary notions of sovereignty. In the year that he became king,

---

from time to time, and similar power was given to his master, the earl of Warwick, in 1428."

90. From *The Literary Remains of Edward VI*, ed. John Gough Nichols (London: J. B. Nichols and Sons, 1857), vol. 1, p. lxx.

91. Ibid., p. lxxiv. Nichols offers the Latin text as follows: "*Cum e coaetaneis nobilioribus quidam ad jurandum, et ad ferociora verba regem hortaretur, sic inquiens decere regiam majestatem denotare ac juramentis fulminare. Ille, ut sunt puerorum ingenia ad quidvis imitandum prona, suum hortatorem secutus, cum a suis institutoribus deprehenderetur praeter consuetudinem juramentis et blasphemiis uti, rogatus ecquid sic praeter morem juraret atque insolenter loqueretur, ingenue confessus est suum coetaneum docuisse sic decere loqui. Puerum igitur illuum, auctorem, in conspectu Regis virgis acriter castigarunt, Regemque monuerunt, hanc esse hujus insolentiae mercedem, atque ut meminerit ea se quoque commeruisse, quare deinceps abstineat ab ea insolentia.*"

Edward is pictured as being punished for imitating the "sovereign" style of swearing. Any humanist pedagogue would have frowned on such behavior, which was yet a "right-royal" accomplishment. Edward's own attempts to act like a king are punished not, however, by chastising his body but by a subject and friend's humiliation, which suggests his royal immunity yet makes him responsible for the act. Behind the other's whipping, however, lies the threat of Edward's own bodily harm. The scene thus at once supports and undermines the concept of sovereign privilege by punishing Edward for behaving immorally, while protecting him from the subjection of pain and humiliation.

In 1605, the playwright Samuel Rowley staged a similar scene in *When you see me, you know me*, his own imaginative reconstruction of the life of Henry VIII, the education of Edward, and the fall of Cardinal Wolsey. Like Heresbach's anecdote, Rowley's play locates the whipping-boy incident in a network of images of authority, ambition, and rebellion. The play intertwines competing power struggles between the king and Pope, the king and Wolsey (who sees himself as overruling "Counsel, Court and King"[92]), and the king and his fool Will Somers. (Wolsey's career is made to coincide with Edward's upbringing, and Cranmer becomes Edward's tutor.) The play is filled with violence connected with the king: for instance, when Henry goes out incognito, he fights with Black Will and is imprisoned as a result. The monarch also frequently threatens to whip Will Somers, who acts as his advisor.

Set within this frame is Cranmer's whipping of "Ned Browne" because the young prince Edward will not "ply his book." This beating is judged effective on two counts: first, that "the fearful boy to save his breech, / Doth hourly haunt [the prince], wheresoere he goes," that is, Ned Browne enforces the schoolmaster's will; and second, that the prince "as loath to see him punished for his faults, / Plies it of purpose to redeem the boy." Edward says that he is sorry for his namesake Ned's punishment but then crafts a witty syllogism:

92. Samuel Rowley, *When you see me you know me or the famous Chronicle Historie of king Henrie the Eight, with the birth and vertuous life of Edward, Prince of Wales* (London, 1605; 2nd ed. 1613), sig. A3v.

Bona virgia facit bonum puerum:
Bonum est, te esse bonum puerum:
Ergo, bona virgia, res bona est: And that's this, Ned.
A good rod makes a good boy: t'is good that thou shouldst
be a good boy: (ergo) therefore a good rod is good.[93]

Will Somers quickly dismantles this prim logic: "Nay berlady [by our Lady], the better the rod is, it's the worse for him, that's certain: but dost hear me, boy; since he can prove a rod to be so good, let him take it himself the next time." The prince instantly repents, saying to Ned, "In truth, I pity thee, and inwardly I feel the stripes thou barest, and for thy sake, Ned, I'll ply my book the faster." He then knights Ned for his service, an act that his father the king approves as a sign of "kingly spirit." As in the Heresbach anecdote, the device of the whipping boy circumvents the physical insult that would be offered to the royal dignity while it whispers a threat against him. This whipping, in turn, provokes the prince to act like a king—in this case, however, in the dignified act of conferring a knighthood rather than the low one of swearing.

Despite these tales, however, documentary evidence does attest to at least one occasion when a tutor did strike Edward, the model pupil. The evidence comes from a letter Edward's early tutor Richard Cox wrote to William Paget in the summer of 1544, when the prince was six and a half years old. Edward had been recently handed over to Cox, leaving the company of the women who raised him, as was customary when a boy reached his seventh year. In the letter, Cox explains how he set up Edward's studies as a kind of military campaign or series of "valiant conquests," in which the young prince might emulate his father's recent capture of Boulogne. The objects of his learning were figured as territory to besiege and capture, which, when they surrendered, became the prince's "subjects and servants." His enemies were named "the captains of ignorance." Edward was told that, having "beaten down" the parts of speech, he should reconstruct them "like as the King's Majesty framed up Boulogne after he had beaten it down." According to Cox, he was also taught the proverbs of Solomon, from

93. Ibid., sig. G2r–v.

which he was to learn "how good it is to give ear unto discipline, to fear God [the word God is inserted above the line as an afterthought, it appears], to keep God's commandments, to beware of strange and wanton women, to be obedient to father and mother, to be thankful to them that telleth him of his faults, etc." This sentence is followed, however, by Cox's complaint about "Captain Will," an "ungracious fellow whom to conquer I was almost in despair." Apparently in this lesson of obedience Edward was not so pliant. Cox complains to Paget that he tried both "fair means" and threats to conquer Edward's "Will," but Edward "thought my meaning to be nothing but dalliance." Finally, before they came from Sutton, Cox wrote, "I took my morris pike [*pyke*] stand at Will. I went and gave him such a wound that he wist not what to do, but picked [*pyked*] him privily out of the place that I never heard of him since. Me thought it the luckiest day that ever I saw in battle." "I think," Cox triumphantly concludes, "that only wound shall be enough for me to daunt both Will and all his fellows." Hereafter, Cox decided to change the game from one of siege to a tournament, conjuring up a new antagonist in the form of "Captain Oblivion," and this time the child readily obeyed: Cox ends by praising him as "a vessel most apt to receive all goodness and learning, witty, sharp and pleasant."[94]

This extraordinary report of the chastening of the young prince demonstrates the master's ambivalent power. At first, as we have seen in the two other scenes involving Edward's punishment, the child tried act like a king, in this case as a warrior. He was positioned against the parts of speech as the sovereign seeking to regain a rightful territory. However, when it came to memorizing and reciting texts meant to humble him and to remind him of the need for self-restraint (especially in the case of "strange and wanton women"), the prince apparently rebelled. Set up as the sovereign conqueror and possessor, he refused to subject his will. When this happened, the master transformed the scenario: Edward's own sovereign resistance, his "Will,"

---

94. R. Cox to William Paget, December 10, 1544; PRO SP1/95, fol. 201–202. On this letter, see Hester W. Chapman, *The Last Tudor King: A Study of Edward VI* (London: Jonathan Cape, 1958), pp. 60–61; I have used Chapman as a guide in reading this sometimes difficult manuscript.

became the antagonist that so many writers on monarchy and resistance feared.[95] Whereas the "captains of ignorance" had earlier opposed the prince, now Cox set himself up as attacking the prince's sovereign will: the victory was *Cox*'s, not Edward's, and Cox expressed his pleasure at his charge's defeat and conversion into a "vessel."

At stake in this battle, then, was how the young prince defined his authority in relation to his master, his father, and his subject—grammar. This struggle took place before Henry's death, but the problem became more acute when Edward himself ruled under the protectorships of Somerset and Warwick. In his brief reign as king Edward showed that one thing he learned well from his tutors was how to use education to control the subject.[96] In his "Discourse on Reform of Abuses in the Church and State," drafted in 1551, the young Edward himself proposed education as the first recourse in reforming a commonwealth endangered by disobedience and idleness at the lower end and greed and ambition at the higher end. According to Edward, if children were trained from the first in work appropriate to their degree, a whole host of social ills could be avoided. Listing "good education" as the first "medicine" or "plaster" to heal the social sores, the young king theorized that insofar as education is "in order first, so it seems to be in dignity and degree. For Horace says very wisely, *Quo est imbuta recens servabit odorem testa diu*, with whatsoever thing the new vessel is imbued it will long keep the savor, says Horace, meaning that for the most part men be as they be brought up, and that men keep longest the savor of their first bringing-up."[97] Here the "vessel" that Cox saw in his prince becomes the vessel of the obedient subject whom Edward would govern.

---

95. On the king's will, see Franco Moretti, *Signs Taken for Wonders: Essays in the Sociology of Literary Forms*, trans. Susan Fischer, David Forgacs, and David Miller (London: NLB, 1983), p. 47.

96. See Joan Simon, *Education and Society in Tudor England* (Cambridge: Cambridge University Press, 1966), pp. 279, 276. The period saw significantly increased interest in education for social advancement, a trend evident in the emerging vernacular literature of instruction on topics ranging form shooting to arithmetic.

97. From *The Chronicle and Political Papers of King Edward VI*, ed. W. K. Jordan (Ithaca: Cornell University Press, 1966), p. 165. See also Quintilian, *Institutio oratoria*, bk. 1.1.5, on the image of a child as a vessel.

Edward's protectors and advisers needed to represent him simultaneously as the ideal schoolboy and the imperious master.[98] In 1553 Edward himself authorized the publication in Latin and English of *A short catechisme, or playne instruction, conteynynge the sume of Christian learninge, sett fourth by the kings maiesties authoritie, for all Scholemaisters to teache* (most likely written by the bishop John Ponet, who advocated resistance to tyrants in his own *Shorte Treatise of Politike Power* while a Marian exile). The English edition bristles with different forms of sovereign authorization emanating from the young Edward. We first encounter the king's command to teachers that "we will therefore and command, both all and each of you, as ye tender our favor, and as ye mind to avoid the just punishment of transgressing our authority, that ye truly and diligently teach this catechism in your schools." This statement is followed by the king's letter patent authorizing John Day as the sole printer with "license and privilege" to publish this catechism. The catechism itself is a Socratic dialogue, for "this is the plainest way of teaching: . . . that both by certain questions, as it were by pointing, the ignorant might be instructed: and the skillful put in remembrance, that they forget not what they have learned."[99] This dialogue form carefully balances the schoolmaster's superior knowledge with the often superior social position of his students. The master's tone is gentle, and the scholar demonstrates careful but affectionate deference towards his "good master": he claims throughout, "I shall do (good master) with a good will as you command me."[100] Yet the scholar holds the floor in the catechism; after all, it is the master who asks the short questions and the student who supplies the long answers. The student may parrot the master's voice—so the master praises him for how he "hast applied thy mind to those things that I have taught"[101]—but the formal effect is that the student instructs the teacher (the opposite of the impression given by Socratic dialogues, where most often Socrates' long "ques-

---

98. Simon, *Education*, p. 281.

99. *A short catechisme, or playne instruction, conteynynge the sume of Christian learninge, sett fourth by the kings maiesties authoritie, for all Scholemaisters to teache* (London, 1553), sig. B1.

100. Ibid., sig. B4v.

101. Ibid., sig. K1r.

tions" are given a short, perfunctory response). The catechism's rhetoric could thus simultaneously shape and subdue authority in the child of a high social rank—even a prince.

Edward asserted his authority most significantly in 1549 during the rebellions against enclosure and the use of the new prayer books. When some landowners refused to observe the new anti-enclosure laws imposed by Somerset's government, the peasants of Norfolk and Suffolk led by Robert Kett revolted, tearing down fences and killing deer and sheep. At the same time, the government proscribed the celebration of mass and instituted the use of the liturgy from the first prayer book, provoking riots in Devonshire and Cornwall.[102] The rebels' rhetoric and the government's response both point to the scholar-king's problematic authority. The rebels continued to insist that they were Edward's "very humble and obedient subjects, whose desire is to be the dogs appointed to keep your house and your kingdom, and the oxen to cultivate your lands, the asses to carry your burdens."[103] At the same time, however, in the articles that "the commons of Devonshire and Cornwall" sent to the king protesting the new religious policy, they invoked his dead father's authority against him, asking that "the six articles, which our sovereign lord king Henry the eighth set forth in his latter days, shall be used and so taken as they were at that time."[104] The government's reply came in the form of a message from Edward himself. This document, it appears, was drafted by the humanist schoolmaster who succeeded Cox in Edward's household, John Cheke, the author of *The Hurt of Sedition*.[105] This schoolmaster's document aimed directly at the problem of Edward's authority in his minority. In it Edward was made to refer to himself explicitly as a father confronted by rebellious children and implicitly as a teacher opposed by a willful and ignorant charge: "Wherefore as to you our subjects by ig-

102. See Chapman, *Last Tudor*, pp. 158–59.

103. Ibid., p. 157.

104. Raphael Holinshed, *Holinshed's Chronicles: England, Scotland and Ireland* (1808; reprint, ed. Vernon Snow, New York: AMS, 1965), vol. 3, p. 919.

105. Chapman, *Last Tudor*, p. 158–59. According to Chapman, by drafting this document Cheke sought to regain his position at Edward's side, from which he had been banished for his supposed links to the disgraced Seymour. However, W. K. Jordan, *Edward VI: The Young King* (Cambridge: Harvard University Press, 1968), chap. 15, makes no mention of Cheke's authorship of this text.

norance seduced, we speak and be content to use our princely authority like a father to his children, to admonish you of your faults, not to punish them; to put you in remembrance of your duties, not to avenge your forgetfulness."[106] This is the language of humanist pedagogy. The cause of the subject's rebellion is "ignorance," the king seeks to admonish, not to punish, and his position is that of the loving father. But behind the love is the threat of bodily punishment, a warning that "if ye provoke us further, we swear to you by the living God, ye shall feel the power of the same God in our sword, which how mighty it is, no subject knoweth." The young prince's exercise of authority is thus implicitly identified with that of the schoolmaster and father, where, as Vives recommended, the threat of violence bolstered the rule of love.

But when Cheke wrote for Edward in this vein he was aware that, being a boy, the king might not be believed to speak with the father and master's voice. In response to the rebels' request that Edward restore Henry VIII's "six articles," the text burns with self-righteous fury. First, it insists that not only were these articles passed imprudently, being "too bloody" and "quickly repented," but that they were also repealed by an act of parliament. Only then does the text recognize the implicit accusation against the young king's authority. To the rebels' request that Edward wait until he is of age before taking such actions, the young king is given to retort: "Be we of less authority for our age? Be we not your king now as we shall be? . . . If ye would suspend and hang our doings in doubt until our full age, ye must first know, as a king we have no difference of years, but as a natural man and creature of God we have youth, and by his sufferance shall have age. We are your rightful king, your liege lord, the sovereign prince of England, not by our age, but by God's ordinance."

As Holinshed's chronicle points out, this rhetoric did not impress the rebels: "although the rebels received this princely message and wholesome admonition from the king's majesty, yet would they not reform themselves, as dutiful subjects ought to have done, but stood still in their wicked begun rebellion, offering to try it at the weapon's point. . . . The rebellious rout were grown to an obstinacy, seeming so

---

106. Holinshed, *Chronicles*, p. 920.

far from admitting persuasions to submission, that they became resolute in their pestilent actions; willfully following the worst, which they knew full well would redound to their detriment; and avoiding the best."[107] The schoolroom scenario was repeated with a bloody difference. When the master wielded the rod in the battle against "Captain Will" willfulness was duly broken in the prince; however, according to the chronicle, when the willful subject refused to recognize "gentle" argument and reason, he brought the rod down upon himself. Only when thousands of rebellious subjects were killed was the uprising finally suppressed.

In these schoolroom and national conflicts we see the duality of the humanist schoolmaster's role. Chastising the prince was supposed to subject his royal will. As a later defense of corporal punishment put it, "It is a generally recognized principle that persons of high estate who are destined to rule whole nations must learn the art of governance by way of first learning obedience. *Qui nescit obedire, nescit imperare* [who knows not how to obey, knows not how to rule]: the reason for this is that obedience teaches a person to be zealous in observing the law, which is the first quality of a ruler."[108] In this sense the prince was to be fashioned paradoxically as a monarch with a subject's demeanor. However, chastisement also offered the prince a model for the exercise of monarchical power, whereby he would kindly forgive his subjects' ignorance while harshly punishing their willfulness. This duality is even more clearly articulated in the stories surrounding the education of James VI, who grew up to think of himself as Britain's father and schoolmaster while remembering the punishment he had received from his own humanist tutor. These stories of the relationship of the domineering tutor and the willful royal charge bring into vivid relief the paradoxes at the heart of the humanist education of the prince.

With his radical politics and irascibility, James's tutor, George Buchanan, appears to have been far more formidable than either of those

---

107. Ibid., pp. 923–24.

108. J. Sulzer, *Versuch von der Erziehung und der Unterweisung der Kinder* (1748), cited by Alice Miller, *Am Anfang war Erziehung* (Frankfurt Am Main: Suhrkamp Verlag, 1980), trans. by Hildegarde and Hunter Hannum as *For Your Own Good: Hidden Cruelty in Child-Rearing and the Roots of Violence* (New York: Farrar, Straus, Giroux, 1983), pp. 12–13.

restrained royalists, Cox and Cheke. An internationally known neo-Latin poet, teacher, and humanist scholar, Buchanan taught James from 1569 to 1578. Unlike Edward, James was already king when he began his education, having been crowned king of Scotland in 1567 when he was a little more than a year old. James himself never knew his own father, Darnley, nor had any memories of his mother, Mary Stuart. As he said in explaining to the Scottish people why he had so long delayed marriage, "The reasons were that I was alone, without father or mother, brother or sister, king of this realm and heir apparent of England. This my nakedness made me to be weak and my enemies stark."[109] Instead of parents, the "fathers" of this patriarchal king were a series of protectors, often violently removed, and his master Buchanan, whom he also came to address as "father."[110]

It is likely that James's written expressions of filial affection for his tutor were conventional, for reports of Buchanan's pedagogical behavior suggest that Buchanan was more tyrant than loving father to him. While James expressed appreciation for his Latin training, mostly his memories of Buchanan were fearful. At the end of his life James is said to have dreamt that Buchanan's ghost appeared and prophesied his death.[111] In 1584 James had his revenge on Buchanan, directing the Scottish Parliament to condemn his teacher's writings. As one report tells it, however, Buchanan cared little: "When he was upon his Death-Bed, they told him that the King was highly incensed against him, for writing his Book *de jure Regni* and his History, and he told them, *That he was not very much concerned about that, for he was shortly going to a Place where very few Kings were.*"[112]

James's condemnation of Buchanan reflected more than personal antipathy. The condemned writings included the notorious *De jure regni apud Scotos*, a dialogue first published in Edinburgh in 1579, which ar-

109. "Letter to the people of Scotland," 22? October 1589, in *Letters of King James VI & I*, ed. G. P. V. Akrigg (Berkeley: University of California Press, 1984), p. 98.

110. See James's letter to Buchanan from the mid-1570s, in which he refers to him as his father, reprinted in *Letters of James VI & I*, pp. 41–42.

111. I. D. McFarlane, *Buchanan* (London: Duckworth, 1981), p. 449, cites Francis Osborn, *Advice to a Son* (1656), p. 19: "King James used to say of a person in high place about him, that he even trembled at his approach, it minded him so of his pedagogue."

112. George Mackenzie, *Lives and Characters of the Eminent Writers of the Scots Nation* (1722; reprint, New York: Garland, 1971), vol. 3, p. 180.

gued for limiting a king's authority and defended tyrannicide. The book justified a people's rebellion against a tyrant on the grounds that he is a criminal and rebel, who has ceased to restrain his will and desire.[113] In his preface to the *De jure* Buchanan offered his text directly to the young king, as a "witness of my zeal toward you," that it might admonish him of his obligation to his subjects. The book was intended to keep away that "soothing wet nurse of vice (*blanda vitiorum altrix*)," bad company, which might seduce the prince from his duty. Therefore the book is not only a "monitor" (*monitorem*), but also an "importunate exactor" (*flagitatorem*, a word echoing the Latin *flagrum*, for whip) to keep him away from the dangers of flattery.[114] The book was thus to function as Buchanan's surrogate, to defend the child from the effeminate lures of vice and flattery, and the rhetoric recalls the contrast of the schoolmaster's male authority with the "foster mother's" or nurse's laxness and cultivation of sensual pleasures.

The image of the stern book reigning over feminine disorder, flattery, and vice while justifying violent rebellion against a sovereign encapsulates the central paradox of Buchanan's mastery over the young King James. Later accounts of Buchanan's pedagogic conduct all attest to the tutor's violent outbursts of temper and beating of the young king while pursuing a humanist education that advocated temperance and self-control.[115] The list of the items in James's library indicate a curriculum based on classical literature and a heavy dose of statecraft, including Elyot's *The Governour*.[116] James's reading, like Edward's be-

113. See Bushnell, *Tragedies,* chap. 2, pp. 45–46, 53–54, on Buchanan's definition of a tyrant.

114. George Buchanan, *De jure regni apud Scotos* (Edinburgh, 1579; facsimile reprint, Amsterdam: Da Capo, 1969), sig. A2v.

115. James spoke later in his life of "the violence of [Buchanan's] humor and heat of his spirit"; see David Harris Willson, *King James VI and I* (London: Jonathan Cape, 1956), p. 21. See also McFarlane, *Buchanan*, p. 448: "We have reports on Buchanan's comportment as a tutor, though they may not all be very reliable. Certain it is that his ill health made him irritable, he may have found teaching increasingly irksome, and he was little inclined to suffer fools gladly; according to Sir James Melville he was 'a stoic philosopher, and looked not far before the hand.' "

116. McFarlane describes it as "the pedagogic curriculum of the French Renaissance geared to the needs of a monarch living at a rather later period" (McFarlane, *Buchanan*, p. 448). See also Caroline Bingham, *The Making of a King: The Early Years of James VI and I* (London: Collins, 1968), p. 53.

fore him, offered ample models of the cultivation of princely virtues. But in the schoolroom Buchanan seems never to have forgotten that he was training the son of Mary Stuart, whom he had had a role in deposing. When the prince did not live up to the ideal of statecraft, Buchanan would remind him of his scandalous royal parentage with a beating: "At another time, the Master of Erskine having a tame sparrow, the King would needs have the sparrow from him, and he refusing to give it, they fell a struggling about it, and in the scuffle the sparrow was killed, upon which the Master of Erskine fell a crying, Buchanan being informed of the matter, gave the king a box on the ear, and told him, *That what he had done, was like a true bird of the bloody nest of which he was come.*"[117] The several accounts we have of Buchanan's tutoring of James resemble this story. We cannot be certain of their authenticity, but the stories are consistent enough in their plots and details to indicate clearly what was seen to be at stake, then and in later years, in the relationship between the politically radical schoolmaster and his proto-absolutist charge.[118]

In his rather indignant life of Buchanan,[119] George Mackenzie relates another beating incident, which he claims to have gotten from the earl of Cromarty, who had it from his grandfather, who was schooled with James:

> The king one Day had got prescribed for him his theme, the history of the conspiracy at Lauder Bridge in King James the III's time, where Archibald Earl of Angus obtained the name of Bell the Cat, from his telling them the fable of some rats that had combined against a cat, whom they resolved to

---

117. Mackenzie, *Lives*, vol. 3, p. 180. See Bingham's comment: "The significant thing about that story is that it was the King who was wholly blamed, and the King whose ears were boxed; and that is not Buchanan the scholar who is speaking, but Buchanan the author of the *Detectio*" (*Making of a King*, pp. 84–85).

118. As Steven Berkowitz pointed out to me at a Renaissance Society of America conference in April 1995, it is likely that such anecdotes reflect a later age's image of Buchanan, filtering history to emphasize his irascibility and dominance in James's life. Rather than discarding these anecdotes because of their uncertain veracity, I continue to be interested in how they suggest ways in which the humanist pedagogic tradition structured the relationship between James and Buchanan.

119. Mostly Mackenzie is infuriated with Buchanan's pattern of ingratitude, which began, he fumes, with his writing a scurrilous epigram on his own teacher, John Major (*Lives*, p. 157).

seize, and to tie a bell about his neck, to warn them for the future, by the ringing of that bell of their danger, but as they were going to put their project in execution, one of the old rats asked which of them would be the first that would seize upon the cat? This question put them all in a profound silence, as it did likewise the conspirators, which the Earl perceiving, told them that he would bell the cat. The king having I say got this for his theme, as he was diverting himself after dinner with the Master of Erskine, the Earl of Mar's eldest Son, Buchanan desired the king to hold his peace, for he disturbed him in his reading, the king taking no notice of this, he reproved him for a second time, and told, *That if he did not hold his Peace, he would whip his breech*, the king answered, *That he would gladly see who would bell the cat*. Upon this, in a passion Buchanan throws the book from him, and whips the king severely, the old Countess of Mar who has her apartment near them, hearing the king cry, runs to him, and taking him up in her arms, asked what the matter was? The king told her, that the master (for so Buchanan was called) had whipped him, *She asked how he durst put his hand on the Lord's Anointed*? To which he made this unmannerly reply, *Madam, I have whipped his Ar[se], you may kiss it if you please*.[120]

As we saw in Cox's report of Edward's punishment, the master's authority was tested in a conflict between himself and his charge. First the teacher exerted moral compulsion but the child refused to heed; then he used violence against the apparently surprised child. But while Cox's strategy was cast indirectly in military metaphors, in Mackenzie's account Buchanan and James's battle was played out explicitly in terms of the language of sovereignty, tyranny, and rebellion. Buchanan gave a writing exercise on James III, illustrating an argument for the right of rebellion against a king whom he called the "Scottish Caligula." That lesson's subtext was surely the potential identity between James VI and his namesake forbear. Perversely, the child James reversed the equation so that the schoolmaster became the tyrant and the child-king the rebel. James, in identifying himself with the conspirator Archibald, at once undermined his own authority while challenging his tutor's. Buchanan was quick to reestablish his mastery, but through exactly the kind of eruption of violence which he would condemn in a king. The wounded

120. Ibid., pp. 180–81.

child then turned to Buchanan's feminine counterpart (his *blanda altrix*), who recognized his sovereignty as the same time as she soothed and comforted him. Buchanan rudely opposed this act to his own as the kind of sycophancy that he warned turns kings into tyrants. The story puts the modern reader in the impossible position of abhorring Buchanan for his brutality and admiring him for his ability to resist the young king.[121]

Another account of the education of James reinforces the impression that the schoolroom was the locus of a struggle for sovereignty between the "master" subject and the "scholar" prince, even when the master did not hit the boy. In this case Buchanan played a trick on his young charge:

> Buchanan had noticed that the young king had a tendency to grant favors to all who asked, without taking proper notice of what was being requested; and he decided that it was time to give the King a lesson. So with two books of requests in his hand he went up to the King; in one of them the suppliant begged that he might be King for a fortnight—with the King's permission, and for that time he have unfettered control of the country. The young king signed the books and granted the various requests contained therein without closer scrutiny. Buchanan then went about saying that he was King for the next fortnight and asked the King to confirm that this was indeed the case. James was in some wonderment and even thought that his tutor's mind might be disturbed; but Buchanan then showed him his signature to the request contained in the book. Well, he said, here is the letter signed in your hand in which you have handed over the kingdom to me. And he began to reproach the King, as a tutor reproves his pupil sternly, instructing him that he could not grant whatever was requested without careful deliberation, otherwise considerable damage to him might follow.[122]

Once again, the story suggests that when Buchanan wanted to teach a lesson in royal wisdom to his charge he did so in a way that threatened

121. On the James III episode, see Maurice Lee, Jr., *Great Britain's Solomon: James VI and I in His Three Kingdoms* (Chicago: University of Illinois Press, 1990), p. 35.

122. I cite McFarlane's telling of the story in *Buchanan*, pp. 448–49: the source is Nathan Chytraeus, *Collectanea*, 3–4, in *Psalmorum Dauidis* (Herborn: C. Corvinus, 1600). The anecdote disappeared from later editions of this text.

James with Buchanan's potential superiority. Moreover, Buchanan did so by portraying himself as a tyrant with "unfettered control." The king's lack of self-control and carelessness were thus mirrored in the master-subject's imitation of absolute sovereignty.

What were the consequences of this education? Some of the results are only too well known. After Buchanan's death, James reacted violently to those teachings that had been imposed on him with violence. Not only did he ban Buchanan's books, but in developing his own absolutist doctrine James also responded in kind with a political theory that opposed Buchanan's. Yet when James rejected his tutor he also modeled himself on him as well.[123] While countering his education with his own written exercise in the *institutio principis*, or statecraft, the *Basilikon Doron* (1599–1603), James adopted for himself the persona of the British realm's "schoolmaster," exercising what Pope called "a pedant reign"[124] and presenting his many treatises as instructions to his readers and subjects.

In the preface to *The Trew Law of Free Monarchies* (1598), written to enlighten his people of their duties, for example, James defended the treatise's brevity as the most effective pedagogy, "the true grounds, to teach you the right-way, without wasting time upon refuting the adversaries. . . . For my intention is to instruct, and not irritate, if I may eschew it. The profit I would wish you to make of it, is, as well so to frame all your actions according to these grounds, as may confirm you in the course of honest and obedient subjects to your king in all times coming." The *Trew Law* thus became a text comparable to the "textbook of Persian Grammar" by which Cyrus had to square his decision,

123. See Roger A. Mason, *"Rex Stoicus*: George Buchanan, James VI and the Scottish Polity," in John Dwyer, Roger A. Mason, and Alexander Murdoch, eds., *New Perspectives on the Politics and Culture of Early Modern Scotland* (Edinburgh: John Donald, 1982), pp. 9–33. See also Mason, "George Buchanan, James VI and the Presbyterians," in Mason, ed., *Scots and Britons: Scottish Political Thought and the Union of 1603* (Cambridge: Cambridge University Press, 1994), pp. 112–37.

124. See Bingham, *Making of a King*, on James's own reputation as a pedant: "The flavor of his learning . . . was not so much pedantic as pedagogic. Both in speaking and writing he delighted to instruct. Given the slightest opportunity he would settle down, motivated by a kindly desire to enlighten, to teach anything which interested him to anyone who was prepared to listen: to Esme Stuart he taught theology, to the favorite of his middle years Robert Ker, Latin, to England he was the Schoolmaster of the Realm!" (p. 98).

proof against the arguments and texts of those—like Buchanan—"that shall praise or excuse the by-past rebellions." Further, echoing and reversing Buchanan's admonishing the king to steer clear from the rocks of effeminate flattery James offered the *Trew Law* as a protection against the "siren songs" of resistance tracts.[125]

James also gave the *Basilikon Doron* to his son as a "teacher" in his absence, just as Buchanan had offered books to James using much the same rhetoric. James asked his son to

> Receive and welcome this book then, as a faithful preceptor and counselor unto you: which, because my affairs will not permit me ever to be present with you, I ordain to be a resident faithful admonisher of you: And because the hour of death is uncertain to me, as unto all flesh, I leave it as my testament, and latter will unto you. Charging you in the presence of God, and by the fatherly authority I have over you, that ye keep it ever with you, as carefully, as Alexander did the Iliad of Homer. Ye will find it a just and impartial counsellor; neither flattering you in any vice, not importuning you at unmeet times.[126]

For James the book combined the schoolmaster's rule with the father's authority, at once a textbook and a testament underwritten by both inheritance and learning. Like Buchanan's *De jure*, the *Basilikon Doron* "admonished" its young reader: in his description of his own book James offered it as the perfect schoolmaster who replaces the absent father. As a king, as well, James believed himself to be a better schoolmaster for his son than any hired tutor, by the benefit of his experience. For the particular "precepts" to his son, he wrote, "it became me best as a King, having learned both the theory and practice thereof, more plainly to express, than any simple school-man, that only knows matters of kingdoms by contemplation."[127]

At the same time, the image of the schoolmaster-book echoes James's reaction to the example of his own education. The book is a "faithful

---

125. *Political Works of James I* (1616), ed. Charles Howard McIlwain (Cambridge: Harvard University Press, 1918; reprint, New York: Russell and Russell, 1965), p. 53.

126. James I, *Basilikon Doron* (1599; reprinted, with revisions, 1603), in McIlwain, ed., *Political Works*, p. 4.

127. Ibid., p. 10.

admonisher" that does not flatter, but it also does not importune (once again echoing the *De jure*). He wrote to his son that—unlike James's own imperious teacher—this book "will not come uncalled, neither speak unasked (*unspeered*) at."[128] The text explicitly and implicitly condemns Buchanan: Prince Henry was to eschew "such infamous invectives, as Buchanan's or Knox's chronicles: and if any of these infamous libels remain until your days, use the law upon the keepers thereof: For in that point I would have you a Pythagorist, to think that the very spirits of these archibellouses of rebellion, have made transition in them that hoards their books, or maintains their opinions; punishing them, even as it were their authors risen again."[129] James's odd neologism, "archibellous," denotes "arch-bellows" yet also combines the Greek root for "chief" or "ruling" (*archi*) with the Latin word for war (*bellum*), thus recognizing Buchanan's and Knox's preeminence and their capacity for violence and rage, difficult to suppress even in death. The word also echoes "rebellious" while juxtaposing it with "archi," suggesting sovereignty.[130] "Archibellous" thus encapsulates the contradictions inherent in Buchanan's status as the sovereign advocate of rebellion, who had now changed places with his former willful charge. James also criticized Buchanan implicitly for undermining parental authority in asserting his own. In the *Basilikon Doron* he asked that Henry never forgive any one who dishonors "your princes or your parents" or any predecessors, "for how can they love you, that hated them whom-of ye are come? . . . It is therefore a thing monstrous, to see a man love the child, and hate the parents: as on the other part, the infaming and making odious of the parents, is the readiest way to bring the son in contempt."[131] The resentment against Buchanan, the author of the virulent *Detectio* against Mary Stuart, shows clearly here. But, more generally, it also recognizes the scandal of the schoolmaster's op-

128. Ibid., p. 4.

129. Ibid., p. 40; note the uncanny prophecy of James' dream of Buchanan's ghost.

130. In the limited (seven-copy) 1599 edition of the *Basilikon Doron*, the word was spelled "archi-bellowces," which the Roxburghe Club edition glosses as "arch-bellows" (*Basilikon doron: or His Majestys instructions to his dearest sonne, Henry the Prince*. [Edinburgh, 1599; ed. Charles Edmonds for the Roxburghe Club, London: Lea & Co., 1887]) p. li.

131. James I, *Basilikon*, in McIlwain, ed., p. 21.

position to the authority of the parents. James tried to reunite the two forms of authority when he set himself up as both the father and the master of his country. This supreme uniting of the sovereign, the teacher, and the father in James was meant to resolve the tension in the opposition of the parental, pedagogic, and political authority evident in the earlier discussions of teaching. James's own education was itself informed by such conflict, which figured the teacher simultaneously as the image of absolute power and its radical opponent. In reaction James took it upon himself to combine rather than divide the master, the father, and the king, so that each role would reinforce the other. In his construction, the student-subject had no escape or alternative.

Buchanan's schoolroom was a place for oppositional thinking and politics at the same time that it was meant to fashion a king. The remaining evidence shows no evidence of Buchanan's awareness of the difficulties implicit in this approach. In his case the practice of his pedagogy united the medium with the message of containing sovereign power. In the common schoolroom, however, what would there have been to distinguish him from any other petty despot of the rod? Buchanan's powerful example brings into relief the paradoxes underpinning the image of the humanist teacher as it developed in England in the sixteenth century. In the town, household, and court, the teacher might be either a social equal or inferior, yet pedagogic tradition made him the monarch of his schoolroom. On the one hand, the analogy between the schoolroom and the state suggests that the classroom was meant to inculcate obedience, preparing the child to serve the state as an adult; on the other hand, the real tensions of the typical schoolroom, where the master was often little respected by parents or students, surely undermined that process. So, the master was the prince if his authority was accepted as socially legitimate. If not accepted he became the tyrant. In that case the violence of corporal punishment, rather than reinforcing absolutism, disabled its premise by rendering it illegitimate.

The alternative humanist vision of a schoolroom of play and pleasure and "a sanctuary from fear" was similarly riddled with contradictions. This schoolroom—however much a dream—would offer a place for both the master and the child to escape the cruel hierarchies of family and state (even as the master would lead the child through the pedagogy of emulation). It positioned the master both inside and outside of politics, and it could be a sanctuary not only for the child but for the master as well, where the schoolmaster might feel safe to criticize and even attempt to redress social and political corruption. In doing so, however, the schoolmaster could not escape the dynamics by which the schoolroom mirrored political structures and thus operated to reproduce them. The humanist schoolroom may have offered the seduction of freedom to both the master, who would see himself as free from his own restricted social position, and to his student, who would become a free man and not a slave. Yet in practice, such a freedom was always limited by the bargain struck: the master free only if he stayed in his schoolroom, the child free only to emulate him there.

CHAPTER 3

Cultivating the Mind

T he early modern humanists' desire to replace the flogging master with the loving father was riddled with contradictions. Certainly, they wanted to make their charges free—free from the tyranny of passion and ignorance and free to act in society—rather than servile, fearful, and blind. At the same time, it can be argued, the last thing they wanted was for their children to be free. Rather, education would bring children into willing bondage, teaching them self-control and loving obedience to parents, the monarch, the law, and the norms of civil society through emulation of the teacher who learned those lessons well for himself. The recent anti-humanist accounts of early English education foreground the student's restraint rather than freedom. These studies tend to connect this kind of restraint with a pessimistic interpretation of "liberal humanism." Catherine Belsey's construction of such a "liberal humanism" tells a story of its birth when the English killed their king in 1649 only to replace him with their own subjection.[1] At this moment, Belsey argues, "liberal humanism is installed, and with it the autonomous subject, the 'free' individual, subject to and subjected by new but equally ruthless mechanisms of power."[2] However, descriptions of the early humanist teachers' repres-

---

1. Catherine Belsey, *The Subject of Tragedy: Identity and Difference in Renaissance Drama* (London: Methuen, 1985), p. 7.
2. Ibid., p. 119. See also p. 8, on the relationship of liberal humanism to a market economy, and p. 125, on the relationship of humanism to the English Civil War: "Liberal humanism, conceived as autonomy for the subject and as control by the social body, but also as violence, in the imagined revenge, insurrection and regicide produced by the

sion of their students by inculcating decorum and mindless conformity have extended this narrative into an earlier age.[3] I am indeed inspired by Belsey's vision of individualism's birth in the resistance to tyranny, insofar as I sense that the child's subjectivity was fashioned through resistance; however, I do not see that the "despotic" conformity that eventually might have flowed from humanism subsumed its birth in resistance to absolutism. On the contrary, humanist education, in its formative stages in sixteenth-century England, could generate authoritarianism and resistance simultaneously.

In reading early modern educational literature for notions of the subject, I have asked myself whether these early teachers attributed an inalterable and particular nature to each child that resists change or whether they believed that they could completely mold his or her body, mind, and soul. I have also considered whether these two beliefs were complementary or incompatible. If each child was seen as different and resistant at some point to the teacher's shaping hand, what were the implications of that belief? Most importantly, was the teacher's recognition of essential differences and a limited freedom in children liberating or repressive for them? I cannot easily still Foucault's voice, murmuring to me that "power is exercised only over free subjects, and only insofar as they are free. By this we mean individual or collective subjects who are faced with a field of possibilities in which several ways of behaving, several reactions and diverse comportments may be realized. Where the determining factors saturate the whole there is no relationship of power."[4] Was the child imagined to be free from the

---

drive of absolutism towards tyranny and born in 1649 when 'bloody hands' applauded the spectacle of tyrannicide on another 'tragic scaffold' . . . still bears in its maturity the marks of its entry into the world."

3. See Richard Halpern, *The Poetics of Primitive Accumulation: English Renaissance Culture and the Genealogy of Capital* (Ithaca: Cornell University Press, 1991), chaps. 1–2; Jonathan Goldberg, *Writing Matter: From the Hands of the English Renaissance* (Stanford: Stanford University Press, 1990), and Anthony Grafton and Lisa Jardine, *From Humanism to the Humanities: Education and the Liberal Arts in Fifteenth- and Sixteenth-Century Europe* (Cambridge: Harvard University Press, 1986). Mary Thomas Crane, in *Framing Authority: Sayings, Self, and Society in Sixteenth-Century England* (Princeton: Princeton University Press, 1993), qualifies this view, opposing humanist practices of reading, writing, and education to "individualistic" aristocratic paradigms (p. 4). By these practices, the humanists constructed a collective, dispersed subjectivity.

4. Michel Foucault, "The Subject and Power," in *Michel Foucault: Beyond Structuralism*

master and to have an essential nature only enough to offer matter for the master's shaping hand? Can resistance be disentangled from "essentialism"? More broadly, as many have asked when facing Foucault, does the teleology of power empty freedom and resistance of any political significance—or any meaning at all?

This chapter returns to the nature versus nurture debate that pervaded arguments over manners, statecraft, gardening, poetics, and wet-nursing, among many other topics. This debate focused on whether virtue and character were taught or innate and, complementing theological arguments over predestination and works, it defined the terms for the discussion of agency and social difference.[5] I take the metaphor of nurture or cultivation at its face value, examining how educational and gardening theory and practice intersected in the gardening tropes that were used to describe a child's development and training. In Chapter 4 I will look at how gardening metaphors permeated images of books and humanist reading, but here I consider the use of metaphors of cultivation to describe the educational process as a whole.[6]

When a teacher was compared with a gardener it could mean many things ranging from violent mastery to tender regard; similarly, a student was imagined in different ways when compared with a seed, a

---

and Hermeneutics, ed. Hubert L. Dreyfus and Paul Rabinow (Chicago: University of Chicago Press, 1982), p. 221.

5. See Edward William Tayler, *Nature and Art in Renaissance Literature* (New York: Columbia University Press, 1964), for a general overview of this issue. For a deconstruction of the opposition of nature and art, through a reading of Renaissance poetics, see Derek Attridge, "Puttenham's Perplexity: Nature, Art and the Supplement in Renaissance Poetic Theory," in Patricia Parker and David Quint, eds., *Literary Theory/Renaissance Texts* (Baltimore: Johns Hopkins University Press, 1986), pp. 257–79.

6. See Crane, *Framing Authority*, chap. 3, for a parallel discussion of gardening tropes in relation to the use of commonplace books. In her incisive analysis Crane contrasts the organic metaphors for the student (as plant or fountain), which see "the psyche [as] an integrated whole that can be cultivated into a productive, powerful, rational being," with inorganic metaphors, related to engraving and sculpting, that envision "the rational self as a wall containing and controlling an unruly unconscious" (p. 54). Crane remarks that the humanists "try repeatedly to imagine an interaction between text and student that would achieve a delicate balance between empowerment and control, but their attempts to do so almost always end in self-contradiction and rupture" (p. 61). I am also grateful to Barbara Riebling for sharing with me her stimulating work on early modern theories of counsel and subjectivity, which differentiated between the developing and mature selves.

plant, or soil. On the one hand, such comparisons suggested that the teacher/gardener could plan and cultivate the pupil's mental garden for greater profit. On the other hand, such analogies also conveyed resistance on the child's part, for they granted the child a specific property or nature that the teacher/gardener could not alter. Thinking about humanist pedagogy as gardening thus pointed two ways, just as gardening practice itself did in the sixteenth and early seventeenth centuries. The first direction called for imposing order and uniformity on England's moral landscape, pruning and weeding it of all superfluity (what we will see in Chapter 4, for example, in Richard Mulcaster's project for uniformity in books and the curriculum of English education). The second direction highlighted the teacher/gardener's lack of control and his need to respect the particularity of each child's development. Whether respect for the child's distinctness was a good thing, however, remains unclear. Such respect may have granted a child power to resist the teacher, yet, just as gardening books could invoke essential nature in the name of innate status differences among plants, pedagogues could use natural difference to justify discriminatory treatment of children on the basis of status or gender.

In early modern England, differences among people were doubly tied to a notion of "property." For example, Shakespeare's "The Phoenix and the Turtle" used the language of property to celebrate love as an eradication of difference: "Property was thus appalled, / That the self was not the same: / Single Nature's double name, / Neither two nor one was called."[7] The primary meaning of "property" here is "distinctiveness, peculiarity, or exclusivity," which marks the difference between self and other. What makes the verse sound slightly strange, however, is the resonance of property's second sense as "that which is owned": a piece of land or a material possession. The first meaning usually denotes difference in pedagogical and gardening literature (as well as many other contexts), that is, it defines the distinctive characteristics and functions of a plant, person, or any natural thing; the latter sense occurs in legal and political contexts, where it signifies ownership by a distinct person.

Some recent studies of early modern identity have argued that what

---

7. In Robert Chester, *Love's Martyr: or, Rosalins Complaint* (London, 1601), p. 171.

made one particular then was what one owned, or "in what" one had "property" or "propriety." In his essay "Psychoanalysis and Renaissance Culture" Stephen Greenblatt found such a connection implicit in sixteenth-century legal records, which betray "a powerful official interest in identity and property, and identity *as* property."[8] At the time, such a notion was not purely individualistic: a farmer might understand a piece of land to be his, or that he had "property in it," when what he meant was, in E. P. Thompson's words, that he had inherited "a place within the hierarchy of use-rights" (customary rights of passage, grazing, and foraging). In this context property defined who he was in terms of his relationship to his community.[9] With increasing enclosure of common land and greater competition for land, property was further reified: Thompson sees that by the eighteenth century, "property must be made palpable, loosed for the market from its uses and from its social situation, made capable of being hedged and fenced, of being owned quite independently of any grid of custom or of mutuality."[10] When conceived of as freehold, landed property provided a mode of identification defined by boundaries marking what is mine from what is yours. Further, when thus enclosed, landed property was also unique.[11] By the middle of the seventeenth century, the linkage of iden-

8. Stephen Greenblatt, "Psychoanalysis and Renaissance Culture," in Parker and Quint, eds., *Literary Theory/Renaissance Texts*, p. 220. In his *Renaissance Self-Fashioning: From More to Shakespeare* (Chicago: University of Chicago Press, 1980), Greenblatt notes how in Thomas More's *Utopia* "private ownership of property is causally linked . . . to private ownership of self," so that "to abolish private property is to render such self-conscious individuality obsolete" (pp. 38–39).

9. E. P. Thompson, "The Grid of Inheritance: A Comment," in Jack Goody, Joan Thirsk, and E. P. Thompson, eds., *Family and Inheritance: Rural Society in Western Europe, 1200–1800* (London: Cambridge University Press, 1976), p. 337.

10. Ibid., p. 341. Andrew McRae has described the ways in which in sixteenth-century England "a growing insistence on the demarcation of land and property rights is documented in early surveying manuals, which proclaim the imperative 'to know one's own.' In the parallel textual tradition of husbandry manuals we can note a gradual rejection of the traditional model of local communities bound by a network of social duties and responsibilities" ("Husbandry Manuals and the Language of Agrarian Improvement," in Michael Leslie and Timothy Raylor, eds., *Culture and Cultivation in Early Modern England: Writing and the Land* [Leicester: Leicester University Press, 1992], p. 49).

11. When property was conceived of not as land but as money and "movables," new systems of exchange raised new problems about identity and self. See also Jean-Christophe Agnew, *Worlds Apart: The Market and the Theater in Anglo-American Thought,*

tity and property extended to the notion that every man has a property in or owns his own person. Richard Overton wrote in 1647, in *An Appeal from the Commons to the Free People*, that "to every individual in nature is given an individual propriety by nature, not to be invaded or usurped by any . . . for every one as he is himself hath a self propriety— else could he not be himself—and on this no second may presume without consent; and by natural birth all men are equal, and alike born to like propriety and freedom, every man by natural instinct aiming at his own safety and weal."[12]

While in the sixteenth century law may have loosely connected property to identity, political resistance theory also directly linked the two. Intermixed with the theological arguments that defended resistance on the basis of conscience, some sixteenth-century Protestant resistance theorists identified the subject with a complementary form of "property" protected by natural law, which a king may not abrogate.[13] For example, in his *A Shorte Treatise of Politike Power* (1556), John Ponet's insistence on the private man's duty to resist matches his obsession with the tyrant's violation of the rights of private property.[14] He thus

---

1550–1750 (Cambridge: Cambridge University Press, 1986), on the interaction of social, economic, and political changes with the changing "measure of a self" (p. 10); and Phyllis Rackin, *Stages of History: Shakespeare's English Chronicles* (Ithaca: Cornell University Press, 1990). I have also profited from reading an unpublished essay by James P. Saeger, "Illegitimate Subjects: The Performance of Bastardy in *King John*."

12. Cited in *Puritanism and Liberty: Being the Army Debates (1647–9) from the Clarke Manuscripts with Supplementary Documents*, ed. A. S. P. Woodhouse (Chicago: University of Chicago Press, 1951), p. 327. C. B. Macpherson, *The Political Theory of Possessive Individualism: Hobbes to Locke* (Oxford: Oxford University Press, 1962), sees the beginnings of the central difficulty in modern liberal-democratic theory in the "conception of the individual as essentially the proprietor of his own person or capacities, owing nothing to society for them," whereby "the human essence is freedom from dependence on the wills of others, and freedom is a function of possession" (p. 3). See Alain Renaut's distinction between humanism's stress on autonomy and the theory of individualism's stress on independence in *L'ère de l'individu* (Paris: Gallimard, 1989).

13. It is important to maintain a distinction between the notion of property as protected by natural law and property as a natural right. See Richard Schlatter, *Private Property: The History of an Idea* (New Brunswick: Rutgers University Press, 1951), chaps. 5–7, on the difference between John Ponet's stress on natural law and John Locke's on natural right.

14. Ponet argued for the subject's right to resist his sovereign, with subjects defined by their subjection to the *law*'s authority, and sovereigns themselves imagined as "sub-

defends the biblical Naboth's refusal to sell King Ahab his land, "as he might do, for by God's law he had a property (*propretie*) therein, from which without his will and consent, he could not be forced to depart."[15] In the context of sixteenth-century thinking about property, Ponet's argument made explicit what was largely implicit: this kind of "property" defined an autonomous identity specific to an adult, primarily male, property-owning class. The legal vestiges of the "feudal theory of dominion"[16] insisted, as John Rastell put it, that "all the lands through all the realm, are in the nature of fee and held mediately or immediately of the Crown."[17] This doctrine contrasted, however, with the complex realities of post-feudal land ownership, for, as John Guy observes, "servile villeinage" was in effect obsolete by 1500.[18] Terms of feudal property law were revived in the early seventeenth century both to defend the king's claim to absolute *dominium* and to defend the subject's claims against him. In 1610 Thomas Hedley declared to the House of Commons that "there is great difference betwixt the king's free subjects and his bondmen, for the king may by commission at his pleasure seize the lands or goods of his villeins (*villani*), but so can he not of his free subjects": thus, "to take away the liberty of a subject in his profit or property, you make a promiscuous confusion of a freeman and a bond slave."[19] As J. P. Sommerville comments on this passage,

---

ject to God's laws, and the positive laws of their countries" (*A Short Treatise of Politike Power*, in *John Ponet [1516?–1556]: Advocate of Limited Monarchy*, ed. Winthrop S. Hudson [Chicago: University of Chicago Press, 1942], p. 35). As Barbara Peardon has noted, this reaction was most likely fueled by "the efforts by the crown in 1555 to remove the right of ownership of private property from those it regarded as delinquents: the Protestant exiles." Barbara Peardon, "The Politics of Polemic: John Ponet's *Short Treatise of Politic Power* and Contemporary Circumstance, 1553–1556," *Journal of British Studies* 22 (1982): 35.

15. Ponet, *Short Treatise*, p. 88.

16. Schlatter, *Private Property*, p. 76.

17. G. E. Aylmer, "The Meaning and Definition of 'Property' in Seventeenth Century England," *Past and Present* 86 (1980): 90, cites John Rastell, in his *Les Termes de la ley: or Certaine Difficult and Obscure Words and Termes of the Common Lawes of this Realme* . . . (London, 1624), fols. 254 r–v.

18. John Guy, *Tudor England* (Oxford: Oxford University Press, 1988), p. 33.

19. Thomas Hedley, speech to the Commons on June 28, 1610, in *Proceedings in Parliament 1610*, ed. Elizabeth Reed Foster (New Haven: Yale University Press, 1966), vol. 2, p. 192.

such arguments use "the law of the land" to justify an anti-absolutist position: since most men were "free," "to strike at their property was to deprive them of this status."[20] Clearly, the logic of this argument demands that a deprived group exist in order to protect another. Similarly, in the later Civil War debates over suffrage freedom was the criterion for suffrage, thus excluding servants, beggars, and criminals; like freedom, "property" was what you had that someone else did not.[21]

Such a notion returns us to the first meaning of "property," the definition associated with particularity and difference. While it is clearly linked to the meanings of use-right or ownership, the other meaning of "property" as a distinctive trait was not limited to certain people. Instead, plants, minerals, and animals, as well as people, were attributed certain "properties"; herbalists and botanists wrote, for example, of the "virtues and properties" of different flowers,[22] or husbandmen of the "properties of a horse" or of a woman.[23] As Thomas Wilson defined it in his *Rule of Reason*, "property is a natural proneness and manner of doing, which agreeth to one kind, and to the same only, and that evermore."[24] Thomas Spencer wrote that "Properties be not adjuncts . . . for adjuncts do outwardly befall the subject . . . [they] are necessary emanations from the principles of nature."[25] This stream of meaning traversed the field of nature rather than that of law, defining the distinctive characteristics of things as they exist in nature. In analogy to other things in nature (which was how they were treated) children could be seen both as their parents' "property" and as having

20. J. P. Sommerville, *Politics and Ideology in England, 1603–1640* (London: Longman, 1986), p. 148; see also pp. 165–66. In general, I am indebted to Constance Jordan and Gordon Schochet for sharing with me their unpublished work on property.

21. See Macpherson, *Possessive Individualism*, p. 124. For example, in the Putney debates, Henry Ireton spoke against equal suffrage in defending private property, saying that to alter the suffrage would "destroy all kind of property and whatsoever a man hath by human constitution"; to which Thomas Rainsborough replied: "Sir, I see that it is impossible to have liberty but all property must be taken away" (*Puritanism and Liberty*, pp. 69–71). See comments on this exchange in Schlatter, *Private Property*, pp. 136–37.

22. John Parkinson, *Paradisi in Sole: Paradisus Terrestris* (London, 1629), Epistle, p. 3.

23. See *Here Begynneth a newe tracte or treatyse moost profytable for all husbandemen* (London, 1523), fols. 31–2, on the properties of different animals and of women.

24. Thomas Wilson, *The Rule of Reason, conteyning the Arte of Logique, set forth in English* (London, 1551), sig. B7v.

25. Thomas Spencer, *The Art of Logik* (London, 1628), p. 62.

"properties" or a "natural proneness and manner" to be cultivated. In this language of property lies a different way of constructing the self: not in terms of the legal/political status of the propertied adult, but rather in the image of the child with natural "properties," an image located in the discourse of natural history.

Comparisons of people and plants recur with surprising frequency in early modern writing. Both secular and theological texts observed a distinction between people and natural things (in particular, animals) and were concerned, as Keith Thomas describes it, "to define the special status of man and to justify his rule over other creatures."[26] At the same time, while dividing man from nature allowed for nature's exploitation, plants and animals also served as emblems of human beings.[27] In this way of thinking, people and plants grow, flourish, and fade; or the human mind and body resemble a garden, composed of soil planted with seeds, which grow into flowers or fruit (or weeds) that blossom and thrive, or crowd each other out, sicken, and die. As Foucault put it, the "fulcrum" of such analogies is always "Man."[28] However, just as the definition of man was in flux, the language of horticulture and husbandry also changed, particularly in relation to the discourses of agency and social order. Thus, comparisons between humanist pedagogy and gardening were historically unstable. Tracking the discursive shifts where the two fields of "man" and "garden" met reveals how variously the self could be imagined as cultured or cultivated.[29]

The frequent comparison of a teacher and a gardener underlines the

26. Keith Thomas, *Man and the Natural World: A History of the Modern Sensibility* (New York: Pantheon, 1983), p. 25.

27. As Thomas puts it, "the contemporary capacity to invest the natural world with symbolic meaning for human life was almost infinite" (Ibid., p. 65).

28. Michel Foucault, *Les mots et les choses* (Paris: Gallimard, 1966), trans. as *The Order of Things: An Archaeology of the Human Sciences* (New York: Pantheon, 1970; reprint, New York: Vintage, 1973): "He stands in proportion to the heavens, just as he does to animals and plants, and as he does also to the earth, to metals, to stalactites or storms" (pp. 22–23).

29. Such an implicit connection became explicit indeed by the middle of the seventeenth century in the work of the Hartlib circle, who simultaneously pursued educational and agricultural reform: "place-making and the making of individuals and societies were inextricably linked in their thought" (Leslie and Raylor, eds., *Culture and Cultivation*, introduction, p. 4).

uncertain authority of teachers and thus the fragility of their power to shape the student's self. For example, when Thomas Elyot called his ideal teacher a gardener in *The Governour*, his rhetoric once again indicated his hesitancy in asserting a teacher's mastery over his noble charge. Elyot declared that in the preparation of such "personages" who shall be governors

> I will use the policy of a wise and cunning gardener: who purposing to have in his garden a fine and precious herb, that should be to him and all other repairing thereto, excellently commodious or pleasant, he will first search throughout his garden where he can find the most mellow and fertile earth: and therein will he put the seed of the herb to grow and be nourished: and in most diligent wise attend that no weed be suffered to grow or approach nigh unto it: and to the intent it may thrive the faster, as soon as the form of an herb once appeareth, he will set a vessel of water by it, in such wise that it may continually distill on the root sweet drops; and as it springeth in stalk, under set it with some thing that it break not, and always keep it clean from weeds. Semblable order will I ensue in the forming the noble [*gentill*] wits of noble men's children, who, from the wombs of their mother, shall be made propitious [*propise*] or apt to the governance of a public weal.[30]

Through the gardening trope Elyot carefully balances the teacher's control over the student with the "noble" child's "natural" claim to superiority. At first, it appears that the teacher/gardener considers the garden and everything in it, including the noble child/plant, as his: he cultivates the "fine and precious" herb so that it should be "excellently commodious or pleasant" to "him and all other repairing thereto" — that is, for his own service, pleasure, and profit, or more generally to serve the commonwealth. To this end, the teacher/gardener would seem to be completely in charge. However, after planting the seed, the teacher/gardener never actually *touches* the plant as it grows; rather, he regulates its environment by setting a pot of water *by* it (not even actively watering), weeding the area *around* it, and putting something *underneath* it. A pattern of growth inheres in the "gentle slips," formed

---

30. Thomas Elyot, *The Boke named The Governour* (London, 1531), ed. H. H. S. Croft (1883; reprint, New York: Burt Franklin, 1967), vol. 1, p. 28.

from their mothers' wombs as "propise" to govern. The passage thus implies at once the teacher/gardener's control and his lack of mastery, an ambivalence in concert with *The Governour*'s pervasive oscillation between the teacher/adviser's self-promotion and his subservience.

However, where Elyot linked gardening more directly with governance, and thus obliquely with teaching, he granted the "gardener" a more violent dominion. Just as Elyot compared the teacher's authority to that of the prince while submitting himself to his own king, he also commented on how "it is written to the praise of Xerxes king of Persia" that he planted "innumerable trees."[31] This example repeats a common strategy of the gardening manuals that encouraged gentlemen to see husbandry as a masterful activity. Conrad Heresbach (for whom a man's property was his kingdom) noted that "most mighty kings and emperors were no whit ashamed to profess this trade [of husbandry]."[32] Not only did emperors come to be husbandmen but "husbandmen come to be emperors." Certainly Heresbach did not mean to diminish emperors in this point, as the husbandman's "tearing" the earth is compared with the triumphant conqueror's seizing a new possession.[33]

Indeed, when applied to governors, gardening could signify the violent imposition of order. When Elyot's governor uses "consideration" and "providence," he does so

> like as the good husband, when he hath sowed his ground, setteth up clouts or threads, which some call shales, some blenchers, or other like shows, to fear away birds, which he foreseeth ready to devour and hurt his corn. Also perceiving the unprofitable weeds appearing, which will annoy his corn or herbs, forthwith he weedeth them clean out of his ground, and will not

31. As Elyot put it, "in that in time vacant from the affairs of his realm, he with his own hands had planted innumerable trees . . . and for the crafty and delectable order in the setting of them, it was to all men beholding the prince's industry, exceeding marvelous" (*Governour*, vol. 1, p. 271).

32. Conrad Heresbach, *Foure Bookes of Husbandry, collected by M. Conradus Heresbachius, Counseller to the hygh and mighty Prince, the Duke of Cleve: Conteyning the whole arte and trade of Husbandry, with the antiquitie, and commendation thereof, Newly Englished, and Increased, by Barnabe Googe, Esquire* (London: Richard Watkins, 1577), fol. 5r. On man's property as a kingdom, see fol. 8r.

33. Ibid., fol. 5v.

suffer them to grow or increase. . . . In like manner a governor of a public weal ought to provide as well by menaces, as by sharp and terrible punishments, that persons evil and unprofitable do not corrupt and devour his good subjects.[34]

Elyot's teacher's garden is an enclosed plot of tender flowers and rich soil; this scene, however, is a field roughly weeded and policed by "menacing" shows. The "husbandman"/governor is tough, though he does not touch the "good" subject, who is allowed to flourish. Instead, he erects defenses to frighten enemies and uproots what is "evil and unprofitable." The good subject/corn is inviolable; the bad (not even named a subject, but a person), morally reprehensible and socially useless, is "cleanly" tossed aside.

The well-known gardening scene from Shakespeare's *Richard II*, in which the gardener discourses on Richard's failure to cultivate his land, sets the gardener against the governor, even as the one is compared with the other. The gardener is brutal: he directs his men to "like an executioner / Cut off the heads of too fast growing sprays, / That look too lofty in our common-wealth," while he will "root away / The noisome weeds, that without profit suck / The soil's fertility from wholesome flowers."[35] He judges that the king did not act like a proper gardener, who should "wound the bark" of the "over-proud" trees and lop off "superfluous branches" so that "bearing boughs may live." The king, insufficiently vigilant, becomes a mere plant in that garden, for "he that hath suffered this disordered spring / Hath now himself met with the fall of leaf. / The weeds that his broad-spreading leaves did shelter, / That seemed, in eating him, to hold him up, / Are pulled up, root and all, by *Bullingbrooke*: / I mean, the Earl of Wiltshire, *Bushy*, *Greene*" (the latter two already plants in name). The eavesdropping Queen castigates this "Old Adam" for his boldness, asking "How dares thy harsh rude tongue sound this unpleasing news? . . . / Dar'st thou,

34. Elyot, *Governour*, vol. 1, pp. 247–48. See also William Lawson, *A New Orchard and Garden* (London, 1618), for a discussion on how the arborist must prune to keep branches from rubbing against each other to avoid "civil strife."

35. *Richard II* in *Mr. William Shakespeares Comedies, Histories, and Tragedies* (London, 1623), facsimile ed. prepared by Helge Kökeritz and Charles T. Prouty (New Haven: Yale University Press, 1954), pt. 2, p. 39 (2.4).

thou little better thing than earth, / Divine his downfall?" The Queen blames the messenger, while drawing attention repeatedly to the gardener's being as base as the earth he tends. "Adam's" daring in speech (although he does not at first realize that he is speaking in her presence) mirrors his superiority as a gardener, while Richard has failed. In short, Old Adam the gardener figures as violent authority, yet his rule is also opposed to the king's traditional authority. Adam is at once low as the dirt he mucks but as high as the king himself and wiser.[36] The paradox recalls the often repeated gardening proverb that "the best dung for the ground is the master's foot."[37] This rule boasts that the master's unflagging supervision makes the land work but dirties the master's foot with excrement.

However, the violence that surfaces in the conjunction of gardener/governor/teacher does not tell the whole story. Indeed, Old Adam's ambivalent role marks the indeterminacy of the gardener's social position at this time, resembling the teacher's social insecurity in sixteenth-century court and public culture and in the private home. In the sixteenth century many wealthy landowners began to undertake the study of husbandry and horticulture, driven to attend to their own demesnes by rising prices, food shortages, and a falling income from rents, and many new gardening books underwrote that enterprise.[38] Some of these gardening manuals addressed the land's master himself as the "gardener" (although he was certainly not imagined to use the spade and knife himself),[39] while others fashioned the gardener as the ideal gentleman's servant.[40] But, increasingly, gardening manuals were

36. It is curious that while Quartos 1–5 of this play merely cite the presence of "Gardeners" the first Folio calls for the entrance of "the Gardener and two servants" as if to reinforce this idea of his special authority. On the role of the humanist adviser in analogy to this scene see Crane, *Framing*, chap. 6.

37. See Heresbach, *Foure Bookes*, fols. 3r–4v.

38. See Joan Thirsk, "Making a Fresh Start: Sixteenth-Century Agriculture and the Classical Inspiration," in Leslie and Raylor, eds., *Culture and Cultivation*, pp. 16–17.

39. For an example of this genre, see Heresbach, *Foure Bookes*. On these books, see McRae, "Husbandry Manuals," in Leslie and Raylor, eds., *Culture and Cultivation*, p. 38.

40. William Lawson's *A New Orchard and Garden* (London, 1618; reprint, New York: Garland, 1982), recommends finding "a fruiterer, religious, honest, skillful in that faculty, and therewithal painful . . . Such a gardener as will consciously, quietly and patiently travail in your orchard, God shall crown the labors of his hands with joyfulness, and

written to appeal primarily to less privileged gardeners: to yeomen, country housewives, and the poorer sort set on self-improvement.[41] Gervase Markham identified his intended audience as the "plain English husbandman."[42] William Lawson's *The Countrie Housewifes Garden* was written specifically for an audience of women who had their own small plot of land to tend, and Reynolde Scot's treatise on hop-gardens was aimed even lower, supposedly at men "trained in the open fields to practice the art of husbandry with their limbs, as being placed in the frontiers of poverty, to bear the brunt of travail and labor" (Scot even included illustrations for the illiterate).[43] All these books of instruction were implicated in the changing agrarian economy, which contributed to the developing consumer economy. New agricultural products such as hops, pippins, and flowers were being introduced and promoted as consumer products, while at the same time innovative agricultural projects, such as woad- and flax-growing, took over in the countryside.[44] The gardening books themselves proliferated in con-

---

make the clouds drop fatness upon your trees, he will provoke your love, and earn his wages, and fees belonging to his place. . . . If you be not able, nor willing to hire a gardener, keep your profits to your self, but then you must take all the pains" (pp. 1–3).

41. See, for example, Thomas Tusser, *Five Hundred Points of Good Husbandry* (London, 1573); Reynolde Scot, *A Perfite Platforme of a Hoppe Garden* (London, 1578); Leonard Mascall, *The Government of Cattell* (London, 1596). McRae discusses the importance of these books which "appeal directly to 'thrift-coveting' farmers throughout the social order, and depict an economic structure sufficiently malleable to accommodate the desires and aspirations associated with individual 'improvement'" ("Husbandry Manuals," p. 44).

42. Gervase Markham, *The English Husbandman* (London, 1613; reprint, New York: Garland, 1982) part 1, dedication to Lord Clifton. This "husbandman," distinct from the gentleman farmer, seems to have the status of a yeoman or just one step below, being a man bent on self-improvement in an economy that allowed for it. Recently some scholars have argued that the increase in agrarian capitalism in this period of rising grain prices would have favored the "yeoman farmer" to the disadvantage of poorer farmers. See J. A. Sharpe, *Early Modern England: A Social History, 1550–1760* (London: Edward Arnold, 1987), pp. 132–35. In *The English Yeoman Under Elizabeth and the Early Stuarts* (New Haven: Yale University Press, 1942), Mildred Campbell describes the controversy over whether the term "husbandman" was tied more closely to rank or occupation.

43. Reynolde Scot, *A Perfite Platforme of a Hoppe Garden* (London, 1578), sig. B2v.

44. See Joan Thirsk, *Economic Policy and Projects: The Development of a Consumer Society in Early Modern England* (Oxford: Clarendon, 1978) on the new growing of hops, pippins, apricots, licorice and tobacco in the sixteenth century (p. 13); the woad-growing projects; and the new commercial flower market (p. 46).

junction with the changing agricultural market and with the rise of what Jack Goody has called "the professional nurseryman."[45]

Like teachers, gardeners were reaching for a "professional" identity (no matter how little value they really gained in economic or status terms). Therefore, not only did the gardening books provide practical advice for those who wished to improve themselves through agriculture, but the men who wrote them also used these books to define their own social status.[46] A prolific writer of popular manuals on all subjects, Gervase Markham, boasted self-defensively in *The English Husbandman* that "I am not altogether unseen in these mysteries I write of: for it is well known I followed the profession of a Husbandman so long my self, as well might make me worthy to be a graduate in the vocation: wherein my simplicity was not such but I both observed well those which were esteemed famous in the profession, and preserved to my self those rules which I found infallible by experience."[47] Like the new humanist teachers and schoolmasters, Markham's appeal to his "profession" staked out the position of husbandman in terms of the period's inchoate notions of professionalism—in particular, the acquisition of a specific body of learning and inclusion in a select group of practitioners. His use of the term "vocation" here suggests the kind of secularization of sacred vocation that when applied to lay occupations was the key to defining a new "profession."[48]

45. In *The Culture of Flowers* (Cambridge: Cambridge University Press, 1993), Goody notes the proliferation of gardening books in the late sixteenth and early seventeenth centuries and the rise of "the professional nurseryman and a huge expenditure on plants and seeds," p. 184. See also Ronald Webber, *The Early Horticulturalists* (Newton Abbott, Devon: David and Charles, 1968), who discusses the emigration of continental horticulturalists to England in the 1550s, the response of the Gardener's Company, and the professionalization of nurserymen and seed-sellers (pp. 19–22); and Thomas, *Man and the Natural World*, pp. 224–26.

46. On the controversy concerning the existence of "professions" in early modern England, see Rosemary O'Day, "The Professions in Early Modern England," *History Today* 36 (1986) : 52–55, Wilfrid Prest, ed., *The Professions in Early Modern England* (London: Croom Helm, 1987); and Harold J. Cook, "Good Advice and Little Medicine: The Professional Authority of Early Modern English Physicians," *Journal of British Studies* 33 (1994): 1–31.

47. Markham, *The English Husbandman*, bk. 1, "A former part, before the first part," sig. a2v.

48. See O'Day, "Professions," p. 53.

Like teachers, gardeners defined their sense of authority and professionalism both in relation to a classical tradition and to their own experience and practice. Especially in the sixteenth century, books directed towards the gentleman farmer were influenced by the classical texts basic to a humanist education. In prescribing horticultural practice these books liberally cite Varro, Columella, and Pliny's treatises on agriculture (however inappropriately for sixteenth-century England, since the classical texts referred to a mediterranean climate).[49] Later manuals directed toward the "plain English husbandman" and the poor displayed a more uneasy relationship to classical authority, similar to that seen in some English writing on poetics in the same period. The writers of these books seem impelled to cite the classics, but they also tried to distinguish particularly English agricultural practices from classical or foreign ones. Leonard Mascall, in his *A Booke of the arte and manner, howe to plant and graffe all sortes of trees*, made a typical double move. He first justified both the art of grafting and writing about it in terms of classical precedent, for it is an art that "hath been put in writing of many great and worthy personages, in divers kind of languages, as in Greek by Philometer, Hiero, Acheleus, Orpheus, Museus, Homer, Hesiod, Constantine, Caesar: and in Latin, by Varro, Cato, Columella, Palladius, Virgil, Amilius Macer. . . ." Yet a few lines later Mascall repositioned himself against this tradition by insisting that all this had very little relevance for English gardeners: "for every one hath written according to the nature of his country. The Greeks for Greece, the Barbarians for Barbary, the Italians for Italy, the French men for France, etc., which writing . . . doth very small profit for this our realm of England, the which I can blame nothing more than the negligence of our nation, which hath had small care heretofore in planting and grafting."[50] Like Samuel Daniel, who argued for English poetry that

---

49. As Joan Thirsk has argued, while the new attention to farming among the gentry was certainly stimulated by economic conditions, the justification for the change was underwritten by these classical authorities on farming (Thirsk, "Making a Fresh Start," in Leslie and Raylor, eds., *Culture and Cultivation*, p. 19).

50. Leonard Mascall, *A booke of the Arte and manner, howe to plant and graffe all sortes of trees, howe to set stones, and sowe Pepines to make wylde trees to graffe on, as also remedies and medicines* (London, 1572), Epistle, sig. a3r–v. Gervase Markham severed himself more resolutely when he wrote that in his writing and gardening, "contrary to all other authors, I am neither beholden to Pliny, Virgil, Columella, Varo, Rutillius, Libault, nor

"all our understandings are not to be built on the square of Greece and Italy," gardeners such as Mascall were attempting to create a new professional authority that emanated from practical and local experience.[51] Teachers and gardeners had a traditionally low status in the early modern household; both professions, however, took on new meaning in a culture that valued work, specialized knowledge, and "improvement" for the benefit of one's self and the commonwealth.

Thus, comparing the teacher to the gardener may have resonated differently, depending on what kind of gardener was envisioned: the classical gentleman farmer overseeing his own demesne, the plain English husbandman, the ideal servant, the peasant, or the country housewife. Each had a separate claim to or style of authority in relation to experience, tradition, and social status, and thus a different tie to the land. This multiplicity reverberated through the image of the teacher/gardener. The teacher/gardener might be compared with the patriarch; in this case the "classical" was a suitable style of authority. Or the teacher/gardener might be a professional, the father's rival, who enclosed and tended a privileged space over which he maintained his own sweet dominion. Or the teacher/gardener might be the ideal servant or housewife, showing the traits of decency, piety, industry, and cleanliness that defined his or her subservience to the house's master.

Within this spectrum of roles, often ill-defined or ill-differentiated, they might be imagined to wound, mold, bend, feed, protect, and cherish in the name of profit, commonwealth, beauty, and love. We find an emphasis on surveillance and the control of growing things in

---

any other foreigner, but only to our own best experienced countrymen, whose daily knowledge hath made them most perfect in their professions." These men, he insisted, are better qualified to teach, "being men of our own neighborhood, acquainted with our climate and soil": why, for example, should English gardeners resort to "strangers' help," who recommend the use of asses' dung for manure, when England has few such animals? (*English Husbandman*, bk. 2, pt. 1, p. 13).

51. Samuel Daniel, "A Defence of Ryme" (London, 1603), reprinted in Daniel, *Poems and A Defence of Ryme*, ed. Arthur Colby Sprague (Chicago: University of Chicago Press, 1965), p. 139. For the argument in English poetics of the vernacular vs. classical models, and how it might be correlated with attention to local place and custom, see Richard Helgerson, *Forms of Nationhood: The Elizabethan Writing of England* (Chicago: University of Chicago Press, 1992), chaps. 1 and 3. While I will argue in Chap. 5 that the parallels are not as strict as Helgerson constructs them, I am indebted to his discussion of the politics of "localism" in early modern England.

the many references to weeding, pruning, and the manual training of the young child / plant. Mary Thomas Crane has observed of humanist pedagogy that, while the teacher was seen as generously planting the seeds of learning in the young mind, "in fact, most examples of this metaphor stress pruning and weeding as heavily as they do the sowing of proper seeds and nurturing of the plant"; for Crane emphasis on the "restrictive side of humanist horticulture" indicates a fear that the rhetoric will "grow out of control." As a result of this fear, "nurture" becomes "conflated with correction."[52] While fully recognizing this effect, I also believe that repression is only one side of the teacher/gardener's stance. I see a persistent and productive tension between a compulsion to order and a respect for nature's claims, understood as the plant and child's inviolable properties.

Gardens and schoolrooms overlapped most clearly where the human body and mind were understood to emulate or even share a plant's nature. William Lawson wrote in *A New Orchard and Garden* about the necessity of reforming both plants and people:

> Such is the condition of all earthly things, whereby a man receiveth profit or pleasure, that they degenerate presently without good ordering. Man himself left to himself, grows from his heavenly and spiritual generation, and becometh beastly, yea devilish to his own kind, unless he be regenerate. No marvel then, if trees make their shoots, and put their sprays disorderly. And truly (if I were worthy to judge) there is not a mischief that breedeth greater and more general harm to all the orchard . . . that ever I saw, . . . than the want of the skilful dressing of trees.[53]

52. Crane, *Framing Authority*, pp. 68–70. For a discussion of the comparison of agriculture and education in More and Erasmus, in the context of the writings of Vittorino da Feltre and Aeneas Silvius, see Wayne A. Rebhorn, "Thomas More's Enclosed Garden: *Utopia* and Renaissance Humanism," *English Literary Renaissance* 6 (1976): 140–55. Rebhorn argues that "where the humanists thought of education as a kind of agriculture and longed for a world transformed at least metaphorically into a garden of innocence, More's artistic imagination treats these metaphors literally, making the Utopians into a race of farmers and the Utopian state into an immense walled garden" (p. 141); at the same time, "*Utopia* simply expands the humanist schoolhouse until its walls reach the borders of the entire state" (p. 155).

53. Lawson, *New Orchard*, pp. 32–33.

Insofar as certain common principles of development—especially the tendency to degenerate—were thus observed in plants and people, similar treatments or "dressing" could apply to them both. Keith Thomas has observed that "so close was the relationship of trees to human society that their treatment, like that of horses or children, fluctuated according to changing educational fashion": when trees were clipped, lopped, or pleached, so were children beaten and violently restrained, and when attitudes towards pruning changed, so did educational theory.[54]

Although I think that Thomas's view must be qualified, it does appear that when bodies and plants were compared, what was most at stake was the control of superfluity and the regulation of form for health and profit. Lawson pointed out how early cutting makes a tree grow larger (and one can use the waste for fuel),[55] and Hugh Platt recommended that his readers bend tree branches to take the shape in which they would use them for building.[56] The arborist might shape any tree according to his own design. Lawson granted that "trees have their several forms," but insisted that

there is a profitable end, and use of every tree, from which if it decline (though by nature) yet man by art may (nay must) correct it. No other end of trees I never could learn, than good timber, fruit much and good, and pleasure. Uses physical hinder nothing a good form. Neither let any man ever so much as think, that it is unprobable, much less impossible, to reform any tree of what kind soever. For (believe me) I have tried it. I can bring any tree (beginning by time) to any form. The Pear and Holly may be made to spread, and the Oak to close.[57]

54. See Thomas, *Man and the Natural World*, p. 220. Thomas argues further that: "in the eighteenth century, when educational theories became less repressive, the cultivation of trees moved from regimentation to spontaneity. There was a reaction against 'mutilating' trees or carving them into 'unnatural' shapes" (p. 221).

55. Lawson, *New Orchard*, p. 35.

56. Hugh Platt, *Floraes Paradise, Beautified and adorned with sundry sorts of delicate fruites and flowers* (London, 1608): "When your trees are young, you may bow them to what compass you will, by binding them down with packthread to any circular form, or other shape that pleaseth one best. And by this means your timber will grow fit for ships, wheels, etc., whereby great waste of timber in time would be avoided" (p. 153).

57. Lawson, *New Orchard*, p. 35.

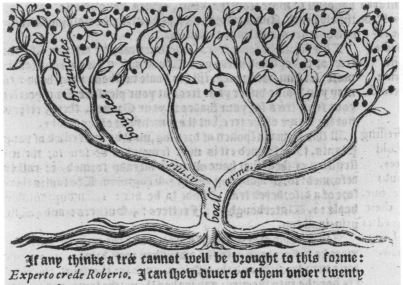

Figure 3. The perfect form of the young apple tree. From William Lawson, *A New Orchard and Garden* (London: 1618; reprint 1631), p. 37. Reproduced by permission of the Folger Shakespeare Library.

Lawson was speaking less of topiary here,[58] than of imposing form as a "reformation" for "uses physical" (see Figure 3 for his image of the perfect form of the young apple tree, "under twenty years of age"). Markham wrote of pruning as if he were a surgeon: he called for cutting away "all those superfluous branches, arms, or scions, which being either barren, bruised or misplaced, do like drones, steal away that nutriment which should maintain the better deserving sinews."[59] Familiar here from early modern anatomy is the fear of excess: in the human body, superfluity must be vented, purged, or cut away.[60] Likewise, the vegetable body should be curbed and made uniform.

58. For the history of topiary and a practical manual, see Charles H. Curtis and W. Gibson, *The Book of Topiary* (London: Bodley Head, 1904). Also see Lawson, *New Orchard*, p. 58.

59. Markham, *English Husbandman*, bk. 1, pt. 2, p. 63.

60. For a discussion of regulating corporal "superfluity" in humoral theory, see Gail

The pedagogical literature, of course, drew mostly on garden images of propagating and raising young plants and trees, which may be trained because of their flexibility (see Figure 4 for an image of gardeners training vines to a trellis, an image that evokes the "skillful experience, and worthy secrets" that such labor entails). Lawson elsewhere undercut his own insistence that he could make a tree do whatever he wanted when he reminded his reader to "begin betimes with trees, and do what you list: but if you let them grow great and stubborn, you must do as the trees list. They will not bend but break, nor be wounded without danger."[61] Such a notion also underwrites Erasmus's analogy between young bodies and young wood, in the matter of training in bodily decorum:

> As so they that for sloth draweth to a custom to crook their body causeth them to be crouch-backed, which nature never brought. And they that use to hold their head upon the one side groweth in to such a custom that in old age they labor in vain to alter it: for young bodies be like unto tender plants which in what fashion you bend them, like a fork or writhen like a cord so they grew and were stiff.[62]

This passage reveals Erasmus's strategy, which proposes a regimen of self-governance guided by the invisible hand of the "rule-setter." At first it seems that only "nature" and the boy's behavior are at stake, but the gardening metaphor slips in the firm hand of the teacher/gardener, who directs and binds.[63] The bending of the body, gesture, and

---

Kern Paster, *The Body Embarrassed: Drama and the Disciplines of Shame in Early Modern England* (Ithaca: Cornell University Press, 1993), introduction. I am also indebted to Christopher James Fassler and his discussion of social "superfluity" in his dissertation, "*Coriolanus*: Community, Theater, and Seventeenth-Century Commonwealth" (Diss., University of Pennsylvania, 1992).

61. Lawson, *New Orchard*, pp. 38–39.

62. Here, for the period effect, I have used the translation by Robert Whittingson from *De civilitate morum puerilium: The lytell booke of good maners for chyldren* (London, 1532), sig.a7v.

63. On the complexities of the "good manners" treatise and its discipline of the body's "nature," see Jacques Revel, chap. 2, in Roger Chartier, ed., *Histoire de la vie privée*: vol. 3, *De la Renaissance aux Lumières* (Paris: Editions du Seuil, 1986), trans. by Arthur Goldhammer as *A History of Private Life*, vol. 3: *Passions of the Renaissance*, (Cambridge: Harvard University Press, 1989), pp. 187–205; see also Norbert Elias, *Über den Prozess der*

THE SECOND PART OF THE

Gardeners Labyrinth, vttering such skilfull experiences and worthie secretes, about the particular sowing and remoouing of the most Kitchin Hearbes, with the wittie ordering of other daintie Hearbes, delectable Floures, pleasant Fruites, and fine Roots, as the like hath not heretofore been vttered of anie. Besides the Phisicke benefits of each Hearbe annexed, with the commoditie of waters distilled out of them, right neneffarie to be knowen.

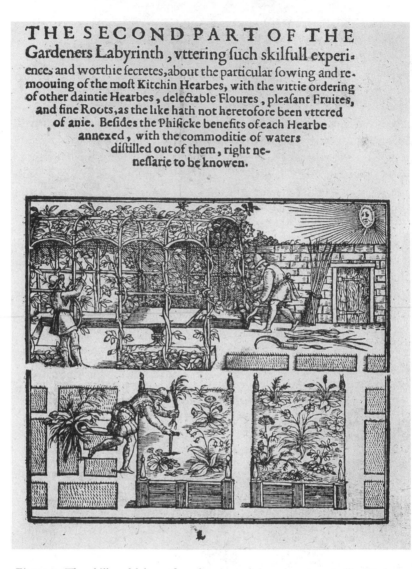

Figure 4. The skill and labor of gardeners, training vines to a trellis. Dydymus Mountain [Thomas Hill], title page to the second part of *The Gardeners Labyrinth* (London: 1577; reprint 1586). Reproduced by permission of the Folger Shakespeare Library.

manners matches the manipulation of the mind, done best when young. From the first the proper must harden into habit, preferably through emulation, just as a vine is bound to a tree.[64] As Erasmus elaborates the point in his thoughts on the early education of children, the teacher should imitate attentive farmers, who rigorously train "the still yielding shoots (*plantulas etiamnum teneras*) to cast off their wild nature (*syluestre ingenium*)" before they harden. They take care lest the plants grow crooked or are damaged, or "if damage had already been done, the farmers haste to fix it, while the plants are still flexible (*dum adhuc flexilis est ac fingentis sequitur manum*)."[65]

For Erasmus, such shaping transformed the young child from a nothing into something human and useful. Keith Thomas has argued that in this period nature was not valued or recognized in itself, but rather only as it resembled and served human beings; the wild had no meaning, and cultivation was a "moral imperative."[66] Analogously, the human being had no value without education. In Erasmus's thinking, nature may have given you a child, but it is only "a raw mass of material (*rudem massam*)"; nonetheless, it is "a compliant mass (*obtemperantem*)" and may be shaped into an optimum form: "If you delay, you will have a wild animal; if you are vigilant, you will have something divine (*Si cesses, feram habes; si aduigiles, numen, vt ita loquar, habes*)."[67] Form or cultivation defined the human; without it, one was unmarked wax,

Zivilisation: Soziogenetische und Psychogenetische Untersuchungen (1939; Berne: Francke, 1969), trans. by Edmund Jephcott as *The Civilizing Process: the History of Manners* (New York: Pantheon, 1982).

64. See Juan Luis Vives, *De tradendis disciplinis*, in *Opera Omnia*, vol. 6 (1745; reprint, London: Gregg Press, 1964), who recommends that teachers follow the husbandman's practice of binding vines to trees in having the students first copy a senior peer and only thereafter the master (*quod consilium agricolas in maritandis vitibus vedemus sequi*) (bk. 4, chap. 4, p. 362). See Quintilian, *Institutio oratoria*, bk. 1.1.26, for the source of this trope. See Halpern, *Poetics*, chaps. 1 and 2, for a discussion of emulation as training.

65. *De pueris statim ac liberaliter instituendis*, ed. Jean-Claude Margolin, in Desiderius Erasmus, *Opera Omnia* (Amsterdam: North-Holland, 1971), vol. 1, bk. 2, p. 28; the translations are my own, but throughout I have consulted the translation by Beert Verstraete, "A Declamation on the Subject of Early Liberal Education for Children," in J. K. Sowards, ed., *Collected Works of Erasmus*, vol. 26: *Literary and Educational Writings*, vol. 4 (Toronto: University of Toronto Press, 1985).

66. Thomas, *Man and the Natural World*, p. 254.

67. Erasmus, *De pueris*, p. 33.

dull clay, uncontained water, or an unwritten book.[68] This "numinous" creature had, of course, to be functional: one became human when one could serve human society. Often, the analogy between farming and education ends up by positioning the object—human, animal, and vegetable alike—as a product for the profit of the teacher/gardener, the family or master he or she serves, or the commonwealth as a whole.[69]

Both pedagogical and gardening handbooks recommended weeding as the complement to pruning and training the plant/child, insofar as weeding controls the seedling's environment. Weeding images occur most frequently in the pedagogical literature in the context of reading and books. Vives used the image frequently when he wrote about expurgating books for student use: classical literature, for example, is "a wide field (*latum . . . agrum*), where grow plants, some useful, some poisonous (*in quo herbae proveniant partim utiles, partim noxiae*)."[70] Extending the distinction between weeds and plants to children, the child's mind becomes soil, and the various thoughts or texts "planted" there, weeds and good herbs; alternatively, the schoolroom or child's society resembles a field, strewn with healthful and harmful companions/plants. "Weeds" were associated with poison or contagion, but also with competition for resources. In *The Countrie Housewifes Garden* Lawson acknowledged that weeds are inherently more vital than "good herbs," the former "strengthened by nature, and the other by art."[71]

---

68. Ibid.: "*Mox tracta ceram dum mollissima est, finge argillam etiamnum vdam, imbue liquoribus optimis testam, dum rudis est, tinge lanam dum a fullone niuea venit, nullisque maculis contaminata.*" Erasmus also mentions Antisthenes' comparison of a student to a new book, pen, and writing tablet (*libro, inquit, nouo, stylo nouo, tabella noua*) (p. 33). Such freshness cannot be maintained, for "without fixing into human form, it will become bestial (*Non potetes habere rudem massam. Nisi finxeris in hominis speciem, in ferarem monstrosas effigies sua sponte deprauabitur*)."

69. So Erasmus asked, "what plant or animal can serve our uses unless our industry adds to nature (*quod autem animal aut quae planta respondet possessorum aut agricolarum votis et vsibus, nisi nostra industria naturam adiuuerit? Id quo fit tempestiuius, hoc succcesit felicius*)," ibid., p. 28.

70. Vives, *De tradendis*, bk. 1, chap. 6, p. 269. See Vives on the difficulty of the process of disentangling the good and bad, in bk. 3, chap. 5, p. 322: "How are we to collect the healthy plants among the poisonous ones? (*quomodo colligendae salutares herbae inter tot noxias?*)."

71. William Lawson, *The Countrie Housewifes Garden, Containing Rules for Hearbes of Common Use, Together with the Husbandrye of Bees, Published with secrets, very necessary for every Housewife* (London: Alsop, 1617; reprint, New York: Garland, 1982), p. 2. See also

Thus, weeds must be extracted with delicate violence, not only because their roots intertwine with the good plant's, but also because the fine plants are weaker than the weeds. In *The Gardener's Labyrinth* Thomas Hill recommended that the husbandman weed "in a soft and tender manner," just as the humanist pedagogues were to treat their charges with compassion: the weeds must be "purged" tenderly, "that the roots of the young plants be not loosed and feebled in the soft earth."[72] As was true in Elyot's comparison of gardening and governance, such recommendations assume a clear difference between the good and bad plants, when the bad must be removed to foster the growth of the good (however difficult in practice). By 1629, however, we find John Parkinson complaining in his *Paradisi in Sole* that none of the earlier botanicals "have particularly severed those that are beautiful flower plants, fit to store a garden of delight and pleasure, from the wild and unfit: but have interlaced many, one among another, whereby many that have desired to have fair flowers, have not known either what to choose, or what to desire."[73]

Pruning, bending and weeding in gardening and their translation in pedagogy all depicted the teacher/gardener's strength and obligation to produce. The teacher/gardener imposed uniformity on a disorderly nature in order to foster the chosen child/plant and increase his/its social value. From the first one should be able to distinguish the good from the bad, and treat them accordingly. When he did so the teacher/gar-

---

Dydymus Mountain (Thomas Hill), *The Gardener's Labyrinth* (London, 1594; reprint New York: Garland, 1982), with his qualification that "All the field plants, flowers and roots, are stronger in nature, but in substance inferior to the garden plants, etc. Among the wild plants, those growing on the mountains or high hills, do excel the others in property. Among all plants, those also are of a stronger nature which shall be of a livelier color, better taste and savor" (p. 59).

72. Ibid., p. 47.

73. Parkinson, *Paradisi in Sole*, Epistle, p. 3. Terry Comito argues that the "practical gardening manuals" emphasize the need to control the "earth's untutored fruitfulness" (pp. 20–21), whereas to botanists presenting nature to an aristocratic audience, "there are no 'weeds' among the 'several Tribes and Kindreds of Nature's beauty.'" Comito cites Parkinson as an example of the latter type. It seems to me, however, that Parkinson is equally concerned with establishing a hierarchy in nature. See Comito, *The Idea of the Garden in the Renaissance* (New Brunswick: Rutgers University Press, 1978), pp. 21–22. Cf. Thomas, *Man and the Natural World*, p. 269, who cites Parkinson as typical of those who made a distinction between the cultivated and the wild.

dener served the commonwealth, for, as Markham wrote of the husbandman, "a husbandman is the Master of the earth, turning sterility and barrenness, into fruitfulness and increase, whereby all common wealths are maintained and upheld, it is his labor which giveth bread to all men and maketh us forsake the society of beasts drinking upon the water springs, feeding us with a much more nourishing liquor." The resulting profit is justified, for "profit is the whole aim of our lives in this world: besides it is most necessary for keeping the earth in order, which else would grow wild, and like a wilderness, brambles and weeds choking up better plants, and nothing remaining but a chaos of confusedness."[74] Erasmus put a similar pressure on the teacher when he compared his work to a farmer's, "who never ceases to cultivate every part of his land, whether with grain, trees, pasture, or gardens; for a recently plowed field must be sown, unless uncultivated it bring forth thistles (*ne incultis ex se gignat zizania*): for surely it must yield something (*nam omnino aliquid gignat oportet*). Similarly, unless the tender child's mind is engaged in fruitful education, it too will be overgrown by vice (*nisi protinus frugiferis disciplinis occupetur vitiis obducitur*)."[75] In both of these versions of cultivation, without the teacher/gardener's intervention and imposition of order society will decline, the land will revert to the wild, and people turn into beasts.

However, as Erasmus's comparison of a child and a newly plowed field makes clear, intervention is important precisely because without it the field will bring forth a quite different crop on its own; that is, it will not be barren but produce an all-too-prickly fruit. Comparing the child with fertile soil recognizes the child/soil's resistance to the imposition of order and uniformity. Not only does the analogy mark that resistance, but it also signals some respect for it. When, in *The Education of a Christian Prince*, Erasmus compared the infant's mind to a newly plowed soil in which "one sows early the seeds of virtue (*ac protinus in puerilis animi nouale iacienda honesti semina*),"[76] this fresh

74. Markham, *English Husbandman*, Bk. 1, "former part of the first book," sig. A3r–v.

75. Erasmus, *De pueris*, p. 75.

76. Erasmus, *Institutio principis christiani* (1516), ed. O. Herding, in *Opera Omnia*, vol. 4, bk. 1, p. 137; translations from the *Institutio* are my own, but I have consulted Neil M. Cheshire and Michael J. Heath's translation, "On the Education of a Christian

soil is like a blank slate, but it also has a powerful potential. As Erasmus warned parents elsewhere, in bringing forth a child "nature surrenders to you a newly plowed field, empty but fertile (*natura tibi tradit in manus nouale, vacuum quidem, sed soli felicis*); if neglected, it will bear thorns and brambles, which you will root out later only with great labor (*tu per incuriam sinis hoc vepribus ac spinis occupari, vix vlla industria in posterum euellendis*)."[77] The "purity" of the child's mind is also fertility, and its instability must be managed, for indeed, "the better the soil is naturally, the more easily it is corrupted and overgrown by useless plants and crops, unless the farmer is vigilant (*etenim quo melior est soli natura, hoc magis corrumpitur et inutilibus herbis ac fructicibus occupatur, ni vigilet agricola*)"; similarly, the more felicitous a man's nature (*ingenium hominis*), the more easily it is taken over by vice unless nurtured by education. [78]

The gardeners' discussions of soil help to clarify the implication of the comparison, for they combined the drive to improve any soil with attention to its particular "nature" (that to which Erasmus refers). Most gardeners would tend to join in the surveyor John Norden's opinion "that there is no kind of soil, be it never so wild, boggy, clay, or sandy, but will yield one kind of beneficial fruit or other," especially through the thoughtful application of manure.[79] The gardening books at first may appear to tend towards generality rather than specificity, offering uniform rules for imposing order and form on a diverse nature. At the same time, however, the writers looked to regional differences. As Norden put it, "every place" should be cultivated "to his fittest fruit."[80]

Prince," in *Collected Works of Erasmus*, vol. 27: *Literary and Educational Writings*, vol. 5, ed., A. H. T. Levi (Toronto: Univ. of Toronto Press, 1986).

77. Erasmus, *De pueris*, p. 39.

78. Erasmus, *Institutio*, p. 141. Also see Crane's discussion of this trope, *Framing Authority*, pp. 68–72.

79. John Norden, *The Surveiors Dialogue, Very Profitable for all men to peruse, but especially for all Gentleman, or any other Farmar, or Husbandman, that shall either have occasion, or be willing to buy or sell lands.*. . . . (London, 1610), p. 167.

80. Ibid. McRae comments on this passage: "These attitudes inevitably promoted the acceptance of regional specialization. England could not henceforth be represented as a patchwork of self-sufficient manors because the 'rule of reason' dictated specific uses for land in different regions. . . . This model would embrace regional specialization in the cause of 'reason' and depict a nation bound by the 'rational' networks of a market economy" ("Husbandry Manuals," p. 51).

Markham thought that it was the husbandman's duty to "consider the nature of his grounds and which is of which quality and temper" because one could not generalize about the land,[81] and "every man in his own work knows the alteration of climates."[82] In short, the knowledge that the husbandman needed in working with soil was a knowledge of differences as well as of rules of form.[83]

When the pedagogical texts spoke of the particular "nature" of the child's "soil" it was to similar effect. Although elsewhere he calls the uneducated child a meaningless mass, Erasmus also speaks of the child's "nature" as present from the first. As he wrote in his work on early education for children, "each person has a particular nature (*sed est natura huic aut illi peculiaris*)" and is suited for a particular discipline; each may be so drawn to that discipline, that "he cannot be deterred for any reason (*ut nulla ratione possint deterreri*)," and, conversely, he may so vehemently hate another discipline that he would sooner walk though fire than study it.[84] So in *The Education of a Christian Prince* he recommended that the teacher should look for signs of the child's "propensities" and try to steer the child's nature in the right direction. "A proclivity to virtue (*ad honesta procliuem*)" or traits that might be easily turned to virtue, like ambition and extravagance, should be assiduously "cultivated (*cultu*)."[85]

Of all the pedagogical writers, Erasmus seems most divided about the force of the child's nature. He wrote that it is best to start education early, for "a *habitus* will harden when fixed in a mind that is tender and blank (*durat is habitus in quem vacuum ac tenerum animum finxeris*)." He then cites Horace's maxim that "You may expell nature with a pitchfork, but she will always come back (*naturam expellas furca, tamen vsque recurrit*)." Erasmus concurs, yet immediately reminds us that the poet is talking about "adult trees (*arbore adulta*)." So, all the more,

81. Markham, *English Husbandman*, bk. 1, pt. 1, p. 2.

82. Ibid., bk. 1, pt. 1, p. 9.

83. For Markham's directions concerning different soils and their cultivation in a multitude of places, see *English Husbandman*, bk. 1, "former part," sig. e2v; see also Norden's *Surveiors Dialogue*, p. 168.

84. Erasmus, *De pueris*, p. 44.

85. Erasmus, *Institutio*, p. 140.

one should emulate the farmer who sets his shoots as he would wish the tree to be; for "what is implanted in our being at the beginning becomes an integral part of us (*protinus in naturam vertitur, quod omnium primum infuderis*)." Clay may sometimes be too moist to retain any impression, and wax may be too soft for molding; but "no human being is ever too young for learning (*at vix vlla est aetas tam tenera quae disciplinae capax non sit*)."[86] Thus, at the first the passage strengthens the teacher/farmer's hand, acknowledging him as fully able to train the tender and "vacuous" plants, but the passage from Horace implies the contrary in suggesting that "nature" cannot be controlled but will inevitably revert or recur (*recurrit*) to what it was before. Then the text qualifies this observation by insisting it is true only of fully formed or "adult" trees. Yet the next analogy to wax and clay equally undermines the teacher's power. While the teacher's approach must aim at the point of least resistance, he needs *some* resistance to form a character: wax may be too soft, clay too moist, but children must have enough natural substance to take on a shape.

The latter passage, of course, begs for a Foucauldian interpretation whereby resistance is necessary for power to work. Elsewhere, however, Erasmus put the point much more strongly, describing the child as naturally inclined to virtue. Because the seeds planted in us are endowed with "vigorous" or "forcible" strength (*ad quam semina quaedam vehementia naturae vis inseuit*), these seeds of our "natural propensity" need only the addition of teacher's industry (*modo ad naturae propensionem accedat formatoris industria*).[87] Here forcible potential overcomes even particularity—the division between the naturally good and the bad. These are the same Platonic "seeds" that Vives described as a desire and an instinct for the truth, what he says Aristotle called *potestatem* and Plato *semina*, and others (in Greek), *prolepseis*, "preconceptions and admonitions fixed in our minds by nature (*anticipationes, et monitiones animis nostris a natura impressas ac infixis*)." Human nature is innately powerful and good, but vulnerable to cultural decay, for

---

86. Erasmus, *De pueris*, p. 47. The last quoted passage is Verstraete's translation in *Collected Works*, ed. Sowards, vol. 26, p. 310.

87. Erasmus, *De pueris*, p. 38.

"*inertia* and negligence may crush and destroy the seeds (*semina*), but use will produce from them a plant and fruit (*educit vero in stirpem ac fructus exercitatio per usum rerum*)."[88] Such passages articulate two of the most familiar—and potentially conflicting—premises attributed to humanist educational theory: that there is an essential human nature and that each person is particular, with different inclinations or propensities that defy generalization. As Montaigne put the paradox, "Oh ingenious mixture of Nature. If our faces were not like, we could not discern a man from a beast; if they were not unlike, we could not distinguish one man from another man."[89]

Such thinking about the child's nature called for a teaching method at once stern and deferential that allowed for the fact that the child is not in fact a blank slate but rather a force of nature. As Elyot reminded his reader, "the office of a tutor is first to know the nature of his pupil, that is to say, whereto he is most inclined or disposed, and in what thing he setteth his most delectation or appetite." If he is good then the tutor will "commend those virtues"; if not he will loudly deplore his vices.[90] Joining with Elyot in advocating attention to the differences of children was also—perhaps surprisingly—that severe advocate of corporal punishment, Richard Mulcaster. With Elyot, Erasmus, and Vives, Mulcaster thought that "there be both in the body, and the soul

88. Vives, *De tradendis*, bk. 1, chap. 2, pp. 250-51. See also bk. 3, chap. 5, p. 324, on the notion that nature implants in every human mind the seeds of the arts (*semina artium omnum quaedam a natura acceperit*). Cf. Richard Mulcaster, *Positions wherin those primitive circumstances be examined, which are necessarie for the training up of children, either for skill in their booke, or health in their bodie* (London, 1581), reprint, ed. Robert Hebert Quick (London: Longmans, Green, 1888): "For as the powers of the soul come to no proof, or to very small if they be not fostered by their natural train, but wither and die, like corn not reaped, but suffered to rot by negligence of the owner, or by contention in challenge: even so, nay much more, the body being of itself lumpish and earthy, must needs either die in drowsiness, or live in looseness, if it be not stirred and trained diligently to the best" (p. 40). As this book went to press, I consulted a new edition of the *Positions*, ed. William Barker (Toronto: University of Toronto Press, 1994), which lists textual variants and offers a valuable introduction. On the religious dimensions of this argument, see Leah Sinanoglou Marcus, *Childhood and Cultural Despair: A Theme and Variations in Seventeenth-Century Literature* (Pittsburgh: University of Pittsburgh Press, 1978), chap. 2.

89. Michel de Montaigne, "Of Experience," *The Essayes, or Morall, Politike and Millitarie Discourses*, trans. John Florio (London, 1603), p. 636.

90. Elyot, *Governour*, vol. 1, p. 38.

of man certain ingenerate abilities, which the wisdom of parents, and reason of teachers, perceiving them in their infancy, and by good direction advancing them further, during those young years, cause them prove in their ripeness very good and profitable, both to the parties which have them, and to their countries, which use them." The parent/master has some control over the ripening of these abilities "by nature implanted, for nurture to enlarge,"[91] but he does not have complete control over them, for indeed these qualities may not be easy to perceive.[92] Like the empiricist "mechanic" or scientist, the parent and teacher must observe individual phenomena, focusing on the diversity of human experience in contrast to its generality.[93]

The question of how much the teacher controls the child's nature plays into a more general debate over whether "property" or the nature of any living thing can be altered. Horticulturalists, like other experimenters in the natural sciences, were already arguing over the extent of natural resistance to the master's hand. Some writers boasted of their ability to change almost any plant to serve human needs and tastes. Others, however, insisted that the "property" of a living thing cannot be altered by art, and a few argued both ways at once, divided between respecting a plant's natural properties and wanting to exploit them. Thomas Hill, Leonard Mascall, Hugh Platt, and Gervase Markham all offered recipes for changing the tastes of fruit, the colors and appearance of flowers, and the times of ripening by artificial means.[94] For example, Markham praised "the effects of grafting" whereby you will have fruits "to ripen early, as at the least two months before the ordinary time." Further, he advised that "if you will have the fruit to

91. Mulcaster, *Positions*, p. 25.

92. See also ibid., p. 26: "Wherefore as good parents, and masters ought to find out, by those natural principles, whereunto the younglings may best be framed, so ought they to follow it, until it be complete, and not to stay, without cause beyond stay, before it come to ripeness, which ripeness, while they be in learning, must be measured by their ableness to receive that, which must follow their forebuilding."

93. See Hiram Haydn, *The Counter-Renaissance* (New York: Scribner's, 1950), pp. 224–51, on "the science of the particular."

94. Platt, Markham, and Mascall are cited elsewhere in this chapter; see also Thomas Hill, *The Art of Gardening*, of which the earliest edition was printed in London in 1522. See, for example, Hill's discussion of lilies, on p. 97 of the 1608 edition of *The Art of Gardening*.

taste like spice, with a certain delicate perfume, you shall boil honey, the powder of cloves and hoar together, and being cold anoint the grafts therewith you put them into the cleft." Or if you want to change the color, bore a hole in the trunk and fill the hole with saffron to produce a yellow fruit.[95] Yet even the industrious Markham was somewhat critical of such "conceits and experiments," which "concern the curious rather than the wise,"[96] and other gardeners were more doubtful of these efforts. Hugh Platt, who himself published compendia of "secret" ways to master the unreliability and mystery of just about everything, wavered between his admiration of Hill's "experience" in these matters of "changing the color, taste, or scent, of any fruit, or flower" and his belief that "though some fruits and flowers seem to carry the scent, or taste, of some aromatical body; yet that doth rather arise from their own natural infused quality, then from the hand of man."[97] By 1629 John Parkinson contended much more strongly that the hand of man has only a limited power over plants. He insisted that "all double flowers were so found wild, being the work of nature alone, and not the art of any man" and that "there is no power or art in man, to cause flowers to show their beauty divers months before their natural time, nor to abide in their beauty longer then the appointed natural time for every one of them." He emphatically declared that any recipes for changing color or scent "from that they were or would be naturally, are mere fancies of men, without any ground of reason or truth."[98]

The ongoing argument over cultivating gillyflowers (carnations or pinks), which serves as a central metaphor for social mobility in Shakespeare's *The Winter's Tale*, neatly demonstrates how such claims for and against art had a distinct social orientation. Markham and Platt both suggested that you could change a gillyflower from a single to a more valued double bloom or change its color through careful culture. Platt confidently directed the gardener to make a plant double by trans-

95. Markham, *English Husbandman*, bk. 1, pt. 2, p. 58.
96. Ibid.
97. Hugh Platt, *Floraes Paradise, Beautified and Adorned with sundry sorts of delicate fruites and flowers* (London, 1608), pp. 141–42.
98. Parkinson, *Paradisi in Sole*, p. 25.

planting at different phases of the moon,[99] while Markham recommended grafting to make them "exceeding great, double, and most orient of color."[100] However, against Markham and others, John Parkinson claimed that you could not propagate gillyflowers by grafting. He mocked any claims that gardeners made to achieve such results with any flower, deploring "the wonderful desire that many have to see fair, double, and sweet flowers, [which] hath transported them beyond both reason and nature, feigning and boasting often of what they would have, as if they had it."[101] In answer to the question of how some flowers have come to be double, "if they were not made so by art," Parkinson crisply replied that we just do not know, except that they are naturally so: "we only have them as nature hath produced them, and so they remain."[102] He speculated that something added to a plant cannot change it permanently, for such added substances are "corporeal . . . and whatsoever should give any color unto a living and growing plant, must be spiritual: [and] . . . no heterogeneal things can be mixed naturally together."[103] Whereas in works directed to the middling sort the gardeners expressed confidence in the human ability to manipulate or improve nature, Parkinson, who was apothecary to James I and

99. "Remove a plant of stock gillyflowers when it is a little wooded, and not too green, and water it presently; do this three days after the full [moon], and remove it twice more before the change [of the moon]. Doe this in barren ground, and likewise three days after the next full moon, remove again; and then remove once more before the change: Then at the third full moon, viz. 8. days after, remove again, and set in very rich ground, and this will make it to bring forth a double flower" (Platt, *Floraes Paradise*, pp. 78–79).

100. "These gillyflowers you may make of any color you please, in such sort as is showed you for the coloring of lilies, and if you please to have them of mixed colors you may also, by grafting of contrary colors one into another: and you may with as great ease graft the gillyflower as any fruit whatsoever, by the joining of the knots one into another, and then wrapping them about with a little soft sleeved silk, and covering the place close with soft red ware well tempered" (Markham, *English Husbandman*, bk. 2, p. 36).

101. Parkinson, *Paradisi*, p. 22.

102. Ibid., p. 23.

103. Ibid., p. 24: "For scents and colors are both such qualities as follow the essence of plants, even as forms are also; and one may as well make any plant to grow of what form you will, as to make it of what scent or color you will; and if any man can form plants at his will and pleasure, he can do as much as God himself that created them."

royal botanist for Charles I,[104] posited a nature resistant to interference while defining a natural "aristocracy" in the botanical world. Similarly, he valued his own books for distinguishing the common from the rare flowers, whereas earlier herbal and botanical works did not make such a distinction.[105] In this view, which sorts out the better flowers from the unfit, the plants can be nurtured or killed, but their natural place in the aesthetic and "social" order cannot be changed.

In his discussion of altering gillyflowers in *Sylva Sylvarum*, Francis Bacon tried to find the middle ground between respecting an immutable aristocracy in nature and retaining the right to change it—a characteristically artful negotiation of the claims of art and nature. Like Parkinson, Bacon contended that "the altering of the scent, color, or taste of fruit, by infusing, mixing, or letting into the bark or root of the tree, herb, or flower, any colored, aromatical, or medicinal substance, are but fancies."[106] Yet the text goes on to consider all sorts of horticultural curiosities (even though its author may "hate impostures, and despise curiosities").[107] Bacon cared to speculate why some gilly-flowers might be colored or monotone:

> Take gilly-flower seed, of one kind of gilly-flower . . . and sow it; and there will come up gilly-flowers, some of one color, and some of another, casually, as the seed meeteth with nourishment in the earth; so that the gardeners find that they may have two or three roots amongst an hundred that are rare and of great price; as purple, carnation of several stripes: the cause is (no doubt) that in earth, though it be contiguous and in one bed, there are

104. His book's dedication to Henrietta Maria addressed the Queen as the greatest of gardeners: because she was "furnished with them as far beyond others, as you are eminent before them," he asked her to accept "this speaking Garden, that may inform you in all the particulars of your store" (Ibid., Epistle Dedicatory).

105. "To satisfy therefore their desires that are lovers of such delights, I took upon me this labor and charge, and have here selected and set forth a garden of all the chiefest for choice, and fairest for show, from among all the several tribes and kindreds of Nature's beauty, and have ranked them as near as I could" (Ibid., Epistle to the reader, p. 3).

106. Francis Bacon, *Sylva Sylvarum*, in *The Works of Francis Bacon*, ed. James Spedding, Robert Leslie Ellis, and Douglas Denon Heath (1859; reprint, Stuttgart: Friedrich Frommann, 1963), vol. 2, pp. 498–99.

107. Ibid., p. 501.

very several juices; and as the seed doth casually meet with them, so it cometh forth.[108]

Such an explanation thus implies at once rarity by nature and a random material causation, which could then lend itself to manipulation. This Bacon eagerly advocated, advising that one also attempt to make flowers double by "often removing them into new earth" (whereas doubles will revert to singles if neglected).[109] Bacon thus delicately balanced a notion of fixed nature with a recognition of the influence of the local conditions and arrived at an explanation that permits the intervention of the human hand.[110]

The Winter's Tale's interlude on grafting gillyflowers thus concisely records the contemporary sociology of horticulture. At first it does seem odd that it is Perdita, the "shepherdess," who dislikes grafting while Polixenes, the disguised king, defends it and thereby the mixing of degrees. Perdita tells Polixenes that she cares not to get the slips of "streaked Gilly-vors, / Which some call Nature's bastards," because "there is an Art, which in their piedness shares / With great creating Nature." Polixenes justifies the practice as "an art, / That Nature makes" and "an Art / Which does mend Nature: change it rather, but / The Art itself, is Nature."[111] Perdita is in fact a natural aristocrat, a

---

108. Ibid., p. 504. See also p. 502, which suggests that culture can change the color of a flower: "It is observed by some, that gilly-flowers, sweet-williams, violets, that are colored, if they be neglected, and neither watered, nor new molded, nor transplanted, will turn white. And it is probable that the white with much culture may turn colored."

109. Ibid., p. 505.

110. In his essay "Of Gardens," in *The Essayes or Counsels* (London, 1625) Bacon veered between a naturalist aesthetic (suggested in his distaste for topiary and admiration of a heath) and his effort to create a *ver perpetuum* or perpetual spring in this "Royal Ordering of Gardens" (p. 266). In his *New Atlantis* gardens prosper through the art of grafting and "inoculating," so that they are "by art greater much than their nature" (*The Works of Francis Bacon*, vol. 3, p. 158). It could be argued that aristocrats might see in the improvement of nature "a new freedom based on the power they effortlessly wield over the world" (Comito, *Idea of the Garden*, p. 2); yet, at the same time, the naturalism of Bacon's ideal garden itself marks an emerging aristocratic aesthetic at a time when "improvement" might as well be associated with the ambitions of the socially mobile. See Tayler, *Nature and Art*, p. 16. I thank Barbara Riebling and Julie Solomon for their helpful remarks about Bacon's writing on gardens.

111. Shakespeare, *The Winters Tale* in 1623 Folio facs., pt. 1, p. 292 (4.3).

state her low culture cannot alter; Polixenes, in turn, subsumes the art of gardening into a kind of nature. As Terry Eagleton puts it, according to this scene, "these distinctions of class and rank are themselves natural, because somehow produced by Nature; for Nature is at once an amorphous, indivisible process and a structure of precise discriminations."[112] The same effect can be observed in the argument of Andrew Marvell's mower, in "The Mower Against Gardens," when he claims that "fauns and fairies do the meadow till, / More by their presence than their skill." Here labor, art, and agency are erased in a nature that *is* rather than *does*, yet paradoxically tills or cultivates at the same time. In these cases agency is reappropriated for nature, or the given order, against the claims of those artists or upstarts who would deal "between the bark and tree, / Forbidden mixtures there to see."[113] The artificial agency that men like Markham, Hill, and Mascall had celebrated earlier and had endeavored to make accessible to everyone from yeomen to housewives becomes, in an interesting class shift, unseemly luxury and enforcement for Marvell's mower. Elyot's efforts to reconcile his conviction that a child born a gentleman is always already one with his argument that culture gentrifies anticipate this kind of naturalization. In the century between these writers the political and social implications of an argument by "nature" had branched off so that nature stood for the status quo or resistance to repression and art for domination of the natural order or liberation from its rules.[114]

The role of time, or timeliness, in both pedagogy and horticulture compresses this tension, for time is seen as a point of resistance to domination, and the teacher/gardener must make much of time. Gardeners quarreled over whether art could alter natural seasons or the times of flowering and fruiting. While Mascall, Markham, and Hill

112. Terry Eagleton, *William Shakespeare* (Oxford: Basil Blackwell, 1986), p. 92. See also Raymond Williams, *The Country and the City* (London: Chatto and Windus, 1973), on the ideology of "nature" in the seventeenth century.

113. Andrew Marvell, "The Mower against Gardens," in *Andrew Marvell*, ed. Frank Kermode and Keith Walker (Oxford: Oxford University Press, 1990), p. 40.

114. See Frances E. Dolan, "Taking the Pencil out of God's Hand: Art, Nature, and the Face-Painting Debate in Early Modern England," *PMLA* 108 (1993): 224–39, on the early modern debate over cosmetics; while focusing on gender, her general argument is that the quarrel about art and nature encoded tension concerning agency, social mobility and identity.

advised how to work against time (an art primarily the luxury of those who could afford to build greenhouses), Parkinson insisted that "every one knoweth their own appointed natural times, which they constantly observe and keep, according to the temperature of the year, or the temper of the climate."[115] A similar question occurred in the humanist pedagogical discourse when it addressed the timing of the child's education. Teachers wondered whether they could bring a child to learn things early or if they were constrained to respect a natural time for learning, different for each child. The demands of time, set by each child's natural "propensities," might constitute a form of resistance to the master's manipulation; or these demands could merely require increased surveillance to maximize profit; or, finally, timing as a natural difference could serve to justify different treatment of children on the basis of rank and gender.

All the talk about the child as a seedling makes it clear that, like gardening, education was driven by time. Just as the early modern teachers fluctuated between their call for play and their drive to work, they also tried to combine their respect for the child's development with their anxiety about time's passing. They worried that the teacher might miss the critical point to intervene in the child's growth before the green sapling stiffened to hard wood. Erasmus and Elyot fretted about early intervention in the case of the prince or governor, for, according to Erasmus, if what we absorb in the early years is important, it is even more so for the prince.[116] Elyot put this in practical terms, advising that the noble child's instruction in Latin and Greek begin before age seven, for "infelicity of our time and country compelleth us to encroach somewhat upon the years of children, and especially of noble men, that they may sooner attain to wisdom and gravity than private persons."[117] Even though noblemen and princes should be more naturally inclined to virtue than "private persons," it appears that it was even more critical to restrain them early.

115. Parkinson, *Paradisi*, p. 25: "As for example, those plants that do flower in January or February, will by no art or industry of man be caused to flower in Summer or in Autumn; and those that flower in April and May, will not flower in January or February; or those in July, August, etc., either in the Winter or Spring."
116. Erasmus, *Institutio*, p. 137.
117. Elyot, *Governour*, vol. 1, p. 32.

Mulcaster, however, who mostly addressed the education of ordinary children, was more wary that the child not be rushed through his or her education. It is fascinating that Mulcaster, who elsewhere so strongly advocated standardizing education and defended corporal punishment, should be so acutely aware of the master's uncertain control over time as to acknowledge that the moment of the child's "ripeness" for learning is as variable as it is for plants. Regarding the question of when to begin a child's education, he answered: "At what years I cannot say, because ripeness in children, is not tied to one time, no more than all corn is ripe for one reaping."[118] But while not universally predictable, it is important to know that time, for "hasty pressing onward is the greatest enemy, which any thing can have whose best is to ripe at leisure . . . How many small infants have we set to grammar, which can scarcely read? How many to learn Latin, which never wrote [a] letter?"[119] Every type of wit, further, develops in a different pattern prone to changes, "for in each wit there is likelihood, and yet error in each. For as there be fair blossoms, so there be nipping frosts. And till the danger of revolt be past, the quick must be held in hope, the dull without despair, the mean the meetest."[120] Mulcaster's use of the word "revolt" here reveals that he saw underneath the calculation of timing a conflict in which the child's "nature" momentarily has the upper hand.[121]

Yet when Mulcaster turned to the same issue in the matter of the education of girls, "nature" and timing took on a different cast. Mulcaster believed in educating girls, given the custom of the country and girls' natural "towardness" (although he did not recommend their attending universities or grammar schools, as this was *not* "the custom of the country"). Nature, he argues, has given girls "abilities to prove excellent in their kind," and thus "young maidens deserve the train[ing]: because they have that treasure, which belongeth unto it, bestowed on them by nature, to be bettered in them by nur-

118. Mulcaster, *Positions*, p. 18.
119. Ibid., p. 256.
120. Ibid., pp. 140–41.
121. But see Goldberg, *Writing Matter*, for a deconstruction of Mulcaster's "nature," where "nature" can only be that which is already "marked" or written (pp. 32–33).

ture."[122] "Nature" calls for parents' tending to their daughters' education with "the same regard to the weakness and strength of their wits and bodies, the same care for their womanly exercises, for help of their health, and strength of their limbs, being remitted to their considerations, which I assigned them in their sons." In what follows, however, attention to "nature" and "property" ultimately worked to the disadvantage of girls, who were seen by nature to follow a different life cycle. Girls, Mulcaster wrote, are also naturally different, for while they may seem to be more intelligent at first, "their natural weakness which cannot hold long, delivers very soon, and yet there be as prating boys, as there be prattling wenches. Besides, their brains be not so much charged, neither with weight nor with multitude of matters, as boys' heads be, and therefore like empty casks they make the greater noise."[123] At first it seems as though Mulcaster was ready to allow for equal education of girls and boys, on the basis of a respect for the individual child's nature. By the end of the passage, however, the argument by nature also allows for dismissing girls, who are by nature weak and "lighter" than boys. Mulcaster noted Aristotle's view of the natural differences in male and female "uses in nature," "condition," and "virtues" and concluded that, while boys and girls may be "of one kind," education brings each to perfection through these differences.[124]

Arguments about the education of girls, as well as of the poor, thus tended to orient themselves doubly—to the nature inherent in gender and rank and to social function.[125] As was the case for different kinds of boys, the humanists' arguments about the usefulness of educating women weighed both the pragmatic end of their social role and a notion of their nature. For the most part, the minimal schooling of girls was to prepare them for their domestic role, and

122. Mulcaster, *Positions*, pp. 169–71.
123. Ibid., p. 175.
124. Ibid., p. 170.
125. See Grafton and Jardine, *From Humanism to the Humanities*, chap. 2, on how the claims of social function restricted the humanist education of women in Italy. On women and humanist education in England, see Retha M. Warnicke, "Women and Humanism in England," in *Renaissance Humanism: Foundation, Forms and Legacy*: vol. 3, *Humanism and the Disciplines*, ed. Albert Rabil, Jr. (Philadelphia: University of Pennsylvania Press, 1988), pp. 39–54.

this practice was altered only in the cases of noble women or women like Mary and Elizabeth Tudor who were destined to rule. Several humanists certainly advocated and undertook the education of élite women: Thomas More provided for the education of his daughters, Vives wrote his treatise on the education of women for the instruction of Mary Tudor, Ascham instructed Elizabeth Tudor, and Aylmer tutored Jane Grey. More once wrote to his children's tutor, William Gonnell, that he believed his girls' nature justified their education, for as human beings they are naturally endowed with reason and thus distinguished from animals. In both boys and girls, he believed, "training in letters will cultivate (*colitur*) reason": "If you would sow teaching of virtue in both, you will produce fruit (*seminibus frugem progerminat*)." But, More wrote, if the "soil" of women is indeed by nature bad and more productive of weeds than fruits (as say those who would deter women from letters), then he thinks that it should all the more diligently cultivated, so that "labor may correct natural vices (*quo naturae vicium corrigatur industria*)."[126] Like other humanists, More thus appealed to nature in two different ways: he presumed a universal, rational human nature, which can be cultivated equally in boys and girls; yet woman's different nature does intrude (via another agricultural metaphor) only to justify more training for girls, who are more naturally in need.

Attention to female nature could also affect the content of girls' education, if they received any at all. Richard Hyrde, in his preface to a translation of Erasmus's *Treatise Upon the Pater Noster* (1524) by More's daughter, Margaret Roper, acknowledged the views of those who thought that women should not learn Latin and Greek,

> alleging for their opinion that the frail kind of women, being inclined of their own courage unto vice and mutable at every novelty, if they should skill in many things that be written into the Latin and Greek tongue compiled and made with great craft and eloquence, where the matter is haply

126. Letter to William Gonnell (1518?), in *The Correspondence of Sir Thomas More*, ed. Elizabeth Frances Rogers (Princeton: Princeton University Press, 1947), p. 122; on this letter see Kenneth Charlton, *Education in Renaissance England* (London: Routledge and Kegan Paul, 1965), p. 207.

sometime more sweet into the ear than wholesome to the mind, it would of likelihood both enflame their stomachs a great deal more to that vice that they say they be too much given unto of their own nature already, and instruct them also with more subtlety and conveyance to set forward and accomplish their froward [perverse] intent and purpose.[127]

Such an argument (which Hyrde would here reject) whereby children's natural proclivities or propensities call for reading different sorts of books is extended to the entire female species, for whom the classics would fuel an inborn tendency to vice and cleverness. In his brief instructions on the plan of studies for girls (*De ratione studii puerilis*, 1523), Vives himself did not proscribe girls' reading Latin. He recommended their use of Cicero, Seneca, Plutarch, Plato, More's *Utopia*, and Erasmus, as well as the Christian historians and poets, plus the pagan poets Lucan, Seneca, and some Horace.[128] Yet his treatise on "The Education of the Christian Woman" (*De institutione feminae Christianae*, 1523) is riddled with restrictions on a woman's reading, bodily behavior, dress, grooming, demeanor, and every aspect of her life from childhood through widowhood. These prohibitions are driven first by his social expectations, based on his belief that unlike men, who have many roles in both home and state, a woman's sole duty is care for her chastity (*pudicitiae*).[129] Yet Vives also assumed that "women were by nature weak in mind and judgment (*infirmum animans est femina, judicio invalido*)"[130] and "prone to instability (*lubricus est feminae cogitatus*)."[131] Just as in the new experimental sciences, in which Nature was seen to be gendered female and so to be molded and mastered,[132] the education

127. Richard Hyrde, dedication to *A devout treatise upon the Pater Noster [of Erasmus] turned into englisshe by a yong vertuus and well lerned gentyllwoman of xix yeres of age* (London, 1525?), sig. A2r.

128. Juan Luis Vives, *De ratione studii puerilis* (1523), in *Opera Omnia*, vol. 1, p. 269.

129. Juan Luis Vives, *De institutione feminae Christianae* (1523), in *Opera Omnia*, vol. 4, p. 66. This text was translated into English by Richard Hyrde as *The Instruction of a Christian Woman* (London, 1540).

130. Ibid., p. 85.

131. Ibid., p. 118. See Josephine Kamm, *Hope Deferred: Girl's Education in English History* (London: Methuen, 1965), p. 44.

132. See Evelyn Fox Keller, *Reflections on Gender and Science* (New Haven: Yale University Press, 1985), chap. 2, on science mastering a feminine Nature.

of women should mold inferior female nature either to better it or to channel it in suitable directions.

Similar restrictions operated in the education of children of lower ranks. Mulcaster pointed out, in the case of the education of girls, "I allow them learning with distinction of degrees, with differences of their calling, with respect to their ends, wherefore they learn, wherein my country confirmeth my opinion." The same measure, it would appear, would pertain to all children.[133] Mulcaster constantly tried to balance the argument that all people can be improved by the appropriate education with his concern to maintain an ordered society in which neither too many nor too few are educated: for "in admitting to uses only such as be fit, as seem to be made for them, pairs off the unfit and lesseneth the number," an important effect where superfluity is the greatest danger to the commonwealth.[134] Neither too many rich nor too few poor should be taught: the "middle sort" seem the most suitable. Thus for Mulcaster the keynote was decorum, in which the education suits the wit and the wit must be fit to social function and rank, and to calling within ranks. He thus effectively elided the contradictions implicit in the conflict of nature and nurture by appealing to a natural decorum.

Such arguments epitomize the conflicts underlying the teacher's playing to the natural properties of the child. Accepting the child's nature may weaken the master, who can only adjust himself to the properties of what he cultivates, intervening at those key moments of crisis before the child becomes hardened to external influence.[135] That teachers granted such properties to children, acknowledging differences among them, would seem to undercut the usual assertion that humanism sought above all to impose a uniform character on the child in the name of revealing the individual's "true humanity." To grant someone

133. Mulcaster, *Positions*, p. 167.
134. Ibid., p. 137.
135. See Mulcaster on the responsibility of the master (ibid., p. 259): "The canker that consumeth all, and causeth this evil is haste, an unadvised, rash, headlong counselor, and then most pernicious when it hath some appearance in reason that the child is ripe: or the heartening of some master, which either is disposed to follow where he seeth replying past cure: or that cannot discern colors, because he is that in his degree, which the child is in his: both unripe: the one to teach, the other to remove."

a property when comparing a person with a plant suggests neither that all human beings are essentially alike, nor that all human beings are individuals. In some cases, the teachers seemed to focus on each child as quite different; more often, however, they were speaking of types of children. To have a natural property does marks you as a member of a species or a group with which you are identified. The properties of a flower, animal or person make it distinct from something else, but these properties are also shared with others in its group: the properties are those of gillyflowers, of copper, of girls, and not of any one thing.

However, at the same time that granting the child a "nature" and "properties" might seem to empower him or her, horticultural metaphors could reinforce a hierarchy of natural difference in groups or species, between male and female, between upper and lower ranks, where the one cannot be changed into another. For some this language justified the treatment of people differently according to their different properties—some to be weeded out, others to be cherished. To grant something—and someone—property would give them a substance to resist manipulation, a substance that they shared with others in their species or class. Properties reified difference: to say people or things were different was to erect a platform for justifying hierarchical treatment. In early modern English pedagogical thinking, in analogy with the nascent natural sciences, the notion of having properties, at once "particular" and generalized, caught at both the power and danger of being identified with a species, class or group—the power of having a property that you owe to no one else and the danger of never having anything else; the strength of a group identity and the oppression that can result from it.[136]

136. Also see Michel Foucault, *Surveiller et punir: Naissance de la prison* (Paris: Gallimard, 1975), trans. by Alan Sheridan as *Discipline and Punish: The Birth of the Prison* (New York: Pantheon, 1977), on the technique of the school examination, which "opened up two correlative possibilities: first, the constitution of the individual as a describable, analysable object, not in order to reduce him to 'specific' features, as did the naturalists in relation to living beings, but in order to maintain him in his individual features, in his particular evolution, in his own aptitudes or abilities, under the gaze of a permanent corpus of knowledge; and second, the constitution of a comparative system that made possible the measurement of overall phenomena, the description of groups, the characterization of collective acts, the calculation of the gaps between individuals, their distribution in a given 'population' (p. 190).

Pedagogical attention to "natural" difference could also be seen to validate the description of disciplinary power that Foucault articulated in *Discipline and Punish*:

> Instead of bending all its subjects into a single, uniform mass, it separates, analyses, differentiates, carries its procedures of decomposition to the point of necessary and sufficient single units. It "trains" the moving, confused, useless multitudes of bodies and forces them into a multiplicity of individual elements—small, separate cells; organic autonomies; genetic identities and continuities; combinatory segments. Discipline "makes" individuals; it is the specific technique of a power that regards individuals as both objects and as instruments of its exercise.[137]

Just as resistance is part of the dynamics of power, for Foucault, "individualization" makes possible "normalization" as well as "naturalization": "Disciplinary power has as its correlative an individuality that is not only analytical and 'cellular,' but also natural and 'organic'."[138] However, as this chapter has suggested, in early modern English thinking about students such individuation was unstable rather than airtight: the process of differentiation was based on the acknowledgement of a lack of control as much as it was exercised in the name of control. Similarly, the argument by nature implied active resistance as much as it did a kind of determinist classification. What Foucault describes, in short, seems a phenomenon of a later age and another place rather than the complex beginnings of humanist education in England in the sixteenth and seventeenth centuries.

137. Ibid., p. 170.
138. Ibid., p. 156.

CHAPTER 4

Harvesting Books

E arly modern humanist pedagogy netted the scholar as well as the schoolmaster in a web of contradictions. The schoolmaster, as we have seen, was at once all-powerful and insignificant, the father's double and his antagonist, the tyrant and the lover. The scholar, in turn, was both the shapeless lump of wax and the resistant force of nature, the pliant vine and the immutable flower. Both were caught together between pleasure and pain, freedom and mastery, for the schoolroom could be both a place to flee from the restrictions of social hierarchy and a site for reproducing that hierarchy. In the thinking about curriculum, and in particular in the reading practices that grounded humanist education, we find a similar oscillation between extremes of flexibility and rigid control, between a passion for variety and abundance and a fear of excess. At moments an uneasy balance was struck, but in the process early humanist teachers created expectations for the range and style of reading from which the humanist today cannot easily escape.

Anthony Grafton and Lisa Jardine have argued that, while the ideal of humanist education may have been transmitting classical values and literary style through careful study and imitation of all ancient literature, the reality was a classroom of students ground down by numbing memorization and tiresome close reading that stressed not "argument or technique" but rather the students' collection (in R. R. Bolgar's words) of "uncommon idioms, pithy sayings, colorful anecdotes, anything that might one day serve to pad out a limping paragraph of their own."[1] The early English humanist pedagogues themselves, however, knew what pitfalls lay before them in implementing their programs, and they may not have contested the criticism that their teaching abandoned the pursuit of general knowledge in the face of the material conditions and social needs of education in their time.[2] The early humanist handbooks and curricular plans were shaped by the pressures of training gentlemen destined for careers in public service or the administration of their estates. This professionalism was inseparable from the institutionalization of learning—the founding of new schools and the control of curricula (especially when the English state took a stronger role in regulating education).

More than any other factor, it was the startling proliferation of knowledge and of books themselves that shaped the early humanists' development of their curricula. Books bothered teachers such as Vives, Mulcaster, and Ascham for two basic reasons. First, they believed sufficiently in the power of the word to worry that books might affect the young with ungodliness or bad style. Second, as Vives observed plaintively, if all knowledge is from books, "the number of books is now grown so immense (*ita libri ad immensum numerum excreverunt*)" that "not a few are seized by terror, and a hatred of study, when they confront in every discipline the volumes requiring inexhaustible labor to read. Those who see them become despondent, and these wretches complain to themselves and ask: Who can read these (*Quis leget haec*)?"[3]

1. R. R. Bolgar, "From Humanism to the Humanities," *Twentieth Century Studies* 9 (1973): 11. See Anthony Grafton and Lisa Jardine, *From Humanism to the Humanities: Education and the Liberal Arts in Fifteenth- and Sixteenth-Century Europe* (Cambridge: Harvard University Press, 1986).

2. See James D. Tracy, "From Humanism to the Humanities: A Critique of Grafton and Jardine," *Modern Language Quarterly* 51 (1990): 122–43: "I would suggest, then, that the difference between humanist theory and humanist practice is just that—a not-so-surprising disparity between the ruminations of original thinkers and the practical accommodations deemed necessary by the much larger number of humanists who earned their bread (at least for a time) teaching in the large town schools of transalpine Europe" (p. 127).

3. Juan Luis Vives, *De tradendis disciplinis*, in *Opera Omnia*, vol. 6 (1745; reprint, London: Gregg Press, 1964), p. 267. Translations are my own throughout, but I have consulted *Vives: On Education. A Translation of the "De Tradendis Disciplinis" of Juan Luis Vives*, ed. and trans. Foster Watson (Cambridge: Cambridge University Press, 1913). See also Glenn W. Most, "Canon Fathers: Literacy, Mortality, Power," *Arion* Ser. 3, no. 1

From 1500 to 1550, the number of printers in England more than tri-
pled, with a proportionate increase in every kind of printed material,
ranging from translations of Virgil and Seneca to the ballad of the
"lytell geste of Robyn Hode."[4] People knew that they lived in a "print-
ing age" in which, as one pessimist put it, "every red-nosed rhymester
is an author, every drunken man's dream is a book."[5] By 1586 William
Webbe feared for his whole country weighed down with "innumerable
sorts of English books, and infinite fardles of printed pamphlets,
wherewith this country is pestered, all shops stuffed, and every study
furnished."[6] (His own list of selected readings, beginning with Orpheus and ending with his contemporaries, is in fact quite broad, generously including those of the universities and Inns of Court whose
works he does not know—and those "whose names come not now to
my remembrance"—but excluding the "uncountable rabble of rhyming
ballad makers and compilers of senseless sonnets, who be most busy
to stuff every stall full of gross devises and unlearned pamphlets."[7]) No
teacher believed that every man could read everything, so books, like
any other kind of commodity useful to a busy gentleman, needed to
be consumed prudently and profitably.[8]

The notion of a book as something capable of generating "profit"
made possible the particular compromise that the early humanists and
the reformist teachers sought between the pedagogic demand for coverage and their particular kind of "close reading." The early sixteenth-
century image of the text as a garden from which the reader harvests
material for "fruit" suggests a lack of concern for the appreciation of

---

(1990): 35–60, on the similar pressure in Greek classical culture to produce a canon in
reaction to an overflow of books.

4. See H. S. Bennett, *English Books and Readers: 1475 to 1557* (Cambridge: Cambridge
University Press, 1969), p. 29; on "Robyn Hode" see p. 151.

5. R. W., *Martine Mar-Sixtus* (London, 1591), sig. A3v. See H. S. Bennett, *English
Books and Readers, 1558–1603* (Cambridge: Cambridge University Press, 1965), pp. 3–4; see
also chap. 3, regarding the royal *Injunctions* to the Stationer's Company in 1559, which
directed the regulation of the book trade as an attempt to avert the "great disorder"
caused by "publication of unfruitful, vain and infamous books and papers" (p. 57).

6. William Webbe, *A Discourse of English Poetrie* (1586), in *Elizabethan Critical Essays*,
ed. G. Gregory Smith (Oxford: Oxford University Press, 1904), vol. 1, pp. 226–27.

7. Ibid., pp. 245–46.

8. On the humanist notion of a "profitable" discourse, see Lorna Hutson, *Thomas
Nashe in Context* (Oxford: Clarendon Press, 1989), chaps. 1–2.

complete texts, an appreciation that we currently associate with "humanist reading." For many sixteenth-century readers and teachers seeking wisdom and good Latin, it was enough to sample the sententious and fruitful sayings of a wide range of authors. However, by the end of the sixteenth century, a concern for argument and structure, or the "body" of the text (a concern that also appeared strongly in humanist rhetoric and grammar), created a potential conflict between the admiration of general education and the demand for "close reading" that construes a whole text. The contrast between thinking about a book as a garden and reading it as a body paralleled the developing aesthetics of the garden itself: a switch from appreciating the concatenation of a garden's individual parts to planning a unified design meant to be viewed in perspective. This aesthetic, when applied to texts and reading, endangered the early humanist curricular compromise: for the single perspective of neoclassical form must inevitably exclude anything "superfluous" when it delineates an organic whole.

FROM COPIA TO SUPERFLUITY

It has become a commonplace that the Renaissance humanists were the first to form "selective" literary canons meant to embody the purity of language and style and the ethics of high classical culture.[9] Typical of statements describing such canons is Roger Ascham's claim for his own list:

These books be not many, nor long, nor rude in speech, nor mean in matter, but next the majesty of God's holy word, most worthy for a man, the lover of learning and honesty, to spend his life in. Yea, I have heard worthy Mr. Cheke many times say: I would have a good student pass and journey through all authors both Greek and Latin: but he that will dwell in these few books only: first, in God's holy Bible, and than join with it, Tully in

9. See, for example, Anthony Grafton, *Defenders of the Text: The Traditions of Scholarship in an Age of Science: 1450–1800* (Cambridge: Harvard University Press, 1991); John Guillory, "Canonical and Non-Canonical: A Critique of the Current Debate," *ELH* 54 (1987): 483–527; and Douglas Bush, *The Renaissance and English Humanism* (Toronto: University of Toronto Press, 1939).

Latin, Plato, Aristotle: Xenophon: Isocrates: and Demosthenes in Greek: must needs prove an excellent man.[10]

Yet this passage suggests that while writers such as Ascham believed that the student could be narrowly selective they also preferred that he read everything—except for heresy. Wendell Harris notes that "the breadth of learning that a Renaissance humanist . . . expected of teachers was less a canon than a summons to universal knowledge."[11] As was true in many of the Tudor arts from architecture to gardening, in teaching and reading variety and abundance were generally valued over brevity and simplicity.

Far from excluding any art, the study of rhetoric and grammar included all fields of knowledge except the professional fields of law, theology and medicine.[12] It was understood, further, that pupils could not really grasp one subject without knowing them all: as James Cleland put it in his *The Institution of a Young Noble Man* (1607), "learning is circular, and the Muses stand round about Apollo, having no beginning nor ending more than a geometrical circle, so that he who would enjoy one of the disciplines must labor to be acquainted with them all."[13] Most often the sole, if still quite restrictive, criterion of text selection was language—Latin and Greek, including works outside of the high classical period. Erasmus, for example, accepted models of usage from modern as well as ancient times, acknowledging that "in

10. Roger Ascham, *The Scholemaster* (London, 1570); reprint, ed. Edward Arber (Boston: Willard Small, 1888), p. 258. See also Erasmus, *De ratione studii*, who wrote that "from the beginning nearly all knowledge could be sought in the Greek authors, for from whence could you drink more purely, quickly and joyfully than from the source itself?" (*De ratione studii ac legendi interpretandique auctores*, in Erasmus, *Opera Omnia*, vol. 1, bk. 2, ed. Jean-Claude Margolin [Amsterdam: North-Holland, 1971], p. 116; translations are my own, but I have consulted the translation by Brian McGregor, in Erasmus, *Collected Works*, vol. 24: *Literary and Educational Writings*, vol. 2, ed. Craig R. Thompson [Toronto: University of Toronto Press, 1978]).

11. Wendell V. Harris, "Canonicity," *PMLA* 106 (1991): 110–21; p. 113. For a similar call to universal reading, see Quintilian, *Institutio oratoria* 1.4.1–4.

12. See R. R. Bolgar, *The Classical Heritage and its Beneficiaries* (Cambridge: Cambridge University Press, 1954), p. 295.

13. James Cleland, *The Institution of a Young Noble Man* (London, 1607), facsimile with intro. by Max Molyneux (New York: Scholars' Facsimiles and Reprints, 1948), vol. 1, p. 144.

no time has there been a single rule of correct writing (*orthographiae*)."[14] Apparently embracing everything while implicitly restricting the field, Erasmus in his *De copia* assumed as his audience a student reader who has decided "to move around the entire array of authors (*per omne genus autorum lectione grassari*), as must anyone who wished to be called educated (*eruditus*)."[15] Advice concerned with the general education of a gentleman, however, prescribed an even wider range of texts. Vives, for example, recommended reading modern historians (such as Peter Martyr) and vernacular writers, as well as the modern neo-Latin poets.[16] And the writers of courtesy books advised the student to acquaint himself with modern and ancient history, the civil and the common law, the vernacular languages, and the English poets, at the same time that he studied rhetoric in both the classical languages and in English.[17]

Such calls for comprehensive reading occur most often in discussions of the training of the teacher and the gentleman, whose broad knowledge was meant to be socially or professionally useful. Further, both

14. Erasmus, *De recta Latini Graecique sermonis pronuntiatione dialogus*, ed. M. Cytowska, in *Opera Omnia*, vol. 1, bk. 4 (Amsterdam: North Holland, 1973), p. 100; the translations are my own, but I have consulted the translation by Maurice Pope, in Erasmus, *Collected Works*, vol. 26: *Literary and Educational Writings*, vol. 4, ed. J. K. Sowards (Toronto: University of Toronto Press, 1985). On the issue of style, see Grafton, *Defenders of the Text*, p. 33, who claims that in general humanists were less tolerant regarding stylistic flexibility. On the function of Latin as the language of a "cosmopolitan caste" or new intellectual class, see Antonio Gramsci, *Selections from Cultural Writings*, ed. David Forgacs and Geoffrey Nowell-Smith, trans. William Boelhower (Cambridge: Harvard University Press, 1985), pp. 217–234. See also Guillory, "Canonical and Non-Canonical," pp. 513–15.

15. *De duplici copia verborum ac rerum commentarii duo*, ed. Betty I. Knott, in *Opera Omnia*, vol. 1, bk. 6 (Amsterdam: North Holland, 1988), p. 258; I have consulted Knott's translation in Erasmus, *Collected Works*, vol. 24: *Literary and Educational Writings*, vol. 2, p. 635. Ascham draws attention to this assumption in his *Scholemaster*, p. 256.

16. See Vives, *De tradendis*, bk. 5, chap. 2, on reading historians; and bk. 3, chap. 9, on modern poets.

17. See Foster Watson, *The Beginnings of the Teaching of Modern Subjects in England* (London: Pitman, 1909; reprint Menston, Yorkshire: Scolar Press, 1971), on the introduction of new subjects in the sixteenth-century curriculum. On courtesy theory and its social manifestations, in general, see Frank Whigham, *Ambition and Privilege: The Social Tropes of Elizabethan Courtesy Theory* (Berkeley: University of California Press, 1984); on connections between society and rhetoric, see Patricia Parker, *Literary Fat Ladies: Rhetoric, Gender, Property* (London: Methuen, 1987), chap. 6.

had the luxury to pursue learning all their life and could be trusted in any case to be discriminating. In *De ratione studii* (a plan of study first published in 1511 and written with the English teacher John Colet and his school at St. Paul's in mind), Erasmus insisted that in preparing someone to be a teacher, he would not be "content with the standard ten or twelve authors, but would require a veritable universe of learning (*sed orbem illum doctrinae requiram*)," even if he would teach very little. Thus, for Erasmus, the student-teacher should "wander though the entire *genus* of authors, at first the best, but he should not leave any author untasted, no matter how far short of good (*etiam si parum bonus sit auctor*)." Erasmus's approach at this juncture thus emphasized coverage over "quality." He asserted that if someone has "insufficient time or books (*verum si cui vel ocium vel librorum copia defuerit*)," he may use stylistically impure compilations such as those of Pliny the Elder, Macrobius, Atheneus, and Gellius, even though it would be better to consult the original sources.[18] Here, in contrast to *De copia*, the education of the teacher was strictly divided from that of the student: the teacher needed to know everything in order to lead students in reading the poets and orators, whereas the student's aim was to develop elegant style in Latin and Greek.[19]

Vives, like Elyot, also allowed a wide range of books to his students. For Vives, a gentleman needed to be instructed in every philosophical and practical discipline to order to fulfill his social role. While Elyot was vague about his principles of selection, for adult readers Vives excluded only books that were violent in method (*libri altercatorii, rix-*

18. Erasmus, *De ratione studii*, p. 120. See also William Harrison Woodward, *Studies in Education during the Age of the Renaissance: 1400–1600* (New York: Teachers' College Press, 1967), pp. 44–45, on the wide range of authors in Guarino's plans for teaching, in which "writers practically unheard of in a school or even University course were construed, commented upon and studied as aids to the understanding of classical antiquity."

19. "*Postremo nulla disciplina est, nec militiae, nec rei rusticae, nec musices, nec architecturae, quae non vsui sit iis qui poetas aut oratores antiquos susceperint enarrandos*" (*De ratione*, p. 124). See Emile Durkheim, *L'évolution pédagogique en France*, 2nd ed. (Paris: Presses Universitaires de France, 1969), trans. by Peter Collins as *The Evolution of Educational Thought: Lectures on the Formation and Development of Secondary Education in France* (London: Routledge & Kegan Paul, 1977), who emphasizes that Erasmus required such knowledge mostly for the construing of authors and the teaching of rhetoric (p. 193) and asked the student only to "develop his taste" by following a small number of the best authors (p. 195).

osi, contentiosi) or in content (praising war, tyranny, or cruelty); he regarded "lascivious writings (*rebus lasciviis*)," popular songs, and vernacular writings as texts best left to individual judgment and taste, for "some things agree with some temperaments, just as to their palates and stomachs (*nam alia aliis ingeniis conveniunt, ut palatis, et ventriculis*)."[20] At the same time that he presented a very specific, if long, list of books, Vives also acknowledged the tentativeness of his judgments and the instability of literary reputation.[21] In a more sweeping fashion, Vives also recognized the changes in aesthetic and cultural standards over time. Musing on the rise and fall of literary reputations over the centuries, Vives observed how a book may appear, "at one time and in some places, beautiful, and in others, foul (*idem alio tempore, et allis locis, pulchrum videtur, et foedum*)."[22] Like Erasmus's allowance of mediocre books to the teacher, Vives's reliance on taste may have assumed the gentleman student's inherent capacity to distinguish quality, but it did not presume to exclude anything from his gaze, given the greater good of copious knowledge which, as Vives stressed, was useful in the fulfillment of a gentleman's civic duty.

Roger Ascham's answer to the question of what should be read by the gentleman scholar was, "all for him that is desirous to know all: yea, the worst of all, as Questionists, and all the barbarous nation of schoolmen, help for one or other consideration." Yet Ascham, like Erasmus, inevitably retracted this grand gesture when he turned to the matter of teaching in schools: "But in every separate kind of learning and study, by itself, you must follow, choicely a few, and chiefly some one, and that namely in our school of eloquence."[23] That is to say, the student engaged in formal study (particularly of eloquence), as opposed to lifetime reading, needed to choose quite narrowly. The ideal of general knowledge thus foundered when Ascham and other pedagogues contemplated the institutional or methodical instruction of students intended for other professions. Teachers came to Thomas Lupset's conclusion that "no man (specially of them that have other occupations)

---

20. Vives, *De tradendis*, bk. 1, chap. 4, p. 259.
21. Ibid., bk. 1, chap. 6, p. 267.
22. Ibid., "De vita et moribus eruditi," chap. 1, p. 422.
23. Ascham, *Scholemaster*, p. 274.

can use reading but in very few works, the which I would should be picked out of the best sort: that the fruit of the reader's diligence may be the greater."[24] When humanist learning was thus firmly attached to programs, schools, and the harvesting of "fruit" or profit for men with occupations, time became a matter of anxiety rather than a natural force aiding the development of knowledge.[25]

In a Tudor translation of a treatise by Johan Sturm, a German teacher who corresponded with Ascham, the argument refers several times to the limitation of three years' study, a limitation that prevents the students from reading all that Sturm would wish:

> Howbeit, I wish no writer to be overpassed: but that we taste somewhat of his doings, and run over some part of him, and diligently observe some things in him. But yet in such wise that we have care and regard of the time, with due consideration of the three year[s], and of the end of our study which we have appointed. And for this cause neither have I named all writers: neither bid I you to read all these; neither forbid I you to know those which I have not named.

Sturm goes on to list writers that he has not discussed and ends by insisting that "for those that have written of husbandry, building and of warfare: who denieth but a learned man should be acquainted with them: but my prescription is of three year[s]: and is agreeable to your age, calling and nobility."[26] This patch of rhetoric demon-

---

24. Thomas Lupset, *An Exhortation to yonge men* (London, 1538), fol. 5v. See Grafton and Jardine, *From Humanism to the Humanities*, chap. 6, on the development of "method" in Northern humanist education.

25. See Richard Mulcaster's attempt to reconcile time with the demands of a curriculum: "Time enough is that mean which perfecteth all, the Elementary in his kind, the Grammarian in his, the Graduate in his, and so profiteth the common weal by perfecting all: the prerogative to thought: the mother to truth: the touchstone to ripeness: the enemy to error: man's only stay, and help to advice." Richard Mulcaster, *Positions wherein those primitive circumstances be examined, which are necessarie for the training up of children, either for skill in their booke, or health in their bodie* (London, 1581), reprint, ed. Robert Hebert Quick (London: Longmans, Green, 1888), p. 260. After completing this book, I consulted a new edition of the *Positions*, ed. William Barker (Toronto: University of Toronto Press, 1994), which lists textual variants and offers a valuable introduction.

26. From Johan Sturm, *A ritch storehouse or Treasurie for Nobilitye and Gentlemen, which in Latine is called Nobilitas literata, written by a famous and excellent man, John Sturmius,*

strates the characteristic tension in humanist pedagogy between advocating a "liberal" or broad education and presenting a definite educational program for men who plan to do other things. "Diligent reading" is opposed both to a diligent consideration for the passing of time and to an awareness of the "end" (defined as both termination and purpose).

Even the courtesy books that presume a lifetime education select texts, often by differentiating between "private" and "formal" reading or by establishing a hierarchy of books to be read or "consumed." As Cleland framed the unsavory digestive metaphor that had already become a commonplace, "there are some books which are only worthy to be tasted, others to be swallowed, and the best to be chewed, let down and digested."[27] Vives worried that even a lifetime is too short to read the innumerable books available, and therefore he advocated that in every subject "books should be assigned, some explained in schools, and others read and perused in secret, lest life, so brief and fleeting, be consumed by the superfluous (*supervacaneis*), or . . . the noxious (*noxiis*)."[28] When the value of copiousness was thus diverted into "superfluity," it took on a different value, one anticipated in Erasmus's *De copia*, where the student was warned against overstepping the boundary between rich variety and distracting excess in rhetorical ornamentation.[29] The bounty of books, while a source of pride and an object of consumption, could thus also be seen as an unmanageable and even harmful excess when one pitted

---

and translated into English by T. B. Gent. (London, 1570), sig. D3r–v. Sturm's Latin treatise was published in 1549. Cf. Harris, "Canonicity," on the limitation of texts in our own curricula: "no selection of texts that can be fitted into the one literature course, or perhaps the two or three, taken by the average undergraduate—or into the dozen or so literature courses taken by the baccalaureate major—can adequately provide all that background (literary history, cultural studies, rhetorical training, etc.)" (p. 119).

27. Cleland, *Institution*, p. 147. This differentiation is implicit in the structure of Vives's treatise, where he recommended both formal and private reading. For a modern reflection on this issue, see Katha Pollitt, "Canon to the right of me . . . ," *The Nation*, September 23, 1991, pp. 328–30, who notes that the current debate of the canon question has ignored such a distinction between school and private reading.

28. Vives, *De tradendis*, bk. 1, chap. 6, p. 267.

29. See also Parker, *Literary Fat Ladies*, pp. 13–14, and Terence Cave, *The Cornucopian Text: Problems of Writing in the French Renaissance* (Oxford: Clarendon, 1979), chap. 1, on the value of rhetorical *copia* in Erasmus and the French Renaissance writers.

the importance of control, closure, and profit against the value placed on copiousness.[30]

The strong impulse to organize and control is evident everywhere in humanist pedagogical writing but without any apparent consensus as to the selection of texts, even in the advice of a single writer struggling to stem the flow of books.[31] The sixteenth-century arguments about education allow two different criteria for the choice of texts: exemplary style and content. Ascham recommended a narrow choice for his "school of eloquence" (that is, his project of teaching language through imitation of the "best" or "choicest" authors of both Greek and Latin literature). Similarly, in what appears to contradict completely what he said in *De copia* about the importance of reading everything, Erasmus insisted in *De ratione studii* that he does not like those who comb through every possible author and "consume a whole lifetime, judging as a complete infant (*infantem*—literally, speechless) someone who misses any scrap of text (*chartula*)."[32] Where the end was instruction in classical grammar and rhetoric a very limited selection of texts would suffice (Lucan, Demosthenes, Herodotus, Aristophanes, Homer, and Euripides in Greek; and Terence, Virgil, Horace, Cicero, Caesar and perhaps Sallust in Latin). However, in his *Institutio principis Christiani*, when Erasmus switched the emphasis from style to content his recommendations for reading were quite different. According to this handbook, since through reading mute letters are changed into *mores* (morals) and states of mind, a naturally headstrong and violent boy might become tyrannical if he should read about Achilles, Alexander the Great, Xerxes, or Julius Caesar without a preventative antidote. Therefore the student is to be steered away from Homer, Caesar, and the historians advocated in *De ratione studii* because they offer a host of bad examples.[33] (T. W. Baldwin also notes

30. See Hutson, *Thomas Nashe*, p. 38, for further discussion of the implications of the economic analogies: "Translated into the terms of humanist education the paradox seems to be that the young man who has been equipped by literature with the ready money of discursive ability is simultaneously rendered more susceptible to the expenditure of his talents."

31. Harris contends that, today, "if The Canon no longer lives, the reason is that it never did; there have been and are only selections with purposes" ("Canonicity," p. 119).

32. Erasmus, *De ratione*, p. 116.

33. Erasmus, *Institutio principis christiani*, ed. O. Herding in *Opera Omnia*, vol. 4, bk.

that Erasmus's "personal" canon [Virgil, Horace, Ovid, Juvenal, Statius, Martial, Claudian, Persius, Lucan, Tibullus, Propertius, Cicero, Quintilian, Sallust, and Terence] would have hardly been acceptable as a school canon.[34]) Elsewhere some effort was made to reconcile the criteria of style and content: Richard Mulcaster expressed his hope that students should be given texts only "where the honesty and familiarity of the argument is honored and apparelled with the fineness and fitness of speech."[35] The humanists' opponents, of course, were not convinced. One John Stockwood complained about "what horrible beastly authors are taught in some schools" in the name of style.[36]

In the end, in concert with the increasing state regulation of the book trade, the pedagogues' drive to control the increasingly unmanageable number of books and their concern with specific ends, value, and profit overcame their admiration of copiousness in words and things. Just as he was otherwise concerned with regulating a superfluity of young scholars in his commonwealth (see Chap. 3), Richard Mulcaster worried about the excess of textbooks. Ostensibly concerned with the expense of needless schoolbooks, Mulcaster proposed imposing uniformity in curricula and publishing anthologies in which "whatsoever is needful to be used in schools, may be very well comprised in a small compass, and have all his helps with him being gathered into

1 (Amsterdam: North-Holland, 1974), p. 179; translations are my own but I have consulted the translation by Neil M. Cheshire and Michael J. Heath, "On the Education of a Christian Prince," in Erasmus, *Collected Works*, vol. 27: *Literary and Educational Writings*, vol. 5, ed. A. H. T. Levi (Toronto: University of Toronto Press, 1986). Vives also felt that the teacher should make sure that a boy is kept away from any author that might encourage or nurture any vice that he suffers; thus Ovid should be kept from the lustful, Martial from the mocker, Lucian from the slanderous, Lucretius or Epicurus from the impious—and even Cicero will not do much for a conceited boy (*De tradendis*, bk. 3, chap. 5, p. 320).

34. T. W. Baldwin, *William Shakspere's Small Latine and Lesse Greeke* (Urbana: University of Illinois Press, 1944), vol. 1, p. 108.

35. Mulcaster, *Positions*, pp. 270–71.

36. John Stockwood, *A very fruiteful Sermon preched at Paules Crosse the tenth of May last* (London, 1579), sig. K5r. In the seventeenth century William Prynne railed against schoolmasters who teach "amorous wanton Play-books, Histories, [and] Heathen Authors," among these Plautus and Terence, whom the humanists so often recommended as stylistic models and opposed to the vernacular drama (William Prynne, *Histrio-mastix, The Players Scourge, or Actors Tragedie*, pt. 2 [London, 1633], p. 916).

some one pretty volume compounded of the marrow of many."[37] The result, he hoped, would be that, with "planting uniformity and pointing out fit books, besides many and infinite commodities which will grow thereby to the whole realm, assuredly the multitude of many needless volumes will be diminished and cut off."[38] Beside the financial benefit to the student and his parents, who would need to purchase fewer books, the "infinite" commodity or profit to the state would be a finite number of books, strictly controlled. Cutting books into pieces and compressing the pieces in a "small compass" (like infinite riches in a little room) would create the conditions in which the superfluous multitude would wither away. In Mulcaster's vision intellectual profit was thus closely linked to financial profit, which in turn was concentrated in a few hands and regulated by the state.

FROM HARVESTS TO ANATOMIES

Mulcaster's proposal to publish anthologies would seem to violate the fundamental principles usually associated with humanist reading: in particular, the insistence on using original sources and the often interminable construing of a single text. Part of his reasoning can be explained by his concern with teaching grammar school students, where Mulcaster's "profession [was] not to perfect but to enter [to start]" them.[39] However, Mulcaster's willingness to rely on anthologies also marks the humanists' combination of an obsession with "close reading" of texts with a disintegrative approach to those texts. Unlike New Critical close reading, which undertakes to demonstrate how the elements of a literary text function to produce an aesthetic unity, humanist reading addressed the parts in great detail but was little concerned with seeing them as a whole. The point of reading a book was not to provide an "anatomy" or an understanding of its argument or structure; rather, the end was a harvesting or mining of the book for its functional parts—useful to borrow for the reader's own writing or to serve as practical conduct rules or stylistic models.[40] This approach served the concern

37. Mulcaster, *Positions*, p. 268.
38. Ibid., p. 271.
39. Ibid., p. 268.
40. For a general discussion of this effect, see Mary Thomas Crane, *Framing Authority: Sayings, Self, and Society in Sixteenth-Century England* (Princeton: Princeton Univer-

for the "profit" of learning. What was sought was what would serve the student in his profession. Such reading provided a solution to the problems surrounding the choice of school texts: students could be exposed to a broad range of authors while handling only pieces of texts. In turn, they would cover those pieces scrupulously.

Grafton and Jardine disapprove of the prodigious and fragmented nature of the humanist teaching of textual commentary, which they conclude would keep the students spending months on one book and prevent them from retaining "any sense of the import of the work as a whole."[41] Such behavior was common enough in Northern European schools that Erasmus advised the teacher that he should explain to the student only what was needed for the passage at hand, and not digress, unlike "the vulgar lot of teachers today who because of some twisted desire for glory (*quod praua quaedam ambitione vulgus professorum facit*), try to say everything about every single passage (*vt omni loco coneris omnia dicere*)."[42] In reaction to the teaching of logic, humanist scholarship resuscitated the art of encyclopedic commentary to serve the practice of literary scholarship and the teaching of grammar.[43] Of

---

sity Press, 1993). In her excellent book, which focuses on the rhetorical and educational practices of "gathering and framing" texts in commonplace books, she also observes, in much more detail, that in humanist education students were "not to be concerned with the interpretation of the whole, but with the identification of the parts" (p. 88). Rather than focusing on the implications of this for the development of the canon, however, she examines the effect of this practice on the fashioning of a "socially constituted subject, common ownership of texts and ideas, and a collective model of authorship" (p. 6). Also see Marion Trousdale, *Shakespeare and the Rhetoricians* (London: Scolar Press, 1982). For a discussion of this attitude in the context of pedagogy, see Richard Halpern, *The Poetics of Primitive Accumulation: English Renaissance Culture and the Genealogy of Capital* (Ithaca: Cornell University Press, 1991), chap. 1: while I agree with Halpern's characterization of the "disintegrative effects of copia" (p. 47), I do not think that it necessarily entailed a "destruction of content" (p. 49); rather, "content" was reduced to *sententiae* or apophthegms.

41. Grafton and Jardine, *From Humanism to the Humanities*, p. 67. After looking at notes from Guarino's lectures on rhetoric, Grafton and Jardine concluded that "to cover texts in the gruelling detail shown here, given an hour's lecturing per day per text, can hardly have taken less than an academic year for each book" (p. 20).

42. Erasmus, *De ratione*, pp. 136–37. Vives also thought that the teacher should not concern himself too much with petty details (*De tradendis*, bk. 3, chap. 2, p. 306).

43. See Anthony Grafton, *Joseph Scaliger: A Study in the History of Classical Scholarship*, vol. 1, *Textual Criticism and Exegesis* (Oxford: Clarendon, 1983), on how the early hu-

course, the more a teacher comments on a text in a lecture, the fewer texts the teacher can "cover" in a limited period of time. Yet while the habit of commentary must have indeed retarded the students' progress through a book list, the pedagogic interest in the "parts" often enabled teachers to present many different authors by anthologizing.[44]

Typical is the cheerful attitude conveyed by Erasmus in the preface to his collection of witty and sententious sayings culled from the classics, the *Apophthegmes*. There he argued for the utility of his book, asking "what one man among many thousands (yea though he be nothing clogged nor letted with any public office or ministry) hath so much vacant time, that he may be at leisure to turn over and over in the books of Plato." The preface goes on to declare that much of Plato (the "subtle knacks" and "long inductions") is superfluous, much of Aristotle is interesting only to the learned, and that even among Cicero's works we find matters "not much to the purpose, nor anything at all necessary, that princes know them."[45] Absent was any sense of the integrity of the literary or philosophical text: what was important was the stuff of service to the governing class. The pedagogical use of such books reflected a reading habit evident in much pedagogic advice. As Francis Meres put it in his own commonplace collection, "as little bees from every place bring home that which is profitable: so a student doth excerpt from every author

---

manists' "line-by-line commentaries inevitably bulk as large as or larger than the texts they deal with" (p. 16). Cf. Durkheim, *The Evolution of Educational Thought*, on the scholarship of the twelfth century, when "whether the subject was grammar or logic or ethics or law or medicine it had the same character throughout: it always consisted in a commentary on a specific book" (p. 113).

44. See Bolgar, *Classical Heritage*, pp. 271–75, on this notion of the book as a collection of parts. See also Marion Trousdale, "A Possible Renaissance View of Form," *ELH* 40 (1973), 179–204; and her *Shakespeare and the Rhetoricians*.

45. Erasmus, *Apophthegmes*, trans. Nicholas Udall (London, 1542). Here I offer Udall's translation, especially because this also seems to reflect Udall's attitude (see below on his edition of the "flowers" of Terence). The Latin text can be found in Erasmus, *Opera Omnia*, bk. 4 (Leiden, 1703), in the epistle: "*sed quoto cuique ne privato tantum est otii, ut apud Platonem Socraticarum argutationum, ironiarum, e Isagogarum ambages ac labyrinthos evolvere vacet. Aristotilis autem copiose quidem scripsit de moribus, sed Philosophis scripsisse videtur, non Principi . . . Tam in philosophiciis et Marci Tulli de Philosophia libris pleraque sunt ejus generis, ut non admodum referat Principium ea scire.*"

that which is for his purpose."[46] Elyot describes the reader's "picking out" "good sentences" from the prescribed poets (while ignoring the "light matter"),[47] a talent amply demonstrated in his citation of Virgil's erotic passage on Dido and Aeneas's venery as one which will delight the child interested in hunting.[48]

In the sixteenth century, commonplace books and rhetorical manuals proliferated both in print and in manuscript continuing a tradition of the medieval encyclopedias, *florilegia*, and collections of *exempla* once intended for students and sermon composers but now useful for the over-taxed secular writer and reader as well.[49] Many of these Renaissance commonplace books, including *Tullies Sentences* (a translation of *Sententiae Ciceronis*), the *Sententiae Terentius*, *Sententiae Pueriles*, and the medieval distichs of pseudo-Cato, were mainly for lower grammar school uses. Such books had the dual purpose of teaching proper Latin in short "sentences" and inculcating moral or "sententious" principles in the impressionable child. However, we also find Erasmus's *Adagia* and *De copia* frequently listed in the book inventories of English universities, where they functioned as repositories of useful phrases and rhetorical formulae, or, as in the case of the *Adagia*, as collections of the proverbial wisdom of classical and popular culture.[50]

The humanists' students also compiled their own commonplace books when they perused their authors. When the students read, they were meant to take notes, recording "a story, a fable, an *exemplum*, an unusual event, a *sententia*, an elegant point, or some other admirable saying."[51] This activity did not serve the purpose of providing a reading of the whole but rather the compilation of items that they could use

46. Francis Meres, *Palladis Tamia. Wits Treasury, Being the second part of Wits Commonwealth* (London, 1598; reprint, New York: Garland, 1973), fol. 268r.

47. Thomas Elyot, *The Boke named The Governour* (London, 1531), ed. Henry Herbert Stephen Croft (New York: Burt Franklin, 1967), vol. 1, p. 129.

48. Elyot, *Governour*, pp. 63–64.

49. See Walter J. Ong, "Commonplace Rhapsody: Ravisius Textor, Zwinger and Shakespeare," in R. R. Bolgar ed., *Classical Influences on European Culture, A.D. 1500–1700* (Cambridge: Cambridge University Press, 1976), pp. 91–126, on the Renaissance's inheritance of the "medieval addiction to texts as such" (p. 108).

50. See Lisa Jardine, "Humanism and the Sixteenth-Century Cambridge Arts Course," *History of Education* 4 (1975):16. See also T. W. Baldwin, *Shakspere's Small Latine*, vol. 1, chaps. 23 and 26–30.

51. Erasmus, *De copia*, p. 261.

themselves in composition. The method of recording these snippets was at once methodical and unsystematic. According to Vives, in his *De ratione studii puerilis* (1523), the student's notebooks should be divided into separate parts, "like nests; in one you would note down words of everyday use: of the mind, body, our duties, games, clothes, times, dwellings, food; in another rare or exquisite words; in another idioms and ways of speaking;. . . . in another *sententiae*; in another humorous and witty sayings; in another proverbs; in another difficult passages, and whatever other things seem noteworthy to you or your teacher."[52] Typically, the "topics" conflated categories of content with rhetorical categories in an almost random way.[53] Similarly, what was worth recording was often judged more by what was unusual than by what was particularly wise. After having mastered the fundamentals of grammar, Erasmus's ideal student would watch for any "remarkable word (*insigne verbum*)," looking for novel or archaic diction, adages, historical parallels or imitations.[54] For both Erasmus and Vives what was worth noting was marked by its difference from ordinary discourse and by its aptness for the student's writing.

The transformation of the text into notebooks converted these pieces of writing into counters or currency, spatially distinct, usable, and exchangeable. The materiality of the textual fragment was fully realized in Erasmus's advice that, as an aid to memory, "the student should inscribe apophthegms, proverbs, and *sententiae* at the front and back of books,

52. Juan Luis Vives, *De ratione studii puerilis* (1523), in *Opera Omnia*, vol. 1, p. 272.

53. Also see Ong, "Commonplace Rhapsody," pp. 110–11, on the random selection of headings in the commonplace books. Cf. Michel Foucault, *Les mots et les choses* (Paris: Gallimard, 1966), trans. as *The Order of Things: An Archaeology of the Human Sciences* (New York: Pantheon, 1970; reprint New York: Vintage Books, 1973), on the encyclopedic project of the sixteenth-century naturalist Aldrovandi, in which the reader finds "an inextricable mixture of exact descriptions, reported quotations, fables without commentary, remarks dealing indifferently with an animal's anatomy, its use in heraldry, its habitat, its mythological values, or the uses to which it could be put in medicine or magic" (p. 39). Bolgar once saw a certain advantage to such lack of systematization, insofar as "the multiform and disjointed citations bring into prominence facets of the ancient world that its systematic historians too often miss" (*Classical Heritage*, p. 300).

54. "*His itaque rebus instructus, inter legendum auctores non oscitanter obseruabis, si quod incidat insigne verbum, si quid antique aut noue dictum, si quod argumentum aut inuentum acute aut tortum apte, si quod egregium orationis decus, si quod adagium, si quod exemplum, si qua sententia digna quae memoriae commendetur*" (Erasmus, *De ratione*, p. 117).

and engrave them on rings and cups, and paint them doors and walls and even on window glass, so that nowhere could one avoid what would add to learning."[55] Here the fragments of text became furniture—the cluttered movables of the ordinary house and the educated mind. The more were accumulated, the richer were the discursive resources: what belonged to an author (that attribution often indicated marginally) also belonged to the student, encased in the "treasury" of a book (to parrot Meres' title).[56] Those riches, in turn, often could be easily accounted for: for example, Meres' own book, organized topically in categories ranging from "Bishops" to "Virgins," "Pettifoggers *vide* lawyers" to "Prince of Darkness *vide* Devil," could be mined easily by means of an alphabetical index that served as an inventory of linguistic possessions.

By the mid-sixteenth century, however, the teachers' attitudes toward textual unity came into conflict with another set of textual and aesthetic values. Condemnations of anthologies and "epitomes" became more prevalent. Ascham, for example, conceded in 1570 that while commonplace books "be very necessary, to induce a man, into an orderly general knowledge," a man should above all "bind himself daily by orderly study, to read with all diligence, principally the holiest scripture and withal, the best doctors" and not rely on "epitomes."[57] Yet Ascham was clearly still excited about putting together his own anthology of imitations, "containing a certain few fit precepts, unto the which should be gathered and applied plenty of examples, out of the choicest authors of both the tongues."[58] Clearly, he did not see any conflict between his reservations about commonplace books and his admiration of anthologies.[59] Similarly, Nicholas Udall's compilation of "flowers" from

55. Ibid., p. 119.

56. See Hutson, *Thomas Nashe*, pp. 38–44, on the notion of the stockpiling of rhetorical "treasuries."

57. Ascham, *Scholemaster*, pp. 222–23.

58. Ibid., p. 256.

59. As early as 1538, Johan Sturm deplored the use of anthologies, even when he published anthologies himself and relied on them for his classes. See Lawrence V. Ryan, *Roger Ascham* (Stanford: Stanford University Press, 1963), p. 266, who cites Sturm's *De litterarum ludis recte aperiendis liber* (Strasbourg, 1543), fol. 23r. But cf. Baldwin who notes "how heavily Sturm relies upon anthologies. To preserve purity, moral but especially linguistic, he puts within the reach of the boys only approved excerpts" (*Shakspere's Small Latine*, vol. 1, p. 294). See also Charles Schmidt, *La vie et les travaux de Jean Sturm* (Nieuwkoop: B. de Graaf, 1970), pp. 248–52. Woodward (*Studies in Education*) similarly

Terence offered selected phrases (with translations) of the plays ordered not by topics, as in a commonplace book, but by line number, scene and act, as if they composed a complete text. The general effect—of a complete interlinear translation nibbled randomly by mice—reveals Udall's sense of the whole pulling against his habit of using the parts.[60]

The difference between the text conceptualized as its parts and as a whole was figured in the competing metaphors of the book as a garden—where useful stuff could be collected, displayed, or exploited for social purposes—and the book as a body, a single and inviolable object that might be anatomized but not dismembered without violence. The most frequently cited metaphor for the book in early humanist pedagogy was that of the garden (the obverse of the "Book of Nature" topos). This metaphor conveyed the idea of a book as a collection of elements, each with its individual interest and value, ordered in pleasing contiguity and available for consumption. In reading the text students were thought to be plowing a field[61] or, more frequently, harvesting the work of others or the products of nature, strolling to pick the healthful flowers and to trample the poisonous ones.[62] In Erasmus's terms, the student "flies about like a diligent bee through

notes that Vives "deprecates the use of Excerpta, which were common in schools as cheap text-books" (p. 198), but Vives also had no difficulty with cutting the "immorality" from a text.

60. This popular schoolbook, entitled *Floures for Latin Spekynge*, first published in London in 1533, was frequently reprinted up to 1581; Udall also translated the *Apophthegmes* of Erasmus in 1542.

61. In his *The ritch Storehouse* Sturm first advises that "in reading we must run over the whole book, or oration, or epistle, or some whole work, and after we must take in hand by piecemeal to consider and judge, and weigh every point, lest anything should escape our understanding"; yet he also admits that some passages are of "such difficulty and so obscure" or "not worth the pains," and these it is "best to overpass" just as a plowman steers around stones or thickets (sig. D4v–5r).

62. Elyot and Vives both employed garden metaphors or similes to discuss the "heathen writers'" mixture of wisdom and obscenity. Vives wrote of the book as "a large field, in which grow herbs, some useful, some noxious, some meant for pleasure and ornament" (Vives, *De tradendis*, bk. 1, chap. 6, p. 269). Elyot developed the metaphor of the text as a garden at some length, concluding that "No wise man entereth into a garden but he soon espieth good herbs from nettles, and treadeth the nettles under his feet whiles he gathereth good herbs. Whereby he taketh no damage, or if he be stung he maketh light of it and shortly forgetteth it. Semblably if he do read wanton matter mixed with wisdom, he putteth the worst under foot and sorteth out the best" (vol. 1, pp. 129–30). See Ong, "Commonplace Rhapsody," p. 118, on texts as collections of "flow-

the whole garden of authors (*ille velut apicula diligens per omnes autorem hortos volitabit*), where he would fall on every little flower, collecting a bit of nectar from each to carry to his hive."[63] In his *Palladis Tamia*, under the heading of the "reading of books," Francis Meres most frequently associates texts with flowers used by bees or man, for as "out of herbs and plants the best things are to be extracted: so the best sayings are to be gathered out of authors."[64]

In the contemporary discourse of gardening to speak of the text as a garden was not to say that it lacked design or order. The order of the sixteenth-century English garden, however, was not that of classical architecture but rather an arrangement of geometrical units through which the visitor (or the bee) traveled randomly. The typical Tudor garden superimposed classical elements and a new iconography on the design of the medieval garden (in the same way that the commonplace tradition was adapted to the citation of classical authors), yet symmetry was "of no primary concern in the planning," according to Roy Strong, who describes the garden as "a series of enclosed squares and rectangles, separate visual experiences bounded by walls and hedges."[65] (See Figure 5, for William Lawson's geometric, but asymmetrical garden plan divided into different terraces and square plots enclosing other forms.) In *The Gardener's Labyrinth* (1594), Thomas Hill wrote of the double "commodity" or benefit of garden alleys and walks: "the one is, the owner may diligently view the prosperity of his herbs and flowers, the other [is] for the delight and comfort of his wearied mind, which he may by himself or fellowship of his friends conceive, in the delectable sights, and fragrant smells of the flowers, by walking up and down, and about the garden in them."[66] That is, the garden visitor's eye was meant to be drawn to the details of the parts, to the individual plants and the elaborate knotted beds, rather than to the design of the

---

ers." I am also grateful to Max Thomas for his discussion of this metaphor in an unpublished essay.

63. Erasmus, *De copia*, p. 262.

64. Meres, *Palladis*, p. 269.

65. Roy Strong, *The Renaissance Garden in England* (London: Thames and Hudson, 1979), pp. 14, 60. According to Strong, p. 15, the architectural notion of a garden integrated with the structure of the house did not reach England until the sixteen-twenties.

66. Dydymus Mountain (Thomas Hill), *The Gardeners Labyrinth* (London, 1594; reprint, New York: Garland, 1982), p. 24.

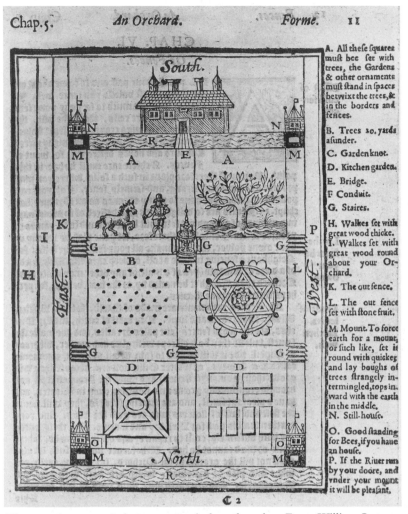

South.

N   N

M   M

A   E   A

R

K

I   G   G   G   P

H   L

B   F   C

East.   *West.*

G   G   G

D   D

M   O   O   M

North.

R

C 2

A. All these squares must bee set with trees, the Gardens & other ornaments must stand in spaces betwixt the trees, & in the borders and fences.

B. Trees 10. yards asunder.

C. Garden knot.

D. Kitchen garden.

E. Bridge.

F Conduit.

G. Staires.

H. Walkes set with great wood thicke.
I. Walkes set with great wood round about your Orchard.

K. The out fence.

L. The out fence set with stone fruit.

M. Mount. To force earth for a mount, or such like, set it round with quickes, and lay boughs of trees strangely intermingled, tops inward with the earth in the middle.
N. Still-house.

O. Good standing for Bees, if you haue an house.
P. If the Riuer run by your doore, and vnder your mount it will be pleasant.

Figure 5. A geometric but asymmetrical garden plan. From William Lawson, *A New Orchard and Garden* (London, 1618; reprint, 1631), p. 11. Reproduced by permission of the Folger Shakespeare Library.

whole perceived in a vista or view. In *The English Husbandman*, after recommending the usual division of a garden into squares, Gervase Markham instructed the reader, "I would not have you to cast every square into one form or fashion of quarters or alleys, for that would show little variety or invention in art, but rather to cast one in plain squares, another in triangulars, another in roundals, and so a forth. . . ."[67] Above all, in the garden, such variety, delight, and "invention" were valued over the pleasures of the design of the whole, just as the text was seen as brimming with remarkable, beautiful, or unusual stuff ready to be admired, plucked out, and used.

The book imagined as a body, however, especially the body constructed in its emergent "classical" conception, was quite different from the "garden" book.[68] The visitor passed from one garden "room" to another, all the while admiring and perhaps gathering the various and abundant plants. By analogy, the reader's experience of the book was like that of the intelligent consumer who could appropriate the best parts from the larger arrangement. The body, however, was conceptualized as a unified structure from which no element could be removed without injuring the others. For example, most prominently, sixteenth-century political writers used the image of the body as a model of the integrated nation state, in which all the hierarchically ordered parts — monarch, aristocracy, commons — functioned to support the whole. While the gar-

67. Gervase Markham, *The English Husbandman* (London, 1613; facsimile reprint, New York: Garland, 1982), bk. 1, pt. 2, p. 112. In giving advice to the country housewife about the design of her garden, William Lawson did not have a great deal to say, but he commends "the wit and art" of a skillful gardener "that can work more variety for breeding of more delightful choice and of all those things, where the owner is able and desirous to be satisfied. The number of forms, mazes and knots is so great, and men are so diversely delighted, that I leave every Housewife to her self . . . lest I deprive her of all delight and direction." (William Lawson, *The Countrie Housewifes Garden* [London, 1617; reprint New York: Garland, 1982], p. 3.) On the early modern aesthetic of detail and variety in ornament, see also Patricia Fumerton, *Cultural Aesthetics: Renaissance Literature and the Practice of Social Ornament* (Chicago: University of Chicago Press, 1991), p. 18, where she describes the aesthetic of the "discontinuous, fragmentary detail."

68. The notion of the "classical" (and male) body here was developed in M. Bakhtin, *Rabelais and his World*, trans. Hélène Iswolsky (Cambridge: MIT Press, 1968); see also Peter Stallybrass, "Patriarchal Territories: The Body Enclosed," in Margaret W. Ferguson, Maureen Quilligan, and Nancy J. Vickers, eds. *Rewriting the Renaissance: The Discourses of Sexual Difference in Early Modern Europe* (Chicago: University of Chicago Press, 1986), pp. 123–44.

den metaphor persisted in description of books, critical discourse increasingly figured the "natural state" of the book, in analogy to the body, as a unified whole.[69] When Jonson recorded his theory of the organic "fable" in his commonplace book, *Discoveries* (thus implicitly distinguishing between disjointed critical and organic "literary" discourse), he clearly delineated this image of the textual body. Jonson first compared the structure of an epic or dramatic "fable" or plot to a house insofar as "nothing in the structure can be changed or taken away, without impairing, or troubling the whole; of which there is a proportionable magnitude in the members."[70] In his comparison, a "whole" and "perfect" literary work had "a beginning, midst and an end," and was evenly proportioned, neither too large or too small, "for as a body without proportion cannot be goodly, no more can the action, either the comedy or tragedy, without his fit bounds."[71] In this kind of critical discourse, tropes and figures were recognized as the clothes of the fable's "body" instead of being counted among the many equally valued discrete elements or parts noted by Vives's or Erasmus's readers. In George Puttenham's words tropes were the "kindly clothes and colors" without which a poem's "limbs" would be left "naked and bare."[72]

69. See Wendy Wall, *The Imprint of Gender: Authorship and Publication in the English Renaissance* (Ithaca: Cornell University Press, 1993), on the body as a metaphor for the text: "Renaissance writers turned to bones and flesh to naturalize a conception of the stable and saleable text. In submitting the text to incorporation as a principle of unity, they also presented a book commodity that had less permeable and provisional borders" (p. 60); she also cites the preface to Thomas Norton and Thomas Sackville's *Gorbuduc* (1570), which presents the play as a violated maiden (pp. 182–84).

70. Ben Jonson, *Timber: or Discoveries* (1640), in *The Complete Poems*, ed. George Parfitt (London: Penguin, 1988), p. 454.

71. Ibid., pp. 455–56. Cf. Vives's use of the body metaphor at the beginning of the sixteenth century, where it is brought up only to justify cutting the text, when he demands that "obscenities should be completely cut off, like a dead thing, and something that would infect anything it touched," just as one would amputate a limb; how, he asked, would a man suffer a loss "if he does in a book, what he would not delay to do in his own body, if necessary" (Vives, *De tradendis*, bk. 3, chap. 5, p. 323).

72. George Puttenham, *The Arte of Englishe Poesie* (London, 1589), in Smith, *Elizabethan Critical Essays*, vol. 2, pp. 142–43. Gabriel Harvey also argued in his *Ciceronianus* (1577) that "merely pointing out, as some have done, the ornaments of tropes and the embellishments of figures, without indicating the stores of arguments, the quantities of proofs, and the structural framework, seems to me tantamount to displaying a body that is surpassingly beautiful and lively but deprived of sense and life" (cited by Jardine, "Humanism and the Sixteenth-Century Arts Course," p. 27).

Unlike the Tudor garden, which thrived on variety and a pleasing excess, the body was thought to be endangered by superfluity of any kind, whether from within (its humors) or from without (in overconsumption of any substance). Moreover, the body was believed to be disfigured by excessive size or disproportion in its limbs. In the second half of the sixteenth century, proportion and control were increasingly valued in both book and body, especially for the body set to study books. For example, Ascham admired most the young scholar "who is fair and comely." Such a scholar has "all other qualities of the mind and parts of the body, that must another day serve learning, not troubled, mangled and halved, but sound, whole, full and able to do their office."[73] Correspondingly, unlike Udall, who deliberately produced a "mutilated" Terence, Ascham worried about the fragmentary nature of extant classical texts—e.g., the "mangled and patched" condition of Varro and the pieces of Menander, which are "like broken jewels, whereby men may rightly esteem, and justly lament, the loss of the whole."[74] What Ascham sought for his "comely" students was an "example to follow, which hath a perfect head, a whole body, forward and backward, arms and legs and all."[75] The "well-grown" text was complete in itself and under control, or in the words of Spenser's E. K., praising *The Shepherds Calendar*, its lines were not "loose" or "ungirt" but rather "well grounded, finely framed, and strongly trussed up together."[76] Such notions of composition predicated new notions of reading and new assumptions about the function of the literary text. Rather than a treasury of textual fragments to be collected and consumed by the reader, the text was to be apprehended and evaluated as a complete and self-sufficient body of work.

In many ways, the shift from thinking about the text as a Tudor garden to imagining it as an integrated body also paralleled a contemporary

73. Ascham, *Scholemaster*, p. 85.
74. Ibid., p. 240.
75. Ibid., p. 317.
76. *Spenser's Minor Poems*, ed. Ernest De Selincourt (1910; reprint, Oxford: Clarendon, 1970), p. 6. See in general, Smith, *Elizabethan Critical Essays*, Introduction, pp. xxxiv–v: "For literature is to be 'well grown,' to show the just proportions of art in subject, technique, and intention, just as the human body and the body politic are to express the ideal harmony of line and plan" (p. xxxv).

change in garden design itself, what Roy Strong has described as an evolution from "a series of separate, enclosed, emblematic tableaux to a sequence of interconnecting spaces whose vital links are in the vista and
point de vue."[77] The differences in garden designs from the sixteenth to
the later seventeenth century are striking. In the sixteenth century the
gardens may be geometric in design, but they are not necessarily symmetrical, nor are they aligned to be viewed from the house (instead, contiguity to the house was a matter of practicality or convenience).
However, in 1677 we see that John Worlidge's *Systema Horti-culturae, or
The Art of Gardening* emphasized the view of the garden from the country house (so that you should "endeavor to make the principal entrance
into your garden, out of the best room in your house"—while there
should be "some other door into your garden for gardeners, laborers,
etc)."[78] The ideal plan is symmetrical, either round or square (see Figure
6, for Worlidge's illustration of a round garden), where "the square is the
most perfect and pleasant form that you can lay your garden into, where
your ground will afford it, every walk that is in it being straight and every
plant and tree standing in a direct line, represents it to your eye very
pleasing."[79] John Lawrence, in the first part of *Gardening Improved*,
called *The Clergyman's Recreation*, also calls for a square or oblong "lead-
ing from the middle of my house, a gravel-walk in the middle, with narrow borders of grass on each side of them for winter-use and each side of
them rows of all the varieties of winter greens set at due distances, which
will appear with an agreeable beauty from the house all the year."[80] An
element may be removed or added to the Tudor "emblematic" garden
without destroying the design. For the late seventeenth-and early eight-
eenth-century garden, however, the emphasis on vistas, controlled by
angles of symmetry, must be designed and maintained as a whole.

From the beginning the humanists' ideal may have been to range
through all books, classic and "pedestrian," where the sum of knowledge like the height of eloquence lay in both breadth and variety. Yet

77. Strong, *Renaissance Garden in England*, p. 11.

78. John Worlidge, *Systema Horti-culturae, or the Art of Gardening* (London, 1677;
reprint, New York: Garland, 1982), p. 20.

79. Ibid., p. 18.

80. John Lawrence, *Gardening Improved*, pt. 1, *The Clergyman's Recreation* (London,
1717; reprint, New York: Garland, 1982), p. 21.

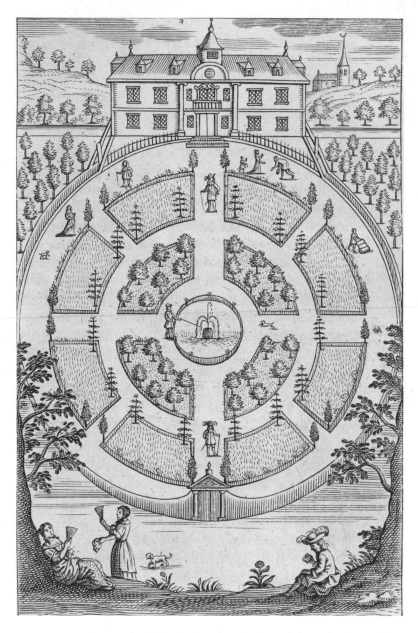

Figure 6. A symmetrical garden designed to be viewed from the house. From John Worlidge, *Systema Horti-culturae* (London: 1677; reprint 1688), p. 14. Reproduced by permission of the Folger Shakespeare Library.

this ideal foundered, for reasons both material and aesthetic. As I have suggested, the humanist educational program was ultimately an institutional one. Its educational institutions — whether the private tutorial, the grammar school, or the university college — demanded curricula that were constrained by time and that had an end in both senses: the purpose of fashioning productive members of society and a boundary marking the termination of formal study. Institutional instruction also ultimately meant regulation and uniformity in the selection of texts, where a tutor's individual choice became a general rule, whether promulgated in printed books or set, as Mulcaster wished, by the state.

But the humanist reading project was also undone, one can argue, by the emergence of a neoclassical aesthetic of symmetry and wholeness. One should not conclude that the study of classical texts per se generated the neoclassical aesthetics of natural order, unified perspective, and the notion of the whole since for years scholars and teachers were content to approach these texts in a fragmentary, disintegrative fashion, whether those texts were in pieces or not. Rather, the "unity" of texts was something that came to be *read into* those books over time. Discipline may have been a keynote of the humanist classroom, with the students driven to focus relentlessly on grammatical rules and the interpretation and copying of bits of texts, but this discipline did not imply the ordering of text as an object of study, nor did it necessarily exclude any object of study. But when texts became seen as whole and schooling became increasingly constricted by time, variety and range had to fall away before the order of symmetry and natural design. As the next chapter will argue, the expectation of finding a given natural and "finely framed" order in art and the world was neither inherently "humanist" nor did it express a coherent political ideology. But it forever changed the role of books in humanist education, where the need to read the whole constantly undermined the desire to read everything.

CHAPTER 5

Tradition and Sovereignty

The aesthetic of "corporal" form, which would transform humanist reading and writing, put new pressures on humanist education when it tried to balance the demands of freedom and control, *copia* and restraint. It was fundamentally a neoclassical aesthetic informing the composition of paintings and literature, buildings and gardens. As such, for artists and poets, teachers and gardeners, it signalled a way of perceiving the natural world and one's relationship to it quite different from that of humanist aesthetics and poetics.[1] This chapter steps outside the walls of the humanist schoolroom to consider the early modern British battles over neoclassical literary form, which was understood either as the copying of antique poetic models or as an aesthetic of unity and symmetry ever present in nature and waiting to be "discovered" through poetic invention. In the end, however, this argument will return us to the schoolroom because such differences over classicism and imitation always involve questions about how the scholar's and poet's freedom may be rooted in the study of the past.

Just as twentieth-century historians have debated whether Renaissance humanism was revolutionary or conservative, sixteenth-century

---

1. For a comprehensive general discussion of notions of a "humanist poetics" in prose, see Arthur F. Kinney, *Continental Humanist Poetics: Studies in Erasmus, Castiglione, Marguerite de Navarre, Rabelais, and Cervantes* (Amherst: University of Massachusetts Press, 1989) and *Humanist Poetics: Thought, Rhetoric, and Fiction in Sixteenth-Century England* (Amherst: University of Massachusetts Press, 1986).

writers disagreed about whether classical imitation was liberating or constricting, capable of fashioning a new national poetry or limited to aping an alien past. Insofar as the early modern argument about imitating literary classical form was articulated in terms of freedom versus servility and patriotism versus cosmopolitanism, the conflict invoked contemporary political discourses. Just as early modern teachers and scholars negotiated stances of rule and resistance in political language, the contests over the poet's role also used terms of sovereignty and autonomy; in this discourse the poet, like the teacher, both resembled the ruler and resisted limitations. Debates over classical imitation and invention not only appealed to the national consciousness and revised the relationship between present law and past custom; they also reshaped how tradition and history defined the poet's—and the monarch's—sovereignty.

In his *Forms of Nationhood: The Elizabethan Writing of England*, Richard Helgerson has written insightfully of how the argument over adapting classical metrical models to English verse encoded conflicting political discourses of law and authority, time and history.[2] For most literary historians the quantitative verse movement's failure signaled a healthy reaction against the "excesses of Renaissance humanism and Elizabethan taste"—in particular the taste for "artificiality."[3] Helgerson sets up ideological parallels for the argument between rhyme and quantitative verse, aligned along the axes of the "gothic" and "classical," where the "gothic" signifies an appeal to time, custom, and the "ancient constitution," and the "classical" signifies the values of humanist "self-fashioning," absolutism, and Roman law. When Gabriel Harvey rebuked Edmund Spenser for trying to make "your *carpēnter* our *carpĕnter*, an inch longer, or bigger, than God and his English people have made him," since it is against "all order of law, and in despite of custom,"[4] Helgerson reads this accusation as Harvey's setting "a

2. See Richard Helgerson, *Forms of Nationhood: The Elizabethan Writing of England* (Chicago: University of Chicago Press, 1992), chap. 1.
3. Derek Attridge, *Well-Weighed Syllables: Elizabethan Verse in Classical Metres* (Cambridge: Cambridge University Press, 1974), p. 234.
4. Gabriel Harvey, *Three proper and wittie, familiar letters: lately passed betweene two universitie men touching the Earthquake in Aprill last, and our English reformed Versifying*

Gothic, common-law tradition" against Spenser's "version of the absolutist cultural politics of antiquity."[5]

Humanism and neoclassical poetics, however, were not inextricably intertwined. Nor can the historical politics of pedagogical or aesthetic choices be easily fixed, for they varied with each writer and changed according to his or her ends. As many scholars have suggested, in sixteenth-century England a "humanist" aesthetic might little resemble neoclassical formal principles of decorum, order, and verisimilitude.[6] In Britain a neoclassicism that defined a formalist order of nature cut away the historical moorings anchoring early humanist aesthetics, scholarship, and political thought. Just as a neoclassical emphasis on the wholeness of a text restricted humanist *copia*, the humanist belief in artifice clashed with a privileging of natural form — art that rooted its laws in nature. I have argued in Chapter 3 that in the complementary spaces of the garden and the schoolroom a desire to master nature had a double significance, as did nature itself. In the politics of aesthetics, as well, nature could serve both to bind the artist and to grant him power.

While acknowledging Helgerson's politicizing of humanist poetics, I wish to complicate his binaries of the gothic and classical, the medieval and the humanist, by reexamining the negotiation of history, authority, autonomy, and nature in the debate over formal innovation. I focus first on the early stabs at neoclassical dramatic form in England, which most sharply brought into conflict humanist and neoclassical principles of history and tradition. A look at Philip Sidney's wavering between history and poetry, nature and art, and humanist artifice and natural decorum, in his *Defence of Poetry* precedes a closer analysis of these conflicts in the works of George Buchanan — neoclassical poet, humanist tutor, historian, and political polemicist. Buchanan's case neatly illustrates the tension between humanist historicism and classical form because Buchanan, whom Sidney much admired, wrote in the

---

(London, 1580), in *The Works of Gabriel Harvey*, ed. Alexander Grosart (1884; reprint, New York: AMS, 1966), vol. 1, p. 100.

5. Helgerson, *Forms of Nationhood*, p. 28.

6. Cf. C. S. Lewis, *English Literature in the Sixteenth Century, Excluding Drama* (Oxford: Oxford University Press, 1954), who insists that "the neoclassics are the humanists' lawful heirs" (p. 19).

genres of history, political polemic, and neoclassical tragedy. Both authors' ambivalence about history and form contrast with celebrations of natural—and native—poetic form, by Samuel Daniel and the young James VI, in which Daniel associated nature with custom and James invoked nature in the name of his own kingly authority. Both Daniel and James dismissed the classical past as irrelevant to the present, understanding the present order of nature as a kind of universal order. In these cases "neoclassicism" understood as the imitation of past literary models gave way to a new "neoclassicism," a submission to a natural order that could support or undercut hierarchy and authority. The significance of such aesthetic debates thus exceeded that of narrow disputes over poetic meter or dramatic form; rather, they revealed how humanism paradoxically roots human freedom in tradition. The debate posed the question of whether the study of tradition means submission to the past's authority, or whether such knowledge makes one free. On the one hand, awareness of the past can confer a kind of freedom through the knowledge that things can change; on the other, the past may offer a way of defining a self in the context of a traditional community, either for or against the state.

SIDNEY AND BUCHANAN

One cluster of poets in sixteenth-century France and England fervently believed that imitating ancient poetic forms would elevate the writer's own art and vernacular language: backward thinking was, in this view, forward thinking.[7] Jean Dorat's Greek epigraph for Joachim du Bellay's *La deffence et illustration de la langue françoyse* (1549) names the author a patriot for defending France's language,[8] even though—or because—du Bellay vilified his country's old poetry: "the old French poems . . . such as rondeaus, ballads, virelaies, 'chants royaux,' songs and other such spicy items (*episseries*), that corrupt the taste of our language, and serve only to bear witness to our igno-

---

7. See Nancy S. Struever, *The Language of History in the Renaissance: Rhetoric and Historical Consciousness in Florentine Humanism* (Princeton: Princeton University Press, 1970), p. 95, on how "the 'Moderns' thus become those who still cling to the recent barbaric past; the 'Ancients' are the party of renewal and illumination."

8. Joachim du Bellay, *La deffence et illustration de la langue françoyse* (1549), ed. Henri Chamard (Paris: M. Didier, 1948), p. 10.

rance" (*ces vieilles poesies Francoyses . . . comme rondeaux, ballades, vyrelaiz, chantz royaulx, chansons, & autres telles episseries, qui corrumpent le goust de nostre Langue, & ne servent si non à porter temoingnaige de notre ignorance*).[9] Even while they recognized the historicity of language and culture, the French poets of the group called the "Pléiade," bound together by their desire to assimilate the classical into the "native," presumed that poetic form transcended history. Thus, while it subjugates French poetry to classical models, du Bellay's *Deffence* traces the contemporary distaste for the vernacular back to Roman imperialism, to the time when the Romans called the Gauls "barbarous" (*barbares*) and tried "not only to subdue, but also to make all other nations vile and abject next to themselves (*tachoint non seulement à subjuguer, mais à rendre toutes autres nations viles & abjectes aupres d'eux*)."[10] The text does not connect this historical explanation for naming French a "barbarous language" with its own rejection of France's "barbarous" traditions, a preference based on an anachronistic comparison of Latin and French poetic forms. In this blindness, as Margaret Ferguson observes, du Bellay's imagination was inevitably "trapped between an unattainable future and an irrecoverable past"—trapped, indeed, in a present tense of abstract poetic form.[11]

As many recent scholars have noted, the theory and practice of imitation of classical models could bring conflicts in humanist historiography to the surface. Nancy Struever argues that in the Italian Renaissance imitation entailed a *productive* sense of anachronism, stimulating "fresh speculation on general historical premises" and establishing that "one must accept discontinuity as true and comprehend time as a limitation of personal choice."[12] Ideally, formal

9. Ibid., p. 108–9.

10. Ibid., p. 18.

11. Margaret W. Ferguson, *Trials of Desire: Renaissance Defenses of Poetry* (New Haven: Yale University Press, 1983), p. 27.

12. Struever, *Language of History*, p. 96. In *The Light in Troy: Imitation and Discovery in Renaissance Poetry* (New Haven: Yale University Press, 1982), p. 33, Thomas M. Greene writes of France and England: "the advent of humanism conferred a keener historical consciousness upon the literary mind and created an etiological problem: the task of constructing retrospectively a past from which a literary work could visibly emerge without damaging anachronism. For a humanist literature, this past was most commonly ancient and the etiological solution was embraced by the term *imitation*." For other key

imitation thus nurtured historical relativism while it assumed a continuity between past and present.[13] In practice, however, imitation more often generated an *unproductive* conflict between those who assumed that "the ancients had discovered the basic features of the various possible poetic genres and that these should inform all poetry for all time"[14] and those who saw that poetic form might change over time and in different cultures. In the former case, form was detached from history; Antonfrancesco Grazzini put the latter case quite succinctly in the prologue to his play *La Strega* (1566): "Aristotle and Horace knew their own time, but ours is different. We have other customs, another religion, another way of life, and therefore need to create our comedies in another manner."[15]

By situating the conflict in the poets' desire to effect change through and against history, arguments for classical imitation raised questions about the writer's autonomy in the face of the past's authority. In *The Scholemaster*, Roger Ascham used a vocabulary of freedom and servitude in writing of the poet's tie to the antique past, objecting to those who "will say, it were a plain slavery, and injury too, to shackle and tie a good wit, and hinder the course of a man's good nature with such

studies of the complexities of Renaissance theories of imitation, see David Quint, *Origin and Originality in Renaissance Literature: Versions of the Source* (New Haven: Yale University Press, 1983); and G. W. Pigman, III, "Versions of Imitation in the Renaissance," *Renaissance Quarterly* 33 (1980): 1–32. See also Timothy Hampton, *Writing from History: The Rhetoric of Exemplarity in Renaissance Literature* (Ithaca: Cornell University Press, 1990), on the way in which "humanist culture was marked by a radical consciousness of the fragility of tradition" (pp. 11–12); and Anthony Grafton, *Defenders of the Text: The Traditions of Scholarship in an Age of Science, 1450–1800* (Cambridge: Harvard University Press, 1991), chap. 1, on the way in which Renaissance humanist scholarship was divided between historical and ahistorical modes of reading.

13. See Struever, *Language of History*, p. 193, for example: "Rhetorical *imitatio*, with its concept of virtuosity as both a command of past techniques which possess continuous sanctions and a sensitivity to the unique demands of the present situation, provides a model of continuity in change."

14. Marvin Carlson, *Theories of the Theatre: A Historical and Critical Survey, from the Greeks to the Present* (Ithaca: Cornell University Press, 1984), pp. 54–55.

15. Cited in ibid., p. 43. See also Greene, *Light in Troy*, on the debate between the Ciceronians, who were "inclined to believe in pure repeatability, in imitation as secular ritual, and to reduce by implication anachronistic distance," and the anti-Ciceronians, who were "inclined to deny the sacred status of the original text and to stress the creative freedom of the imitator, a freedom which is inescapable given the fact of cultural change" (p. 154).

bonds of servitude, in following another." Yet Ascham could not answer this accusation, except to acknowledge the modern writer's inferiority: "Except such men think themselves wiser than *Cicero* for teaching of eloquence, they must be content to turn a new leaf."[16] When Sidney saw poetry as transcending time and history he set his freedom within the frame of a natural order of verisimilitude and decorum (even though he wrote of escaping nature's "enclosure"), and when Samuel Daniel wrote of the imitation of classical meters his own political and poetic freedom meant submission to the rule of custom and nature.

All arguments about poetic form addressed issues of history in some way, but of all the genres tragedy most deeply involved history: first, because tragedy's subject was characteristically secular or biblical history, and second, because its mimetic form reenacted an historical event in the present moment.[17] Greek tragedy was founded on a conflict between present and past, or, as classicists Jean-Pierre Vernant and Pierre Vidal-Naquet put it, a contrast of "heroic values and ancient religious representations with the new modes of thought that characterize the advent of law within the city-state."[18] On the surface, Greek tragedy focuses on the here and now, on what Vernant calls "a human, opaque time made up of successive and limited present moments," a time that the audience experiences as the present in its enactment.[19] In this brief duration of time, however, Greek tragedy opens up both the mythic past, increasingly inaccessible to

16. Roger Ascham, *The Scholemaster* (London, 1570; reprint, ed. Edward Arber, Boston: Willard Small, 1888), pp. 243–44. For those earlier writers who concerned themselves primarily with the problem of the imitation of texts, in Struever's words, "the essence of Humanistic method is a relationship between freedom and constraint which can be either an easy reciprocity or a difficult ambiguity" (p. 153).

17. As Tom F. Driver put it: "The theater, then, tends to reflect the assumptions of its age regarding time and history because it is on the one hand a narrative of temporal events, and on the other hand, an enactment taking place within a moment of time" (Driver, *The Sense of History in Greek and Shakespearean Drama* [New York: Columbia University Press, 1960], p. 6).

18. Jean-Pierre Vernant and Pierre Vidal-Naquet, *Mythe et tragédie en Grèce ancienne* (Paris: Maspéro, 1972); trans. Janet Lloyd, *Tragedy and Myth in Ancient Greece* (Atlantic Highlands, N.J.: Humanities, 1981), p. 4.

19. Vernant and Vidal-Naquet, *Tragedy*, p. 19.

the present understanding and the scheme of "divine time," incomprehensible to the human mind.[20] In its historical period Greek tragedy played out the horror of living in a circumscribed time of experience when the future was mysterious and the past oppressive.[21] It is thus the genre in which time creates great anxiety for characters and audience alike.

Generally, most northern European humanist drama of the sixteenth century seems far away from this Greek model or anything else conventionally termed neoclassical theater. According to Donald Stone, Jr., the hallmarks of French humanist drama were moral teaching, sententiousness, and the formal elaboration of rhetoric; it did not follow strict "Aristotelian" rules.[22] In England and France the humanists' primary classical tragic model was Senecan tragedy, which had fossilized Euripidean tragedy, reproducing the Greek tragic structure without its life. In Senecan tragedy, the chorus, instead of interacting with the protagonists, merely recited between acts, shaping a five-act structure that was at its most static merely a "collection of formal speeches."[23] While recreating the episodic and agonistic form of Greek tragedy, Senecan tragedy and its Renaissance imitations focused less on the circumscribing of human action in experienced time than on the inexorable progress from the moment of mythic foresight or curse to the fulfillment of that vision.[24] It was later French neoclassical tragedy, in contrast, which shifted the attention to *vraisemblance* and the aesthetics of per-

20. See Vidal-Naquet, "Temps des dieux et temps des hommes: Essai sur quelques aspects de l'expérience temporelle chez les grecs," *Revue de l'histoire des réligions* 157 (1960): 55–80. See also Vernant and Vidal-Naquet, *Tragedy*, p. 19.

21. See Jacqueline de Romilly, *Time in Greek Tragedy* (Ithaca: Cornell University Press, 1968), chaps. 1 and 2. See also Rebecca W. Bushnell, "Time and History in Early English Classical Drama," in Gordon J. Schochet, ed., *Law, Literature, and the Settlement of Regimes: Proceedings of The Folger Institute Center for the History of British Political Thought* (Washington, D.C.: Folger Institute, 1990), vol. 2, pp. 73–86. Some short parts of this essay are borrowed from this source.

22. Donald Stone, Jr., *French Humanist Drama: A Reassessment* (Totowa, N.J.: Rowman and Littlefield, 1974).

23. See Gordon Braden, *Renaissance Tragedy and the Senecan Tradition: Anger's Privilege* (New Haven: Yale University Press, 1985), p. 104.

24. See Bruce R. Smith, *Ancient Scripts and Modern Experience on the English Stage, 1500–1700* (Princeton: Princeton University Press, 1988), who argues that the critical the-

formance, making the theater appear more "natural" through the unities of time, place, and action that collapsed the time of enactment into the story time.[25]

Thus, when George Buchanan, beginning in the 1540s in France, imitated Euripides, and Sidney, in the England of the early 1580s, advocated observance of an Aristotelian unity of tragic time their innovations not only brought into relief the contrast between neoclassical order and humanist *copia*,[26] but they also restored to tragedy a tension between nature and history, the present moment and a long view of the past. Although he began writing before the theoretical formulation of dramatic neoclassicism, Buchanan alone among the early humanist dramatists in France followed the example of Euripides (whom he had already translated).[27] Similarly, Sidney's advocacy of the dramatic unities was the first clear statement of continental neoclassical principles in English criticism. In the intervening decades commentators on Aristotle's *Poetics* had begun to formulate a theory of "realistic" tragic time while misconstruing Aristotle's statement that "as far as its length is concerned tragedy tries as hard as it can to exist during a single daylight period."[28] We see this concern with verisimilar time in all the commentators on the *Poetics*, in Francesco Robortello's *In Librum Aristotelis De arte poetica explicationes* (1548), Giombattista Giraldi's *Discorsi* (1554), the *De poeta* of Sebastiano Minturno (1559), and most notably

---

ories of Horace, describing the play as a rhetorical event, and those of Aristotle, which focused on the play as art object, conflicted in this period (pp. 38–39).

25. See Stone, *French Humanist Drama*, chap. 4.

26. See Smith on how in Dryden's comments on Seneca "we witness the triumph of neoclassical order over Renaissance copiousness" (*Ancient Scripts*, p. 57). He compares such developments with the change in theatrical space from medieval hall to geometric classical theater (Ibid., p. 65).

27. See Raymond Lebègue, *La tragédie réligieuse en France: Les débuts (1514–1573)* (Paris: Honoré Champion, 1929), p. 467; Lebègue sees *Jepthes* as Buchanan's only "true Greek tragedy"; see also pp. 460, 463, 465. On the question of Buchanan's style in relationship to Euripides and Seneca, see *A Critical Edition of George Buchanan's "Baptistes" and of Its Anonymous Seventeenth-Century Translation, "Tyrannical Government Anatomized,"* ed. Steven Berkowitz (New York: Garland, 1992), pp. 213–22: Berkowitz concludes that Buchanan was deeply influenced by Euripides rather than Seneca, although his plays are not strictly Aristotelian.

28. Aristotle, *Poetics* 3849b1, trans. Gerald F. Else (Ann Arbor: University of Michigan Press, 1967), p. 24.

in *Poetices libri septem* (1561) of Julius Caesar Scaliger, which first clearly identified the time of performance with the time of the action represented.[29] The idea of verisimilar time was most notoriously formulated as a rigid "rule," limiting action to the extent of twelve hours, by Sidney's source, Lodovico Castelvetro's *Poetica d'Aristotele vulgarizzata e sposta* (1570). Buchanan's close attention to Euripides' example marks the beginnings of this new notion of tragic form. In the *Defence*, Sidney looked back at earlier English plays like Thomas Sackville and Thomas Norton's *Gorbuduc* (1561) through the lens of the newest Italian criticism.[30]

Some readers find the appearance of Sidney's neoclassical strictures disconcerting, given the *Defence of Poetry*'s celebration of the poet's creative freedom. As O. B. Hardison, Jr. put the case, it is as if we hear two voices in the *Defence*: the first,

> the familiar voice of humanist poetics. . . . Its key ideas are inspiration, the superiority of imagination to reason and nature, and the power of poetry, through its emotional appeal, to cause *praxis* rather than *gnosis*. The second voice is that of incipient neo-classicism. . . . Its touchstones are the subordination of imagination to reason and nature, the need for artistic 'rules,' the interpretation of imitation as copying masterpieces, and the insistence on verisimilitude—with the corollary of the three unities—in drama.[31]

29. Cf. John W. Cunliffe, *Early English Classical Tragedies* (Oxford: Clarendon, 1912), pp. xliv–xlvii.

30. As T. W. Baldwin snorts, "this dogma of Castelvetro's was published only in 1570, several years too late to save the authors of *Gorbuduc* in 1561 from a scolding still some years later by young Sir Philip Sidney for not having obeyed it" (*Shakspere's Five-Act Structure: Shakspere's Early Plays on the Background of Renaissance Theories of Five-Act Structure from 1470* (Urbana: University of Illinois Press, 1947), pp. 362–63.

31. O. B. Hardison, Jr., "The Two Voices of Sidney's *Apology for Poetry*," *English Literary Renaissance* 2 (1972): 92. See also Phyllis Rackin's construction of the difference in terms of two different appeals to nature, in "Shakespeare's Boy Cleopatra, the Decorum of Nature, and the Golden World of Poetry," *PMLA* 87 (1972): 201–12. On art and nature, see also Edward William Tayler, *Nature and Art in Renaissance Literature* (New York: Columbia University Press, 1964). Many readers argue that the apparent duality is merely part of Sidney's irony or rhetorical technique. See Ferguson: "The 'voice of freedom' and the 'voice of censuring' Hardison hears are produced by the diplomatic defensive project whose aim is necessarily double: to establish poetry's power (the *confirmatio*'s 'monarchy') and to protect that power from its potential for abuse (the checks of the *refutatio* and the *digressio*)" (*Trials*, p. 151). See also Martin N. Raitiere, "The Unity

Rather than being simply opposed, the "double voices," however, separate and merge where the powers of nature and art diverge and converge in the text and distort the shape of history. As Daniel Javitch has noted, what may have been seen as restrictive rules from one perspective were understood as empowering from another: "Aristotelian norms of poetics and art . . . were as amenable to champions of new forms and genres of poetry as to the upholders of ancient orthodoxy."[32]

When Sidney deplored how contemporary English tragedies and comedies observed "rules neither of honest civility nor skilful poetry," he drew on the authority of both art and nature embedded in natural reason. So it was that *Gorbuduc*, in which "there is both many days, and many places inartificially imagined, . . . is faulty both in place and time, the two necessary companions of all corporal actions." Instead, "the stage should always represent but one place, and the uttermost time presupposed in it should be, both by Aristotle's precept and common reason, but one day." Sidney ridiculed plays that represent "Asia of one side, and Afric[a] of the other" and are too "liberal" in their telling of time, displaying the course of a prince's life "in two hours space: which, how absurd it is in sense, even sense may imagine, and art hath taught, and all ancient examples justified."[33] Sidney based his judgment in equal measures on example, the precepts of art, and "common" or untutored "reason" and "sense" (the latter term with meanings extending from a faculty of perception or corporal sensation to the function of a sane mind). The poet thus trusts here in a "natural" reason, seconded by art and the authority of the ancient example. In effect, using common sense

---

of Sidney's *Apology for Poetry*," *SEL* 21 (1981): 37–57; and Alan Sinfield, "Sidney's *Defence* and the Collective-Farm Chairman: Puritan Humanism and the Cultural Apparatus," in *Faultlines: Cultural Materialism and the Politics of Dissident Reading* (Berkeley: University of California Press, 1992), pp. 181–213; the latter views the "structural difficulty" in the *Defence* as "arising from the tension in the puritan humanist situation" (p. 200).

32. Daniel Javitch, "Pioneer Genre Theory and the Opening of the Humanist Canon," *Common Knowledge* 3.1 (1994):65.

33. Sir Philip Sidney, *A Defence of Poetry*, in *Miscellaneous Prose of Sir Philip Sidney*, ed. Katherine Duncan-Jones and Jan Van Dorsten (Oxford: Oxford University Press, 1973), pp. 112–13. The *Defence* was first published posthumously in London in 1595. Duncan-Jones and Van Dorsten suggest that it was composed in 1579–80.

naturalized rules, artifice, and the authority of tradition—the same strategy at work in the notion of decorum.[34]

Such recourse to nature, rules, and reason may appear to contradict the *Defence*'s earlier claim that the poet who disdains "to be tied to any such subjection [to nature], lifted up with the vigor of his own invention, doth grow in effect another nature, in making things either better than nature bringeth forth, or, quite anew, forms such as never were in nature." But the latter part of the *Defence* moves closer to the earlier position in suggesting a coalescence of nature and the poet's art. Indeed, even in the first part, in which the *Defence* celebrates the poet's mastery of nature, he still goes "hand in hand" with her: "Nature never set forth the earth in so rich tapestry as divers poets have done; neither with so pleasant rivers, fruitful trees, sweet-smelling flowers, nor whatsoever else may make the too much loved earth more lovely."[35] While Sidney's beginning might seem to oppose the poet to nature, freeing him from her dominion, the language here in fact echoes the praise of horticulture, representing the poet as one who like the consummate gardener makes "the too much loved earth more lovely," fashioning what was never before in nature by working with her.[36]

This collaboration and competition between nature and art match the relationship Sidney saw between poetry and history. Sidney mocked the historian "laden with old mouse-eaten records, authorizing himself (for the most part) upon other histories, whose greatest authorities are built upon the notable foundations of hearsay; . . . better acquainted with a thousand years ago than with the present age, and yet better knowing how this world goeth than how his own wit run-

34. See Norman Rabkin's appendix, "Shakespearean Mimesis, English Drama and the Unity of Time," in *Shakespeare and the Common Understanding* (New York: Free Press, 1967), pp. 239–61.

35. Sidney, *Defence*, p. 78.

36. Sidney's ambivalence here is matched by his even-handedness on the issue of quantitative verse: "Now of versifying there are two sorts, the one ancient, the other modern. . . . Whether of these be the more excellent, would bear many speeches: the ancient (no doubt) more fit for music, both words and time observing quantity, and more fit lively to express diverse passions, by the low or lofty sound of the well-weighed syllable; the latter likewise with his rhyme, striketh a certain music to the ear, and fine, since it doth delight, though by another way, it obtains the same purpose: there being in either sweetness, and wanting in neither majesty, truly the English before any language I know, is fit for both sorts" (*Defence*, pp. 119–20).

neth; curious for antiquities and inquisitive of novelties; a wonder to young folks and a tyrant in table talk."[37] Such rhetoric simultaneously makes the historian the poet's competitor and trivializes him: he is a tyrant—but only of table talk; a wonder—but merely to the young. If the historian's work is worth something, it is only for the poet's use: for "the best of the historian is subject to the poet; for whatsoever action, or faction, whatsoever counsel, policy or war stratagem the historian is bound to recite, that may the poet, if he list with his imitation make his own, beautifying it both for further teaching, and more delighting, as it please him: having all, from Dante's heaven to his hell, under the authority of his pen."[38] The poet is the master, history the subject, like nature; but history like nature again is also the stuff from which the poet fashions his art.[39]

The *Defence*'s aesthetic of tragic time, in turn, intensifies the competition between history and poetry. Anticipating objections to his strictures about tragic time and place, Sidney attributed to such critics ignorance of the difference between history and art. The answer to the question "How then shall we set forth a story which containeth both many places and times?" is: "And do they not know that a tragedy is tied to the laws of poesy, and not of history; not bound to follow the story, but having liberty either to feign a quite new matter or to frame the history to the most tragical conveniency? Again, many things may be told which cannot be showed, if they know the difference betwixt reporting and representing."[40] "Reporting" means the recounting or narrating of real events, the kind of history that Sidney described to his brother Robert as "a narration of things done, with the beginnings,

---

37. Ibid., pp. 83–84.

38. Ibid., p. 89. See Ferguson on Sidney and history: "To gain recognition for poetry, Sidney shows it rising from a position of low esteem to a monarchy based on its 'moving' power" (*Trials of Desire*, p. 145).

39. On Sidney and history, see also Arthur F. Kinney, "Sir Philip Sidney and the Uses of History," in Heather Dubrow and Richard Strier, eds., *The Historical Renaissance: New Essays in Tudor and Stuart Literature and Culture* (Chicago: University of Chicago Press, 1988), pp. 293–314; Elizabeth Story Donno, "Old Mouse-eaten Records: History in Sidney's *Apology*," *Studies in Philology* 72 (1975): 275–98, who argues that Sidney was not "anti-history"; and F. J. Levy, "Sir Philip Sidney and the Idea of History," *Bibliothèque d'humanisme et Renaissance* 26 (1964): 608–17.

40. Sidney, *Defence*, p. 114.

causes, and appendences [there]of," in which "your method must be to have *seriem temporum* [temporal sequence] very exactly."[41] However, "representing"—the "figuring forth of a speaking picture"—produces an aesthetic object that exists according to different temporal laws. In representing a tragic moment, not shown are the "beginnings, causes, and appendences"; for, as Sidney says, "if they will represent a history, they must not (as Horace sayeth) begin *ab ovo* [from the beginning], but they must come to the principal point of that one action which they will represent."[42] Here the tragic poet is liberated from history, which is bound merely to tell "what is."[43] The poet is freed both from history's unedifying immorality and from the burdens of historical time and process.

Representing foregrounds the present moment, obscuring the sequence of events which led up it. In tragedy, according to Sidney, this past may be reported but not represented. In not being enacted on the stage, the beginnings and causes of events (the *ovum*) are thus distanced and even suppressed outright. The *Defence* thus prepares us to see how the tragic representation of time can tip the scale on the uneasy balance achieved between the roles of the historian and the poet in the case of a poet who believed, as his letter to his brother suggests, in the value of studying chronicle history to extract edifying examples. In the *Defence*, the poet is allowed to reshape the materials of history, both for better teaching or moral effect and for a greater aesthetic effect. In doing so the poet's autonomy entails a rejection of the tyranny of history and the installation of the poet as an absolute monarch of truth and beauty.

Sidney thus gives us a vantage point from which to approach the works of George Buchanan, whom Sidney praised for his "piercing wit" and for tragedies that "do justly bring forth a divine admiration."[44]

41. Letter from Sidney to his brother Robert Sidney, dated October 18, 1580, in Sir Philip Sidney, *Complete Works*, vol. 3, *The Defence of Poesie, Political Discourses, Correspondence, Translations*, ed. Albert Feuillerat (Cambridge: Cambridge University Press, 1923), p. 130. Sidney suggests that it will be useful for his brother to extract the good examples and order them in a table for easy reference.

42. Sidney, *Defence*, p. 114.

43. Ibid., p. 85.

44. Ibid., pp. 110, 116.

Sidney admired Buchanan for his politics as well as his art. In October 1579, Sidney wrote to Buchanan, introducing himself and speaking of his "desire to see you, and kiss the hand of the young king, in whom many have laid their hopes. God prosper him and make him learn by you that goodness is the greatest greatness." With this letter he sent his servant, who "can show unto you as much as I of the materials concerning Monsieur and purpose of his marriage." This letter, referring to a common interest in Elizabeth I's potential marriage to the duke of Alençon, encoded a set of shared values, that James E. Phillips sums up as "puritan piety, humanistic learning, and royal subordination to popular sovereignty."[45] As a humanist historian, a neoclassical poet, and a protestant polemicist against tyranny, Buchanan indeed practiced what Sidney preached. For this reason, Buchanan's then much-admired Euripidean tragedies, which depict critical events in biblical history, offer a test case for what happened when a humanist historian adapted classical tragic form to represent history.

Buchanan's own national identity was multiple. As a neoclassical poet his ties were closest to France, but as an historian and polemicist he spoke for Scotland and from there to England and the rest of Europe. Having spent his early career primarily in France, Buchanan composed all of his prodigious literary efforts in Latin. At the same time, he was most distinctly a Scot, embroiled in Scottish politics and engaged in writing a patriotic history of his country.[46] Buchanan freely admitted his lack of interest in the vernacular, professing that he would

perceive, without regret, the gradual extinction of the ancient Scottish language, and cheerfully allow its harsh sounds to die away, and give place to the softer and more harmonious tones of the Latin. For if, in this transmigration into another language, it is necessary that we yield up one thing or

45. See James E. Phillips, "George Buchanan and the Sidney Circle," *The Huntington Library Quarterly* 12 (1948–49): 39. The text of Sidney's letter is reproduced, pp. 33–34.
46. Because Buchanan was a neo-Latin poet and spent so much time in France, scholars of French rather than British literature usually claim the literary Buchanan. See the introduction to his *Tragedies*, ed. P. Sharratt and P. G. Walsh (Edinburgh: Scottish Academic Press, 1983), p. 1. All citations of Buchanan's plays will be from this edition: the Latin texts are cited by line number in the text; translations are my own except where indicated (I cite the page numbers of Sharratt and Walsh's translation in the notes).

other, let us pass from rusticity and barbarism to culture and civilization, and let our choice and judgment repair the infelicity of our birth.[47]

From the perspective of historians of political thought, Buchanan was a Scot whose political writings specifically addressed Scottish controversies and who was committed to Scottish political traditions.

Buchanan did not play out the conflict between the literary neoclassicist and the Scottish traditionalist in a poetic treatise (although he did write a short treatise, *De prosodia libellus*, published in 1595). Unlike England or France, sixteenth-century Scotland was a multilingual culture, with Middle Scots, English, Latin, and Gaelic all in current use and the identity of the "Scottish" language still in flux.[48] Latin verse continued to be popular in Scotland from 1500 to 1650[49] because "Scottis" did not dominate the culture as English did in England and because Scottish literary and intellectual culture was far more international and Latinate than English high culture.[50] But a conflict between the Scottish polemicist and historian and the neoclassical poet did surface within the rhetoric of Buchanan's poetic and historical texts. Like the writers of the Pléiade, Buchanan generally believed in renewing mod-

47. George Buchanan, *Rerum Scoticarum Historia* (1582), trans. James Aikman, *The History of Scotland, from the Earliest Period to the Regency of the Earl of Moray* (Glasgow: Blackie and Sons, 1845), vol. 1, p. 9.

48. See Agnes Mure Mackenzie, "The Renaissance Poets 1 : Scots and English," in James Kinsley, ed., *Scottish Poetry: A Critical Survey* (London: Folcroft, 1973), p. 35; see also Alex Agutter, "Middle Scots as a Literary Language," in Ronald D. S. Jack, ed., *The History of Scottish Literature*, vol. 1, *Origins to 1660*, (Aberdeen: Aberdeen University Press, 1988), pp. 13–26.

49. See James W. L. Adams, "Renaissance Poets 2: Latin," in Kinsley, ed., *Scottish Poetry*, p. 70. See also Introduction by Jack, in *History of Scottish Literature*, p. 2.

50. See Adams, in Kinsley, ed., *Scottish Poetry*, p. 70. Adams also notes that "the Renaissance, with its emphasis on *imitatio veterum*, seems indeed to have penetrated the Arts curriculum in Scotland before it succeeded in displacing the schoolmen in the "higher" studies of philosophy and theology" (p. 71). According to John Durkan, Scottish scholars mostly wandered to Paris and other continental centers of learning rather than England (Durkan, "The Cultural Background in Sixteenth-Century Scotland," in David McRoberts, ed., *Essays on the Scottish Reformation: 1513–1625* [Glasgow: Burns, 1962], p. 278). But cf. Jenny Wormald, *Court, Kirk and Community: Scotland 1470–1625* (London: Edward Arnold, 1981), pp. 102–3, on the importance of England in 1530s as a "haven" for Scots "of unorthodox views." Also see Durkan, "The Beginnings of Humanism in Scotland," *Innes Review* 4 (1954): 5–24. For a broad account, see John MacQueen, ed., *Humanism in Renaissance Scotland* (Edinburgh: Edinburgh University Press, 1990).

ern culture through a return to the old (just as he thought "civilization's" coming to Scotland would be marked by its conversion to
Latin). Yet his political writings took opposing positions on the relationship between the past and present. When he rejected the tyranny
of custom, he showed his acute awareness of historical and cultural
difference; at other points, however, when he resisted the monarch's
claims to make new laws, Buchanan's polemics emphasized the continuity between the past and present. It is in his tragedies that these
contradictions are expressed formally and aesthetically as well as discursively. Buchanan's temporal verisimilitude, which gives the effect of
events compressed into an oppressively truncated moment in time, cuts
off the play's action from its own history. In his tragedy on the death
of John the Baptist, *Baptistes sive calumnia*, in particular, this formal
compression of time becomes a central theme when the characters debate the role of tradition in shaping the present and future even as they
themselves feel the acute pressure of time.

In both his political treatise *De jure regni apud Scotos* (1579; *On the
Powers of the Crown in Scotland*) and his *Rerum Scoticarum Historia* (1582;
History of Scotland), Buchanan invoked ancient Scottish tradition, identified with "eternal" laws, to defend current political practices. As he
tells the story in *De jure*, "the evidence of long-held usage and beliefs
which have never been publicly contradicted" (*accessit praeterea longi
temporis confirmatio, & perpetui iuris a populo vsurpatio, nullo vnquam
decreto publico reprehensa*)[51] confirms that the Scottish people originally
granted their kings a limited authority. This tradition was not the same
as the English common law, but it had a similar resonance. In Scotland,
a country where law was underdeveloped, people respected what Arthur H. Williamson describes as "a body of unwritten traditions which
were neither feudal in origin nor in any sense the law of the land," but
which primarily defined the reciprocal responsibilities of the nobility
and monarch.[52] Buchanan held that tradition to be consonant with
"eternal law," which was the basis of his political theory. At the end

51. George Buchanan, *De jure regni apud scotos, dialogus* (Edinburgh; 1579), facsimile
reprint (Amsterdam: Da Capo, 1969), p. 66. Translations are my own, but I have consulted the translation of Charles Flinn Arrowood, *The Powers of the Crown in Scotland*
(Austin: University of Texas Press, 1949).
52. Arthur H. Williamson, *Scottish National Consciousness in the Age of James VI: The*

of the *Historia*, for example, in the earl of Morton's speech regarding Mary Stuart's deposition (a text Hugh Trevor-Roper believes Buchanan himself composed), the deposition's critics are upbraided because they "do not reflect upon what they owe to the examples of their forefathers; and forget those eternal laws, which have been held sacred since the foundation of the monarchy, and enforced by the illustrious nobles, who set bounds to the despotism of the crown."[53] For Buchanan, divine law and the law of reason dictated the sole injunction that we love God and our neighbors as ourselves.[54] This injunction, in turn, underwrote the Scottish traditions of elective monarchy and the responsibility of the ruler to the electors.[55] All of these traditions and forms of law, it seems, fall under the rubric of the "eternal laws." In effect, then, Buchanan's drawing on custom privileged the past while he assumed that history illustrates timeless principles.[56]

Yet, while the *De jure* thus identifies tradition with "eternal laws" and the law of reason, it demonstrates at key moments a keen consciousness of the dialogue's unique situation in time and space. At such moments, Buchanan often opposes reason against custom rather than assuming that the first underlies the second. In response to the claims of Thomas Maitland (Buchanan's interlocutor in this dialogue)

Apocalypse, the Union, and the Shaping of Scotland's Public Culture (Edinburgh: John Donald, 1979), pp. 6–7.

53. Buchanan, *History of Scotland*, vol. 2, p. 550. See H. R. Trevor-Roper, "George Buchanan and the Ancient Scottish Constitution," *English Historical Review* (1966), Supplement 3: 12–13.

54. Buchanan, *De jure*, p. 11.

55. See Trevor-Roper, "Buchanan," pp. 12–13, on the two cardinal principles of Buchanan's political writing: that Scotland had always had an elective monarchy, and that "this system is no mere Caledonian freak but has its roots in the laws of nature."

56. See Roger A. Mason, "*Rex Stoicus*: George Buchanan, James VI and the Scottish Polity," in John Dwyer, Mason, and Alexander Murdoch, eds., *New Perspectives on the Politics and Culture of Early Modern Scotland* (Edinburgh: John Donald, 1982), pp. 9–33. Mason points out that, "as Buchanan himself implies, Scotland did not possess anything remotely akin to a common law enshrining the rights of the subject and delimiting the sphere of governmental authority. . . . Patently, his conception of the legal framework of the state is neither rooted in nor guaranteed by positive law. He is, on the contrary, appealing solely to divine or natural laws which he believes the ancient Scottish polity to have embodied and exemplified" (p. 26). This is, of course, different from the kind of appeal to the common law that Helgerson discusses in the case of England (see *Forms of Nationhood*). Here the focus is on a kind of natural law rooted in history.

that custom has the force of law and people customarily suffer the government of tyrants, the *De jure*'s Buchanan condemns the "tyranny of custom or precedent (*consuetudinis tyrannis*)" evident in both the present and antiquity and reminds Maitland of the matters in which he follows reason rather than ancient custom.[57] Just as he rejected any appeal to a custom he disliked, Buchanan historicized his interpretation of texts when it suited him. In particular, when confronted by a traditional objection raised to political resistance — Paul's enjoining the Romans to obey their magistrates — the Buchanan of *De jure* cautions that we must read that statement in its context, "considering when, for whom, and why it was written (*non enim verba solum examinare oportet: sed quibus temporibus, ad quos, & cur scripserit*)."[58] Similarly, in response to Maitland's citation of the passage from I Samuel 8, in which God offers the people a tyrant when they beg for a king, Buchanan replies that the passage is irrelevant because history does not mention any legitimate monarchies in Asia.[59] Thus, although elsewhere it invokes the force of custom and ancient tradition, the *De jure* also criticizes the tyranny of custom; further, while it posits that "eternal law" underlies Scotland's ancient constitution, the *De jure* simultaneously draws attention to changes in cultures and political institutions.[60]

Buchanan's history of Scotland similarly lacks a coherent historiography. It faithfully follows Hector Boece's list of legendary monarchs while vilifying other myths of British history. Commentators have reacted accordingly. Hugh Trevor-Roper separates Buchanan from "modern" historians like Machiavelli and Guicciardini, grouping him with the "humanist historians," by which he means historians who "believed in texts" and whose "only originality . . . was to purge their chosen text of barbarous solecisms" and rewrite it in fine Latin.[61] James E. Phillips, however, sees Buchanan as "unreservedly on the side of the

---

57. "*Cogita tecum quot sint res, nec hae exiguae, in quibus rationem secutus ab inueterata tot seculis consuetudine desciueris*" (*De jure*, p. 69).

58. Ibid., p. 71.

59. Ibid., p. 70.

60. See Williamson, *Scottish National Consciousness*, p. III, on Buchanan's perception of the uniqueness of the Scottish situation.

61. Trevor-Roper, "Buchanan," p. 21.

'moderns' in historiography" and capable of "critical skepticism."[62] Such disagreement is naturally produced by a symptomatic contradictoriness in Buchanan's uses of Scottish history. As McFarlane points out, sometimes Buchanan followed his own dicta: for instance, even though Buchanan retained Boece's forty kings because they served his political purposes, "he shows, in theory, a reasonably critical attitude."[63] More fundamentally, his works mix the critical consciousness of the humanist philologist and historian, who differentiated between the past and present and subjected custom to the light of reason, with the needs of the humanist polemicist, who knew how to argue through tradition and how to exploit the myths of Scottish history.[64]

When Buchanan composed a tragedy rather than a political dialogue, pamphlet, or prose history, that tragedy's formal conventions brought out these contradictions in his historical thinking.[65] Buchanan's biographers link the *De jure*'s appearance in 1579 with the publication of *Baptistes* in 1577, speculating that Buchanan rewrote and published *Baptistes* to reflect his current political thinking.[66] When Buchanan chose to dramatize an episode from biblical history, that of Herod's conflict with John the Baptist, to make a political point about tyranny and resistance, the form which he adapted was that of Euripidean tragedy. The *agon* in Greek tragedy reflected the institution of new law for the

62. James E. Phillips, "Buchanan and the Sidney Circle," p. 50. Cf. I. D. McFarlane's final judgment of Buchanan in his biography, *Buchanan* (London: Duckworth, 1981), p. 440.

63. McFarlane, *Buchanan*, p. 426.

64. In his essay "Scotching the Brut: Politics, History and National Myth in Sixteenth-Century Britain," in Roger A. Mason, ed., *Scotland and England: 1286–1815* (Edinburgh: John Donald, 1987), pp. 60–84, Mason argues that for Buchanan "the mythical kings were a convenience, not a necessity. They *were* a necessity, however, if the antiquity and autonomy of the Scottish kingdom were not finally to fall victim to the blandishments of the British History" (p. 74).

65. Buchanan's scriptural tragedies were probably first written in the early 1540s when Buchanan was in Paris and then Bordeaux, although *Jephthes* was not published until 1554 and *Baptistes* not until 1577. McFarlane suggests that when Buchanan wrote these plays "he moved in circles where historiography was very much in evidence." Buchanan was probably thinking about writing a patriotic history of Scotland in the earlier parts of his career (*Buchanan*, p. 416).

66. See ibid., p. 385; see also Sharratt and Walsh, ed., *Tragedies*, p. 13. Cf. Steven Berkowitz, ed. *Critical Edition of "Baptistes,"* who argues against Buchanan's having substantially revised the play in the 1570s (pp. 25–56, 118–23).

city state. In his political writings, however, Buchanan wrote of a Scotland governed by ancient and "eternal" law, which had never changed. Whereas Greek tragedy represented a division between the past and present, Buchanan's history and polemics envisioned the present as part of the past. Yet influenced by humanist scholarship and its insistence on the historical specificity of language and custom Buchanan was aware of living in a specific place and time even as he appealed to eternal law and tradition. His classical plays stage a crisis of characters trapped between past and future who express anxiety about their temporal blindness.

Among Buchanan's plays, *Baptistes* best exemplifies the clash between tradition and historical consciousness both formally and discursively. In the preface Buchanan himself described the play as linking past and present: the event of Herod's execution of John the Baptist may be old (*veteres*) because it happened centuries before, "but if we consider as new what is fresh from recent recollection (*recenti memoria*), this will certainly be new, "for the human race continues to practice fraud and calumny and the wicked oppress the good (ll. 48–51)."[67] Buchanan thus suggested that the past event resembled the present, whether he referred to specific events or the general condition of humankind. However, the play's action is itself compressed, involving the last hours of the Baptist's life sensed as a time of imminent danger. It sets the temporality of crisis against the rhythm of a cyclical history.

Baptistes contrasts the eternal realm of God with Herod's temporal world, and then collapses the distinction as it plays out the story of the martyr's defiance of a tyrant. The following exchange expresses the initial opposition between the antagonists concisely:

HEROD: Speak of matters heavenly when you reach the stars. As long as you dwell on earth, bear with earthly laws.

JOHN: I respect earthly kingdoms and I obey their kings; but the eternal kingdom I consider my native land, and its king I worship.[68]

---

67. Trans. Sharratt and Walsh, in *Tragedies*, p. 134. Note Berkowitz, *Critical Edition*, pp. 105–17, who reads the play as an allegory of contemporary political events, and see pp. 203–13, on the relationship of old and new as stated in the prologue.
68. Trans. Sharratt and Walsh, in *Tragedies* p. 145: HER. *Cum in astra venies, loquere*

From Herod's point of view, the crisis caused by John's reformist preaching is a purely political one, an issue of the king's placating the people or looking after his own safety (ll. 542–4). At the play's end, too, Herod bases his decision to have John killed on his immediate concerns when he apparently gives in to his Queen's urging that he affirm his own authority (although in fact he had already decided to do so). From John's point of view, however, the play's events are enacted before the all-seeing eyes of God. While at first it appears as though John opposes the two kings of heaven and earth, he tells himself and the Chorus that in fact both kings want the same thing; that is, both Herod and God will that he should die. God's will encompasses Herod's wicked intentions. His eternal time enfolds the present moment of Herod's power.

Correlated with the realms of God and Herod are two kinds of temporality. The unenlightened characters see little continuity or relationship between past, present, and future, whereas John the prophet ties himself to both past and future. Even at the very beginning, when the rabbi Gamaliel recalls to the rabbi Malchus the precedent of their forbears' actions in such a crisis, the ambitious Malchus retorts that "old ways are suited to the old, while ours are more proper to us (*vetusta veteres, nostra nos magis decent*)" (l. 175) — even though Malchus has claimed from the beginning to be the sole defender of the ancient rituals.[69] The Chorus, too, mourns the gap between "the splendid exploits of an earlier age (*aevi splendida facta prioris*)" (l. 580) and the present world's desolation. In general in *Baptistes* such temporal constriction in the present marks corruption. The Queen attacks Herod for moving too slowly, insisting that something must be done immediately lest John become too powerful and the king's authority should weaken (ll. 345–46). The Queen's attitude clearly signifies both political and spiritual blindness. Herod, the Queen, Malchus, and the Chorus, harassed by the pressures of time, recognize neither the continuity between the political tradition and the present nor their

---

tum caelestia; / terrena iura patere dum terram coles. / IO. Terrena vereor regna, pareo regibus; / aeterna patriam regna puto, regem colo. (ll. 508–11).

69. See Berkowitz, *Critical Edition*, p. 211, on Malchus as "something of a Sophistic modern"; also p. 115.

actions' meaning beyond the present crisis and its political consequences.

In *Baptistes* John the Baptist unites past, present and future both politically and spiritually. For many early modern historians, the past and present dovetailed with Christian or eschatological time, beginning with the creation and fall of man and ending in apocalypse.[70] Using typology, the symbolic language of prophecy, Christian historians struggled to situate individual human actions in this eternal time.[71] So in *Baptistes* John is careful to state that by defying Herod and continuing to preach and prophesy he only upholds "precedent and ancient rites (*sacra quam pie colam / et instituta vetera*)" (ll. 486–87). He allies himself with the protection of tradition (just as he claims that he scrupulously obeys kings in earthly matters), but he also accepts and understands the future in a way that the other characters cannot. When the Chorus voices its terror at John's coming death, more fearful because it is unknown, John accepts it as his inevitable future to be revealed "in time's passing (*temporis longinquitas*)" (l. 1012). He sees his progress toward death as part of the past and the future of the human race, his journey on "the way set since the world's beginning (*institutam ab initio mundi viam*)" (ll. 1052–53).

With this vision, however, John is not a "prophet" in a conventional or a Greek sense, for in this play he tells us nothing of the momentous events to come except for a brief glimpse of the coming of Jesus, who is named only as one "whose slippers I, his servant, would be unworthy to remove" (ll. 789–90).[72] Although John's actions are political, his vision of salvation is personal rather than communal or historical. The play ends not with future expectations but with the Chorus despondently refusing the Messenger's attempt at consolation: they still fear death and envision a life of misery (ll. 1356–58). As Martin Mueller

---

70. See J. G. A. Pocock, *The Machiavellian Moment: Florentine Political Thought and the Atlantic Republican Tradition* (Princeton: Princeton University Press, 1975), p. 31: "All these propositions denoted temporal events; the past or the future tense must be used in stating them; and yet the significance of every one of them was extrahistorical in that it denoted a change in the relations between men and that which was outside time altogether."

71. See ibid., p. 44.

72. Trans. Sharratt and Walsh, in *Tragedies*, p. 151.

observes, "no writer of scriptural tragedy went further than Buchanan in blocking any vision of transcendence that might mitigate the catastrophe by placing it in a wider context."[73] Only the martyr has an enviable future in this play.

Baptistes thus shows the stress of Buchanan's imitation of classical tragic form in representing a political and spiritual subject. Responding to the formal constraints of time, Buchanan used a limited view of time to define political character. He gave his politically corrupt or vicious characters limited temporal perception; they separate themselves from the past and cannot understand the future. Their time is contrasted with that of the martyr, who allies himself politically with the past and who can know and accept his own future. It is even more significant that Buchanan did not directly invoke the scheme of prophetic or eschatological time; in terms of the playwright's understanding of tragic form, the martyr is freed from the limits of secular time but the community is not. The formal pressures here present a bleak picture of the kingdom's future. In this sense, Buchanan's tragic poetics betray his ambivalence about his own place, balanced between the past and the future of his own country and that of European humanist culture.

JAMES VI AND SAMUEL DANIEL

When Sidney praised Buchanan in the *Defence*, he also praised his pupil, James VI, as a patron of poets, for the young James had indeed offered himself to his court and his people as a prince who would glorify Scotland's literary culture. But James intended to do more than simply support Scottish poets: he was himself a poet. In his essay on the "reulis and cautelis to be observit and eschewit in Scottis poesie," written when James was nineteen and published in 1585 in *The Essayes of a Prentise in the Divine Art of Poesie*, the young king tried to do for Scotland what du Bellay (cited in his preface) and the Pléiade had done for France.[74] In promoting the composition of Scottish vernacular po-

---

73. Martin Mueller, *Children of Oedipus and Other Essays on the Imitation of Greek Tragedy, 1550–1800* (Toronto: University of Toronto Press, 1980), p. 171.

74. James may have learned about du Bellay from Buchanan himself, who associated with members of the Pléiade when he was in Paris. McFarlane suggests that during his sojourn in Paris Buchanan "was in the forefront as a poet, rubbing shoulders with mem-

etry and instructing his "docile" readers in the best practices of writing a new poetry, James was working out his sense of himself as a "free" lawmaker and a Scot, a self-conception that would surface more clearly in his later political works.

In his *Basilikon Doron* (1599–1603) James observed that it is a king's duty and privilege to develop his country's language, for "it best becometh a King to purify and make famous his own tongue; wherein he may go before all his subjects; as it setteth him well to do in all honest and lawful things." Besides, he pointed out to his son, enough "poor scholars would match you" in Latin and Greek (a swipe at Buchanan, to be sure).[75] For James, writing in his own language—at first in the Scottish dialect and later in English—set him apart from mere "poor scholars": it was the essence of his very kingliness as well as his Scottishness.[76] So, too, in his "Reulis" he defended his writing of a treatise on Scottish poetry explicitly on the grounds that the Scottish language was unique and implicitly on the assumption that he was the one to make the laws concerning its poetry. James indeed intended to be both the patron and the lawmaker for his "Castalian band," the group of court poets whom he patronized in Scotland, who would produce a new, purely Scottish poetry.[77]

---

bers of the Pléiade, and particularly with Joachim du Bellay" ("George Buchanan and French Humanism," in A. H. T. Levi, ed., *Humanism in France at the End of the Middle Ages and in the Early Renaissance* [Manchester: Manchester University Press, 1970], p. 299).

75. James VI, *Basilikon Doron* (1599; reprinted, with revisions, 1603), reprinted in *The Political Works of James I*, ed. Charles Howard McIlwain (Cambridge: Harvard University Press, 1918; reprint, New York: Russell and Russell, 1965), p. 48. Note: in this and subsequent citations, I identify the royal author as James VI in reference to works written before he became king of England in 1603 and as James I in reference to works written after 1603.

76. See Timothy J. Reiss, "Poetry, Power and Resemblance of Nature," in John D. Lyons and Stephen G. Nichols, eds., *Mimesis: from Mirror to Method, Augustine to Descartes* (Hanover, N.H.: University Press of New England, 1982), who offers several examples of ways in which, in the late seventeenth century, it was imagined that "the king, with his possession of, and power over, language, can guide all its other users in social action and in natural knowledge" (p. 230), insofar as "the king is both the principal poet of his country and the unique sovereign" (p. 229).

77. On the "Scottish literary Renaissance," see Ronald D. S. Jack, "Poetry and King James VI," in Jack, ed., *History of Scottish Literature*, p. 126.

At the same time, however, while James's effort might resemble the efforts of the Pléiade writers, his poetics also diverged from theirs in its ideas on the uses of imitation. In Italy in the fifteenth century and elsewhere in the sixteenth century the notion of imitation had already begun to move from "copying" classical models to what Sidney calls "a representing, counterfeiting, or figuring forth" of nature.[78] With this diminishing interest in imitating ancient models and with an increasing concern for decorum and verisimilitude, "the historicism of Petrarch and Valla was largely repressed or exhausted and the poet's autonomy was magnified."[79] In short, imitation became "invention." In sixteenth-century poetic theory such invention meant the "discovering" or fashioning of new phrases, tropes, or ideas. Grahame Castor describes the way that invention was construed in early French poetics: "invention was set against imitation, taken in the sense of following literary models. . . . Both in translation and in imitation the poet is drawing upon other authors for his material. When he invents, on the other hand, he is relying entirely upon himself. He becomes the first to tread a particular poetic path, and all credit and honour are due to him for that primacy."[80] Invention differs from imagination, for it uses reason to construct images never thought before but pre-existing in nature and found or discovered rather than created.[81] Above all, invention was seen as anti-traditional while linked to nature: so James wrote in his own treatise, "You must also beware with composing any thing in the same manner, as has been ever oft used of before."[82] James' simulta-

---

78. Sidney, *Defence*, pp. 79–80.

79. Greene, *Light in Troy*, p. 180.

80. Grahame Castor, *Pléiade Poetics: A Study in Sixteenth-Century Thought and Terminology* (Cambridge: Cambridge University Press, 1964), p. 115.

81. See ibid., p. 128. Castor notes that invention was primarily associated not with "imagination" but with the power of reasoning; furthermore, "invention was thus the very antithesis of literary imitation, for it was the process of doing something which had not been done before, of treading *un sentier* hitherto *inconnu*. . . . [yet] To invent was simply to come into something which already existed and to make it manifest for the first time" (pp. 189–90).

82. James VI, "Ane schort treatise, conteining some reulis and cautelis to be observit and eschewit in Scottis poesie," in *The Essayes of a Prentise in the Divine Art of Poesie* (Edinburgh, 1585; reprint, ed. Edward Arber, New York: AMS, 1966), p. 65. Note that I am in effect translating here from the Scots dialect in which the treatise is written; while I have transformed words into English spellings and meaning, I have not revised

neous appeals to nature and originality recall du Bellay, who also declared that poets must be poets "naturally," even though natural talent alone cannot create immortal art. Even when restricted to imitating classical models, du Bellay's poet is directed to develop his natural faculty of "invention" by fashioning new images and ideas. It is this notion of invention that James drew on most strongly in his own poetics, which moved away quite deliberately from imitation to find princely inspiration in never-changing nature.

Buchanan's precedent in this area surely colored James's distaste for classical imitation. James owed a great deal to Buchanan, and not just for his thorough acquaintance with Latin and Greek,[83] but when it came time to formulate a poetics he turned away from Buchanan's example quite resolutely. In the *Basilikon Doron*, James demonstrated his impatience with the writings of the neo-Latinists most succinctly when he recommended composition in the vernacular, for "there is nothing left to be said in Greek and Latin already."[84] A more dismissive note to his teacher could not be imagined. Far from revering Greek and Latin languages and poetic models, at times the king seemed to have had little patience with them. Rather than representing the summit of perfection, the poetry of past ages was in its "infancy and childhood," according to James, but now it had come to "man's age and perfection." James further distinguished his poetic treatise from those written in other languages, either in the present or in the past, by stressing the difference of his time and culture. First, poetic treatises by those of other nations were irrelevant for his country: "That as for them that has written in it of late, there has never any of them written

---

the syntax. One of James's likely sources in this "original" conception, George Gascoigne, construed this stance in more pejorative and class-tinged terms when he advised the writer to study some "good and fine invention" but "to avoid the uncomely customs of common writers" (George Gascoigne, "Certayne notes of instruction," 1575, in G. Gregory Smith, ed., *Elizabethan Critical Essays* [Oxford: Oxford University Press, 1904], vol. I, pp. 47–48).

83. See David Harris Willson, *King James VI and I* (London: Jonathan Cape, 1956), p. 21.

84. James VI, *Basilikon Doron*, in McIlwain, ed., *Political Works*, p. 48. This might echo his resentment, scribbled in a copy book, that "they made [*gar*] me speak Latin ere I could speak Scottish" (Willson, *James VI and I*, p. 23). See also Jack, *History of Scottish Literature*, p. 125.

in our language. For albeit sundry has written of it in English, which is likest to our language, that we differ from them in sundry rules of Poesy, as ye will find by experience." Then he discarded much of what had been written on poetry in the past (belying his later insistence in the *Basilikon Doron* on history's repeatability) by arguing that, "as for them that wrote of old, like as the time is changed since, so is the order of Poesy changed. For then they observed not *Flowing* [euphony], nor eschewed not *Rhyming in terms* [using long words at the beginnings and ends of lines], besides sundry other things, which now we observe and eschew, and do well in so doing."[85]

In pointing out the irrelevance of "them that wrote of old," James also broke away from his tutor on the matter of history and its relations to "eternal" laws.[86] Though both writers, in their historical and political writings, appealed to a kind of eternal or natural law, Buchanan identified eternal law with tradition while James used the notion of natural order to legitimize kings without referring to tradition.[87] This difference is symptomatic of the authors' divergent uses of Scottish political tradition. Both James and Buchanan were interested in the specific character of Scottish politics. Buchanan's important political writings are concerned almost exclusively with the contemporary turmoil in Scotland; James, in turn, in the *Basilikon Doron* advised his son how to rule Scotland and professed ignorance of English customs.[88] However, although James carefully adjusted himself to the particularities of Scottish politics and respected his immediate predecessor's example, he did not use Scottish political history as Buchanan did.[89] The *Basilikon Doron* briefly advises Prince Henry to read history:

85. James VI, "Reulis," in *Essayes*, p. 54.

86. Both drew on the *speculum principis* image of the ideal king for their different purposes: See Mason, "*Rex Stoicus*," on Buchanan's use of the speculum king; also see Rebecca W. Bushnell, *Tragedies of Tyrants: Political Thought and Theater in the English Renaissance* (Ithaca: Cornell University Press, 1990), chaps. 2 and 3.

87. See Williamson, *Scottish National Consciousness*, on the king's reliance "upon the lessons and implications of the natural law" (p. 45); also p. 54, on what emerges from James's writing of the 1590s as a sense of "the timelessness of insubstantial flux superimposed on an underlying eternal order."

88. James VI, *Basilikon Doron*, in McIlwain, ed., *Political Works*, p. 11.

89. Cf. Wormald, *Court*, chap. 9, who claims that James in many ways was quite conservative.

I would have you to be well versed in authentic histories, and in the chronicles of all nations, but especially in our own histories . . . the example whereof most nearly concerns you. I mean not of such famous invectives, as *Buchanan's* or *Knox's* Chronicles. . . . But by reading of authentic histories and chronicles, ye shall learn experience by theory, applying the bypassed things to the present estate, *quia nihil novum sub sole* [there is nothing new under the sun]: such is the continual volubility of things earthly, according to the roundness of the world and the revolution of the heavenly circles: which is expressed by the wheels in *Ezekiel's* visions, and counterfeited by the Poets *in rota Fortunae* [the wheel of fortune].[90]

James's notion of history appears different from that underlying Buchanan's "famous invective": instead of drawing on history to validate present practices, James posited the eternal, cyclical recurrence of events.[91] History's value lay in the comparison of the past with the present, which provides a guide for prudent action, and not in the supposition that the past authorizes the present state of affairs.

James VI's theoretical arguments authorizing patriarchal monarchy rely most frequently not on history or tradition—except for the continuity of hereditary succession—but on natural law and the force of analogy, whereas Buchanan and others turned to "usage" and "long-held beliefs" underwritten by eternal law and reason to explain and legitimize their version of monarchy. When comparing the king to a father and to the body's head, James called on a nature imagined as an eternal and unchanging hierarchy.[92] As Arthur Williamson observes,

90. James VI, *Basilikon Doron*, p. 40.

91. See Achsah Guibbory, *The Map of Time: Seventeenth-Century English Literature and Ideas of Pattern in History* (Urbana: University of Illinois Press, 1986): "The classical view of history included two related concepts: nature is always the same, and history is a series of repetitive cycles" (p. 8).

92. See Gordon J. Schochet, *The Authoritarian Family and Political Attitudes in Seventeenth-Century England: Patriarchalism in Political Thought* (New Brunswick, N.J.: Transaction Books, 1988) (a new version of *Patriarchalism and Political Thought* [Oxford: Basil Blackwell, 1975]). Schochet argues, regarding James's patriarchalism: "James's statements about the nature of kingly power are replete with fatherly images, but they do not contain a clearly defined patriarchal doctrine. While the King frequently argued from the role of the father as the head of the family to his own status as head of the kingdom, his usage was analogical; he never actually *identified* regal and paternal power" (p. 87);

while James did not openly deny the claims of custom and heredity, his "paramount concern when visualizing politics within a purely Scottish context was to demonstrate the natural necessity of his status and authority as king," where "only the timeless, changeless hierarchy of being ultimately withstood 'the continual volubility of things earthly' and legitimated princely authority."[93]

When he did use history to explain the Scottish kings' authority, James's strategy also differed from Buchanan's. When, in his treatise *The Trew Law of Free Monarchies* (1598), James rejected as irrelevant the claim that kings were originally chosen by the people, he defended his point by referring to the conquests of Fergus and William the Conqueror, after which, James wrote, kings have been "the authors and makers of laws, and not the laws of the king."[94] James here called up the past to construct a foundation myth that separates absolute rule from contingency and dependence on the consent of others. What J. G. A. Pocock says of other anti-traditional thinkers was also true of James: he is "one who, having denied that the past authorizes the present by vesting it with continuity, is obliged to create a new past and invest it with an authority which easily abolishes the necessity of referring to a past at all. . . . It tends to become unhistorical in the sense that it devises a mode of authority independent of social continuity."[95]

---

but Schochet also acknowledges James's awareness and circulation of patriarchal doctrine in England and gives as an example Richard Mocket's *God and the King* (1615), which declared: "But the duty of Subjects in obedience to their Sovereign, is grounded upon the Law of Nature; beginning with out first beginning" (p. 90).

93. Williamson, *Scottish National Consciousness*, pp. 45–46.

94. James VI, *The Trew Law of Free Monarchies* (1598), in McIlwain, *Political Works*, pp. 62–63.

95. J. G. A. Pocock, *Politics, Language and Time: Essays on Political Thought and History* (Chicago: University of Chicago Press, 1971), p. 260. In his self-image as the Roman emperor or god James also reached into history to fashion an image which transcended time. As Jonathan Goldberg and others have described it, the iconography of James's reign represented him as reviving imperial Rome with James himself the new Emperor Augustus. But this Stuart revival of Rome acted more to eclipse or suppress history than to use history to ground or clarify the present. See Jonathan Goldberg, *James I and the Politics of Literature: Jonson, Shakespeare, Donne, and Their Contemporaries* (Baltimore: Johns Hopkins University Press, 1983), on how Ben Jonson figured James's "Roman" entrance into London as a moment outside history: in this spectacle, "James's time is extraordinary, time fulfilled, a time out of time; a present state unmoving" (pp. 51–52).

Even when he claimed to write about a particular case at a particular time, James's understanding of his own authority veered away from history.

Thus James's own early conception of the poet's responsibility to nature as opposed to tradition demonstrates the close tie between this kind of political thinking and literary constructions of invention and imitation.[96] Above all, what separates James's treatise from those of the Pléiade is this insistence that one improves poetry not by imitating classical models but rather by following the king's rules and developing one's own power of invention (however contradictory these two injunctions might be). The "Reulis" is primarily a technical treatise on prosody, describing models for writing different kinds of lyric poetry—some borrowed from other national literatures and some native to Scottish poetry (in particular, the genre of "flyting" or poetic invective). Equally important are the king's pronouncements on decorum, which reflect his vision of a fixed hierarchical social order. As Jonathan Goldberg puts it, this poetic decorum is "also a version of social decorum, all things in their place, unmovable, 'ever framing your reasons, according to the quality of your subject.' "[97] Behind this minor form of "lawmaking," however, lies James's self-conception as a "lawmaker" and his desire to control the poetic practices of the self-described Castalian Band.[98] The treatise is directed not to imperious schoolmasters but to the "docile bairns of knowledge," supposedly willingly to submit themselves to his paternal guidance (at all of his nineteen years of age).

Even though James strictly set forth rules concerning prosody and decorum, in his estimate the main virtue of poetry was not to be found in its form. He wrote in the *Basilikon Doron* that the "principal part of a

96. See ibid., pp. 22–23, on the content and style of James's own poetry, as "exercises in freedom and subjection."

97. Ibid., p. 19. Here Goldberg cites James's dialect, which I have translated. James's treatise is also remarkable, as Ronald Jack has noted, precisely in extending the notion of decorum from a "linguistic" to a "social" phenomenon: that is, he recommends that not just style but the form of argument must fit the social position of the speaker (Ronald D. S. Jack, "James VI and Renaissance Poetic Theory," *English* 16 [1967]: 208–11).

98. See Jack, *History*, p. 125. In Buchanan's *De jure*, Maitland is moved to compare the king's power to make the law with those of artists to set the rules for their own art, an equivalence Buchanan vigorously rejects (p. 31).

poem" is not "to rhyme right, and flow well with many pretty words"; rather, its "chief commendation" is "that when the verse shall be shaken sundry in prose, it shall be found so rich in quick inventions, and poetic flowers, and in fair and pertinent comparisons; as it shall retain the luster of a poem, although in prose."[99] That is, James saw as the main attribute of a poem the excellence of its "inventions," or original ideas. He stated this opinion clearly in the "Reulis," where he wrote: "But since invention, is one of the chief virtues in a poet, it is best that ye invent your own subject, your self, and not to compose of seen subjects. Especially, translating any thing out of [an]other language, which doing, ye not only essay not your own ingenuity [*ingyne*] of invention, but by the same means, ye are bound, as to a stake, to follow that book's phrases, which ye translate." (James violated his own rule, however, in translating Du Bartas's *L'Uranie* in the same volume.) It is not surprising, then, given James's emphasis on poetic invention, that he proscribed his poets from "writing any thing of matters of common weal, or other such grave seen subjects (except metaphorically, of manifest truth openly known, yet notwithstanding using it very seldom [*seindil*]), because not only ye essay not your own invention, as I spoke before, but likewise they are too grave matters, for a poet to mell in."[100] That is, poets—except for the king—must *not* try out original ideas about matters of state, apparently either because ordinary people should not have any original ideas about politics or because such invention was the sole privilege of the king as author and poet.

Finally, in his "Reulis," as in his political writings, James brought in nature to serve his invention, insofar as he claimed that one must be a poet "naturally" and that invention must find its source in nature. In the preface, he wrote:

I will also wish you (docile Reader) that ere ye cumber you[rself] with reading the rules, ye may find in your self such a beginning of Nature, as ye may put in practice in your verse many of the foresaid precepts, ere ever ye see them as they are here set down. For if Nature be not the chief worker

99. James VI, *Basilikon Doron*, in McIlwain, p. 48.
100. James VI, "Reulis," in *Essayes*, p. 66.

in this art, rules will be but a band to Nature, and will make you within short space weary of the whole art: Whereas, if Nature be chief, and bent to it, rules will be a help and staff to Nature.[101]

Like Sidney and the Pléiade poets, James here attempted to negotiate the relationship between nature and art in the making of a poet and his poetry. As they did, he suggested that the poet must have a natural talent, which is shaped by art and learning. Indeed, James implied that the true poet by nature will understand and articulate the "laws" he pronounces. In effect, the treatise represents James's own precepts as a kind of "natural law" of poetry. Nature underwrites James's notion of invention: "But because ye can not have the invention, except it come of Nature, I remit it thereunto, as the chief cause, not only of invention, but also of all the other parts of Poesy. For art is only but a help and a remembrance to Nature, as I show you in the Preface."[102] This statement can be read two ways: first, a poet must be a poet naturally; but second, all inventions find their shape in nature. Thus James's poet's true freedom is freedom from artistic precedent. He is subject only to imitating the unchanging present that is nature. Not other men and their laws define truth and authority; rather the timeless rules of nature, in which the king finds his own image, shape them.

Thus the humanistically trained James rejected a kind of neoclassicism by celebrating the vernacular, dismissing Latin and Greek as living poetic languages, and avoiding the precedents of ancient poetic form. Yet the "Reulis" could be said to signal a new form of neoclassicism different from that understood as the imitation of antique formal conventions. James's neoclassicism recognizes natural rules of form, which coincide with the poet-king's laws. These are not seen as laws imposed from the outside, but ones that grow from within. They have always been there, not, as in Buchanan's concept, through custom, which coincides with "eternal" laws, but rather in the order of nature alone. The tension Buchanan held between atemporal form and history is lost in

101. Ibid., p. 55.
102. Ibid., p. 66.

James's gesture of historical relativism, where history is curiously subsumed in an appeal to timeless nature.

James's absolutist poetics of "nature" set into relief the strange mixture of resistance and conservatism in Samuel Daniel's *Defence of Ryme*
(1603). As Helgerson points out, by the late 1580s poetry in rhyme had
become the court style in England, and experiments in imitating classical meters mostly fell to "poor scholars" alone. When Thomas
Campion's *Observations in the Art of English Poesie* appeared in 1602
advocating the imitation of classical meters in English poetry it
sounded like the last gasps of an academic experiment. Daniel's reply
to Campion was thus surprisingly virulent, especially given the fact that
he himself had taken part in the fight of the Countess of Pembroke's
circle against "the tyrant of the North; / Gross Barbarism," a fight he
described as "first found, encountered and provoked forth" by her
brother Philip Sidney.[103] Helgerson suggests that because Daniel's condemnation of Campion's *Observations* involved rejecting "its humanist
and absolutist model of self-making," its force was directed mostly
against political innovation, a fear evoked by the coming of the new
"foreign" king, James. Thus Daniel's plea to his reader to observe custom and immemorial laws "responded directly to the concerns aroused
by the accession of a king who claimed ancestral conquest as the ulti-
mate sanction of his authority, a king who thought his will should be
law."[104] However, Daniel and James shared a view of the politics of
poetry that found poetics and authority together in the natural order.

In the opening lines of *The Defence of Ryme*'s dedication to William
Herbert, Daniel linked custom and nature, just as Buchanan identified
the traditions of the Scottish nation with the "eternal laws." Daniel
then acted surprised that the issue of reviving classical meters should
come up at all: for "the general custom, and use of rhyme in this
kingdom, noble lord, having been so long (as if from a grant of nature)

103. See the dedicatory poem to the countess of Pembroke in *The Tragedie of Cleopatra*, his Senecan tragedy: the dedication, which appeared in the 1594 edition, was
omitted from the editions of 1605, 1607, and 1609, but restored in the edition of 1611
(*The Complete Works in Verse and Prose of Samuel Daniel*, ed. Alexander Grosart [London:
1885], vol. 3, p. 24).

104. Helgerson, *Forms of Nationhood*, p. 38.

held unquestionable; made me to imagine that it lay altogether out of the way of contradiction, and was become so natural, as we should never have had a thought to cast it off into reproach, or be made to think that it ill became our language."[105] Rhyme as he depicted it is "most powerfully defended" by both "custom and nature": "custom that is before all law, nature that is above all art. Every language hath her proper number or measure fitted to use and delight, which, custom entertaining by the allowance of the ear, doth indenize and make natural" ("indenize" here can mean "to naturalize" politically and thus "enfranchise").[106] Whereas for Buchanan the long view of history revealed divine and natural law, and for James the nature that authorized his art and law was separate from history (both because the present was discontinuous from the past and because nature always exists in the present tense), for Daniel custom became nature over time, and nature came before art, just as custom preceded imposed law.[107]

Like James, however, and like Buchanan when it suited him, Daniel was also a historical relativist. While he rooted rhyme in custom and time, the poet's freedom to write rhyme signified the present's freedom from the past. Like James, Daniel cast off the burden of the classical past yet linked rhyme to the English past. So he claimed that "we should not so soon yield our consent captive to the authorities of antiquity . . . we are the children of nature as well as they."[108] This language parallels that which Daniel used to resist the "innovation" of imposed classical meters: the classical old is also new, and the antique bonds of "the tyrannical rules of idle rhetoric" are new fetters.[109] Thus,

105. Samuel Daniel, *A Defence of Ryme*, in *Poems and A Defence of Ryme*, ed. Arthur Colby Sprague (1930; reprint, Chicago: University of Chicago Press, 1965), p. 129.

106. Ibid., p. 131.

107. See Arthur B. Ferguson, *Clio Unbound: Perception of the Social and Cultural Past in Renaissance England* (Durham, N.C.: Duke University Press, 1979), p. 66: "Daniel had, above all else, to reconcile custom and nature. He found it difficult. The two were not, of course, necessarily incompatible; *natura* could be considered as *naturans*, revealing itself in processes of development, just as well as it could be thought of as *naturata*. But Daniel was never quite sure which. As a philosopher he clearly preferred the latter. As a cultural historian, he could not help but identify nature with civilized usage and all the diversity and relativity it implied."

108. Daniel, *Defence*, p. 139.

109. Ibid., p. 135.

awareness of historical difference frees the poet from the past, but tradition authorizes present practice.

Daniel's treatise is hardly a cry for freedom, as is clear when it insists that rhyme is "far more laborious than loose measure," that is, than classical meter. "Art" may be equated with bondage when associated with classical meter, but rhyme, however "natural," proves a more severe disciplinarian. Its superior order binds more strictly than the order of the classical rules, precisely because rhyme is natural. Daniel observed of the "limits" set in sonnets that such limits are not the "tyrannical bounding of the conceit, but rather a reducing it in *girum*, and a just form, neither too long for the shortest project, or too short for the longest." Such a binding of "our imagination, being as a unformed *Chaos* without fashion," he argues, "is it not more pleasing to Nature, that desires a certainty, and comports not with that which is infinite, to have those closes, rather than, not to know where to end, or how far to go, especially seeing our passions are often without measure." According to Daniel, the imposition of classical meters cannot achieve a decorum of "just form," for "we find the best of the Latins many times, either not concluding, or else otherwise in the end than they began." That is, the classical meters are disorderly because they have no closure. Rhyme offers "the certain close of delight, with the full body of the period well carried, . . . as neither the Greeks or Latins ever attained unto. For their boundless running on, often so confounds the reader, that having once lost himself, must either give off unsatisfied, or uncertainly cast back to retrieve the escaped sense, and to find way again into his matter."[110]

The English sonnet's appeal thus lies in its compression and containment, for, Daniel asks, "is it not most delightful to see much excellently ordered in a small room, or little, gallantly disposed and made to fill up a space of like capacity, in such sort, that the one would not appear so beautiful in a larger circuit, nor the other do well in a less: which often we find to be so, according to the powers of nature, in the workman."[111] This insistence on boundaries and compressed order

110. Ibid., pp. 138–39.
111. Ibid., p. 138. I am reminded here of Mulcaster's enthusiasm for his neat and compact anthology of texts, as well as Jonson's image of the well-ordered text.

undercuts the mood of resistance to classical "tyranny": classical meter is denigrated because it is insufficiently regulated or because it gets out of control and loses direction, while rhyme offers the pleasing containment of natural form and law. Furthermore, Daniel saw that any artificial attempt to impose quantitative meter will always end up imitating nature anyway. That is, what may appear to be quantitative verse will lapse into the syllabic rhythms of ordinary English speech, for "not all the artificial coverings of wit . . . can hide [the syllables'] native and original condition, which breaks out through the strongest bands of affectation, and will be itself." Our syllables may have "been ever held free and indifferent in our language, . . . owing fealty to no foreign invention. . . . But every versifier that well observes his work, finds in our language, without all these unnecessary precepts, what numbers best fit the nature of her idiom, and the proper places destined to such accents, as she will not let in, to any other rooms than into those for which they were born."[112]

Custom becomes nature allied with the native freedom of the English people, but the structure of rhyme is a naturalized order, proportion, and decorum, which will not let things into "any other rooms than into those for which they were born." The dilemma resembles that laid out in Chapter 3, in the languages of gardening and pedagogy: the force of the child's nature can be construed as resistance to the master's hand but at the same time the opposition of nature to art could fix people in a ranked social order. Indeed, while the poet Daniel tried to combine the rules of custom and nature, Daniel the historian also endeavored to link his historical relativism with a belief in the cyclical occurrence of human events (much as James did). As Arthur Ferguson puts it, "by fusing the idea of a uniform nature and an eternal recurrence and by dipping the resulting compound in a strong tincture of Christian determinism, [Daniel] sometimes made it appear that the lessons of history were unlikely to avail against the indelible traits of human nature."[113] Daniel's appeal to nature and custom might thus

112. Ibid., p. 151.
113. Ferguson, *Clio*, p. 65. On Daniel and the theory of cyclical recurrence, see also Joan Rees, *Samuel Daniel: A Critical and Biographical Study* (Liverpool: Liverpool Uni-

function as resistance to the foreign "innovation" and imposed laws, but at the same time his argument resembled James's rejection of the classical in favor of the vernacular because the vernacular marks the eternal order of nature.

In his reconsideration of English classicism Don Wayne has argued that in the Tudor and Stuart eras advocating classical subject matter and form could define a position of contesting the status quo. For Ben Jonson, Wayne observes, "in a still rigidly hierarchical social system, [classicism] was the appeal to rigor in method and to an authority in knowledge based on the norms of Nature and Reason that gave the writer a certain freedom and transcendence": for Jonson "to proclaim himself a classicist was to adopt a literary *persona* that allowed him to go beyond the existing hierarchical system for grounding social and psychological identity, to derive his truth and his being from a prior order, a natural order first codified in the texts of antiquity."[114] Yet at the same time, as Wayne briefly notes, such an appeal to "classicism" and natural order could also offer a style of rule to James at the apogee of the traditional hierarchy. Thus, as this chapter has suggested, such categories as tradition, custom, nature, and reason had a remarkable political volatility, whether in the arguments about literary form or in the public arena. The sense of freedom and stance of resistance latent in "nature" and "reason" might be oppositional or "radical" in one context, but in another, reason and nature could serve the ends of absolutist thought. Similarly, the recourse to tradition as political and personal validation was Janus-faced. In different ways tradition and custom functioned to oppose the innovations of absolute rule; yet when tradition was identified with nature it served as a kind of bondage.

Exploring humanist and neoclassical ideologies of tradition and invention thus brings me back full circle to where this book began: the unstable terms of rule, control, and autonomy in humanist education. I have argued that the early humanists set up a paradox of freedom

---

versity Press, 1964), p. 132; also Cecil Seronsy, "The Doctrine of Cyclical Recurrence and Some Related Ideas in the Works of Samuel Daniel," *Studies in Philology* 54 (1957): 387–407.

114. Don E. Wayne, "Mediation and Contestation: English Classicism from Sidney to Jonson," *Criticism* 25 (1983): 219–20.

and mastery in pedagogy: just as they asked how the poet was free when both a servant to tradition and a master of invention, they also wondered how the student was to be fashioned as "free" when the teacher was his master and servant, father and mother. The ongoing discussion of tradition and autonomy in modern humanist pedagogy and poetics underlines the importance of remembering how these paradoxes were defined in the early modern period. In modern-day humanist education we have not escaped the conflict between the assimilation of the past and creative autonomy implicit in early humanist poetics. In its classic liberal version this literary education fashions an individual capable of acting responsibly and independently by teaching him or her those Western cultural values accessible through its literary canon. That is, the student becomes a sovereign individual now by absorbing the truths manifest in the writings of the past.[115]

This formulation of humanist education may be correlated with conventional definitions of modern American political conservatism, to the extent that allegiance to "traditional values"—that is, those of the European élite—is understood as "conservative." Its opponents describe such conservatism as authoritarian because it holds these values as the sole standard for ethical, social, and political behavior. However, politically, such conservatives see themselves as *opposed* to centralized authority and in favor of individual rights (though these absolute individual rights may

---

115. For example, in his "Tradition and the Individual Talent," T. S. Eliot reminded his reader that the word "tradition" had come to be used as a "phrase of censure" for English writing, with most people locating the poet's strength in his power to invent something particular to himself. But Eliot notoriously argued the opposite, that "the most individual parts of his work may be those in which the dead poets, his ancestors, assert their immortality most vigorously" (p. 48). The poet informed by this "past" consciousness, however, hardly resembles the lawyers, humanists, and clergy of the early modern period who allied themselves with tradition in resisting the encroachments of absolute sovereignty. Rather, Eliot understood the poet's relationship to the past and history in terms of an "escape from personality" (p. 58), which is paradoxically a form of power. Eliot's Greek epigraph to the final section of the essay, which refers to the mind as something divine (*theioteron*) and impassive (*apathes*), depicts the poet as godlike in his detachment; he is a creator, whose power is in self-sacrifice and denial of individuality or difference (T. S. Eliot, "Tradition and the Individual Talent," in *The Sacred Wood: Essays on Poetry and Criticism* [London: Methuen, 1920], pp. 47–56). See Geoffrey H. Hartman, *Criticism in the Wilderness: The Study of Literature Today* (New Haven: Yale University Press, 1980), chap. 2, "The Sacred Jungle 1: Carlyle, Eliot, Bloom," pp. 42–62, on the transformations of a notion of tradition by these three critics.

be reserved for those respecting the traditional authority of patriarchy and established religion).[116] Contemporary "radicalism" signifies for many the rejection of Western European cultural and political traditions, understood as embodying the hegemony of white men. For some who would define themselves as "radicals," education means reproducing white, male social control and cultural hegemony. Others, however, have held out hope that education and a different sort of recourse to tradition may provide the tools to critique and thus resist cultural and political domination. Both types of radicals, however, suspect any appeal to individual rights or agency as being contaminated through association with conservatism and a transcendental humanism.[117]

Comparing these current alignments to the early modern political and cultural appeals to tradition and autonomy, however, suggests the instability of such alliances. In early modern England and Buchanan's Scotland, alignment with tradition could ground resistance to the innovations of absolutist doctrine. For James Stuart rejecting or at best redefining tradition (except the past embodied in patrilineal inheritance) at least theoretically bolstered the power of the absolute monarch, who was fettered by no bonds except God's judgment and could remake the world after his own image. Tradition helped to create individual and community resistance against absolutism, while absolute rule was predicated on the supreme individual's power to invent.

In his essay "Integrating the American Mind" Henry Louis Gates, Jr., invokes the more familiar association between tradition and authority when warning against a "rhetoric of liberal education" which "remains suffused with the imagery of possession, patrimony, legacy, lineage, inheritance—call it cultural geneticism (in the broadest sense of that term). At the same moment, the rhetoric of possession and lineage subsists upon, and perpetuates, a division: between us and them, we

116. See Stanley Aronowitz and Henry A. Giroux, *Education under Siege: The Conservative, Liberal, and Radical Debate Over School* (South Hadley, Mass.: Bergin and Garvey, 1985), pp. 210–11, on how neo-conservative discourse about public schooling "embraces elements of community and localism in its support of the family, patriarchal authority, and religion" combined with "the tenets of classical liberalism, with its stress on individualism, competition, and personal effort and reward."

117. See Philip Wexler, Rebecca Martusewicz, and June Klein, "Popular Education Politics," in David W. Livingstone, ed., *Critical Pedagogy and Cultural Power* (New York: Bergin and Garvey, 1987), p. 230, for the discussion of issues of agency.

the heirs of *our* tradition, and you, the Others, whose difference defines our identity."[118] Gates challenges humanists to abandon the "cultural nationalism" that "has been a constitutive aspect of Western education."[119] With this move, implicitly, Gates is also asking us to give up the notion of a self-defining cultural property in favor of "the study of the possibilities of human life in culture."[120] Yet in another essay in the same volume Gates calls on African-Americans to study the traditions of African-American culture, as opposed to the "high canon of Western masterpieces." He admits that "this is one case where we've got to borrow a leaf from the right, which is exemplarily aware of the role of education in the reproduction of values."[121] From this point of view, claiming a tradition through education allows formerly marginalized people to "constitute ourselves as discursive subjects."[122]

Gates's move is thus a characteristically humanist double gesture: on the one hand confronting and disengaging from the canon of Western tradition, which teaches "an aesthetic and a political order, in which no women or people of color were ever able to discover the reflection or representation of their images, or hear the resonances of their cultural voices"; on the other hand recuperating the power of an alternative tradition as a means of "exploring and reclaiming our subjectivity."[123] Having done so, women and people of color may discover political agency, to the degree that "self-identification proves a condition for agency, for social change."[124] Gates's pedagogical return to tradition thus attempts to restore the possibility of fashioning resistance to the present order through identification with the past. He revives the notion of a tradition defining a distinctive community, which in turn grants its members identity in their similar differences. Such revivals are a powerful reminder to us how the past can be used to free us, as much as to burden us, in the double vision of humanist teaching.

118. Henry Louis Gates, Jr., *Loose Canons: Notes on the Culture Wars* (New York: Oxford University Press, 1992), p. 109.
119. Ibid., p. 111.
120. Ibid., p. 114.
121. Ibid., p. 35.
122. Ibid., p. 39.
123. Ibid., p. 35.
124. Ibid., p. 37.

EPILOGUE

Contemporary
Humanist Pedagogy

ontemporary arguments about tradition and authority evoke
the complexity of early modern humanism's survival in the
Anglo-American academy. It is not just a question of pitting
tradition against freedom and autonomy but rather a volatile mixing
and crossing of the claims of past and present, of likeness and difference, freedom and submission—a mixture of the kind that characterized early modern humanist pedagogy and poetics. As David
Bromwich has noted, even today "an appeal to authority is often the
opposite of an appeal to tradition."[1] Rather than seeing the current
situation as one in which traditional humanist education has been
threatened by something alien and new, I believe that such conflict was
present in the humanist educational project from the beginning: in
particular, in the paradoxical relationship between masters and students
and in the ambivalence concerning freedom and control. I do not pre-
tend to offer a genealogy of contemporary humanist education, given
the convoluted history of English and American education since the
seventeenth century, and the differences among elementary, secondary,
and university educational systems.[2] Nor would I want to say with

1. David Bromwich, *Politics by Other Means: Higher Education and Group Thinking*
(New Haven: Yale University Press, 1992), p. 100.
2. On the continuity see John Guillory, "Canonical and Non-Canonical: A Critique
of the Current Debate," *ELH* 54 (1987): pp. 494, 498–99. Also see Anthony Grafton
and Lisa Jardine, *From Humanism to the Humanities: Education and the Liberal Arts in
Fifteenth- and Sixteenth-Century Europe* (Cambridge: Harvard University Press, 1986),
who write that "whether we like it or not, we still live with the dilemma of late human-

James I and Samuel Daniel that "there is nothing new under the sun." Rather, in keeping with this book's overall method, using the framework of historical languages, I will conclude by examining selected examples of the recent debate over humanist education, looking at the role of teachers, the treatment of students, and the shaping of curricula.

TEACHERS

At the heart of the politics of humanist education is the question of freedom: the freedom of the teacher, the student, and the academy itself. We still ask whether the classroom is quite different from the home and the *polis* and whether it must always reproduce political relations and indoctrinate the students into social conformity. We wonder whether it is a place where politics should not be discussed or where nothing *but* politics should be discussed, both alternatives possible in Ascham's vision of the classroom as "a sanctuary from fear" from which to view and even criticize the actions of "great ones" without fear of punishment.[3]

For a sense of the modern confusion about the teacher's and class-

---

ism: we too can only live in hope, and practice the humanities" (p. 200). The route from the humanist educational theory and method to the current debate over the university curriculum is particularly circuitous, for the sixteenth-century debate was devoted almost exclusively to grammar school or private aristocratic education. See Lisa Jardine, "Humanism and the Sixteenth-Century Cambridge Arts Course," *History of Education* 4 (1975): 16–31, on the exclusion of basic grammar training at Cambridge. At the same time, however, starting in the early sixteenth century, humanist educational practices made considerable inroads at Oxford and Cambridge: innovations included the teaching of Greek, an emphasis on the return to classical sources, and the use of reformed dialectic for the study of texts (see Charles G. Nauert, Jr., "Humanist Infiltration into the Academic World: Some Studies of Northern Universities," *Renaissance Quarterly* 43 [1990]: 799–812). Insofar as humanist educational theory concerned the teaching of "grammar" or the study of "literature," broadly defined, it bears on current discussions about reading and teaching literature in universities.

3. While I will not treat the issue of corporal punishment here, since I am focusing on debates over humanist education primarily at the secondary and post-secondary levels, it is fascinating that the debate over corporal punishment in schools continues unabated in the United States. In 1988, *The Humanist* devoted a special issue to the issue of corporal punishment: at that time, it was noted that "corporal punishment is legal in most places in 39 states" (Bob Keeshan, "The Time Is Now," *The Humanist* 48 [November/December 1988]: 7).

room's ideological safety, here is a passage from Gerald Graff's description of the typical picture of American college life:

> Consider our most familiar image of the college, graphically depicted in the photographs of virtually every catalog: an oasis of pastoral serenity, removed from everything that is conflictual or dissonant in adult urban experience. Small intimate groups of students and professors gather under shady trees on the smooth, sloping campus green. The professors are a benevolent lot, formidably learned and strict, of course, if colorfully ineffectual in the real practical world. For like ministers of the church, they presumably live removed from the harsh demands of commercial getting and spending that "real people" must reluctantly graduate into after their college days are over. It is just this otherworldliness that makes the professor's lessons so valuable in retrospect (however often one may have slept through them at the time). These lessons exemplify that realm of "value" that the commercial and industrial world has so little respect for.[4]

Graff's image of the professor's authority recalls the early humanist fashioning of the schoolmaster: "formidable and strict" in matters of learning yet "benevolent" in the seminar, a "small intimate group" that imitates and supplants the family. The teacher is expected to be terrifying yet also loving (and lovable, precisely because he or she is not *really* threatening, being "ineffectual" in the "real world"). Peter Elbow identifies these two poses as "the 'paternal' version, which is to stick up for standards and firmness" and the " 'maternal' version, which is to stick up for students," both the inevitable "contraries in the teaching process."[5] We still combine the authoritarian image of a teacher with those of the playmate and foster-mother, who lure the pupil into the pleasant retreat of learning.[6]

---

4. Gerald Graff, "Teach the Conflicts," in Darryl J. Gless and Barbara Herrnstein Smith, eds., *The Politics of Liberal Education* (Durham: Duke University Press, 1992), p. 61.

5. Peter Elbow, "Embracing Contraries in the Teaching Process," *College English* 45 (1983): 329.

6. See Richard Halpern, *The Poetics of Primitive Accumulation: English Renaissance Culture and the Genealogy of Capital* (Ithaca: Cornell University Press, 1991), p. 30, on the

The instability of the paternal role is clear in Graff's conclusion to his picture of the pastoral seminar: viewed from outside the academy, teachers have no authority at all.[7] When Allan Bloom tried define the source of the power of "authentically great thinkers" in the universities, he found it in those "who gave living proof of the existence of the theoretical life and whose motives could not easily be reduced to any of the baser ones people delight in thinking universal. They had authority, not based on power, money or family, but on natural gifts that properly compel respect."[8] Bloom valued what such teachers impart to their students precisely because it has no material value. The professor's authority is absolute precisely because it appears to be located elsewhere than the "outside" world. Within the institution, the teacher may be granted what we call "academic freedom," a freedom of action, thought and speech—but one bounded by the institution's limits. As Geoffrey Hartman wistfully put the point in 1980, it is a difficult compromise: "Since the academy is, despite everything, a good place, one that protects the scholar's freedom to work on any topic that does not make him rich, we accept the trade-off that substitutes leisure for influence, and shape our lives accordingly. . . . The isolation of the humanist may be a blessing in disguise. Yet there are signs at present that humanists, because of that isolation, have lost their currency, which is about all that was left after they had lost their authority."[9] The passage

---

shift between the paternal and maternal in some early humanist pedagogic rhetoric. On the rhetoric of seduction in pedagogy in its later survivals, see Joan De Jean, "*La Nouvelle Héloïse*, or the Case for Pedagogical Deviation," and Jane Gallop, "The Immoral Teachers," both in a special edition of *Yale French Studies* edited by Barbara Johnson: *The Pedagogical Imperative: Teaching as a Literary Genre (Yale French Studies* 63 [1982]). In the same issue, Shoshana Felman's "Psychoanalysis and Education: Teaching Terminable and Interminable" explores critiques of pedagogy by Lacan and Freud in which the teacher takes on the paternal role.

7. See Bruce Kuklick, "The Emergence of the Humanities," in Gless and Smith, eds., *The Politics of Liberal Education*, pp. 201–12, on the ways in which this position comes from American pedagogy's tie with the church. Also see Bromwich, *Politics*, p. 105, on the isolation of the academy.

8. Allan Bloom, *The Closing of the American Mind: How Higher Education Has Failed Democracy and Impoverished the Souls of Today's Students* (New York: Simon and Schuster, 1987), pp. 244–45.

9. Geoffrey Hartman, *Criticism in the Wilderness: The Study of Literature Today* (New Haven: Yale University Press, 1980), p. 289.

from Graff suggests a similar ambivalence about the classroom's status as a protected—and isolated—space.

Today's conservative commentators on education accuse leftist teachers of politicizing the classroom and abandoning the disinterested search for truth, thus breaking a tradition of salutary isolation.[10] Bloom praises his students of Greek civilization who, during the demonstrations at Cornell in the 1960s, preferred to read Plato's *Republic*, for "they were really more interested in the book than the revolution, which in itself proved what kind of counter-charm the university ought to provide to the siren calls of the contemporary scene."[11] Bloom's opponents retaliate with the claim that all classrooms are political. Echoing Brecht, they would say that yearning for an apolitical classroom in itself makes a political statement. This is not just because they believe that all subject matter is inherently political, but also because, as Henry Giroux puts it, they are convinced that "what we teach and how we do it are deeply implicated not only in producing various forms of domination but also in constructing active practices of resistance and struggle."[12]

For this new breed of teacher, as for the early humanists, there remains the challenge of inventing an alternative pedagogy that avoids "domination." In 1968 Paulo Freire called on teachers to abandon authoritarian pedagogy that "deposits" knowledge into the student and to adopt a pedagogy based on dialogue and "problem-posing": "through dialogue, the teacher-of-the-students and the students-of-the-teacher cease to exist and a new term emerges: teacher-student with student-teachers. . . . In this process, arguments based on 'authority'

10. For a comprehensive statement of this point of view, see Roger Kimball, *Tenured Radicals: How Politics Has Corrupted Our Higher Education* (New York: Harper and Row, 1990).

11. Bloom, *Closing*, p. 332.

12. Henry A. Giroux, "Liberal Arts Education and the Struggle for Public Life: Dreaming about Democracy," in Gless and Smith, eds., *The Politics of Liberal Education*, p. 129. See also Pierre Bourdieu and Jean-Claude Passeron, *Reproduction in Education, Society and Culture*, trans. Richard Nice (London: Sage Publications, 1977). Stanley Fish, in his introduction to *There's No Such Thing as Free Speech . . . and It's a Good Thing Too* (New York: Oxford University Press, 1994), also attacks the neoconservative view of their own pedagogy as "apolitical" or politically disinterested; see also Michael Ryan, "Deconstruction and Radical Teaching," in Johnson, ed., *The Pedagogical Imperative*, pp. 45–58.

are no longer valid."[13] Freire was filled with optimism about the liberating effect of this new pedagogy: "Problem-posing education, as a humanist and liberating praxis, posits as fundamental that men subjected to domination must fight for their emancipation. To that end, it enables teachers and students to become subjects of the educational process by overcoming authoritarianism and an alienating intellectualism; it also enables men to overcome their false perception of reality."[14]

In the postmodern adaptations of Freire's vision, however, the teacher's role in a non-authoritarian classroom is not entirely clear. What exactly is a "postmodern" teacher supposed to *do* in the classroom?[15] Like Freire, Henry Giroux advocates a pedagogy that "replaces the authoritative language of recitation with an approach that allows students to speak from their own histories, collective memories and voices while simultaneously challenging the grounds on which knowledge and power are constructed and legitimated." But in the end Giroux draws on the same alternative proposed by the early modern humanists, who replaced the authoritarian teacher with the teacher as a role model, inculcating social values through imitation. Giroux asks teachers to adopt the role of the "engaged and transformative intellectual," who needs "to encourage students by example to find ways to get involved, to make a difference, to think in global terms, and to act from specific contexts."[16] While Giroux's aim may differ from that of some — but not all — early humanist educators, the strategy is the same: in seeking to avoid overtly authoritarian positions, both involve the student in what Richard Halpern terms the "play of mirrors, a dialectic of imaginary

---

13. Paulo Freire, *Pedagogy of the Oppressed*, trans. Myra Bergman Ramos (New York: Continuum, 1986) p. 67.

14. Ibid., p. 74.

15. In a review of the rhetoric of poststructuralist pedagogy, John Schilb has noted these theorists' habit of erasing any agency for "human subjects" ("Poststructuralism, Politics, and the Subject of Pedagogy," in Maria-Regina Kecht ed., *Pedagogy Is Politics: Literary Theory and Critical Teaching* (Urbana: University of Illinois Press, 1992), p. 55. For a general criticism of the problematic role of the teacher in postmodern pedagogy, see Gregory Jay and Gerald Graff, "A Critique of Critical Pedagogy," in Michael Bérubé and Cary Nelson, eds., *Higher Education under Fire: Politics, Economics, and the Crisis of the Humanities* (New York: Routledge, 1995), pp. 201–13.

16. Giroux, "Liberal Arts Education," pp. 138–39.

capture by a dominant form" that is education by example.[17] Buchanan seems to have believed that he could pursue his radical ends and keep James Stuart from turning into a tyrant while treating him tyrannically. As Alice Miller has suggested in her study of corporal punishment's links with fascism, however, repression used to produce the self-controlled subject will only reproduce itself in the next generation.[18] Any radical pedagogy must ask how to teach students to resist if being taught must always constitute a form of obedience or adherence to the teacher's "superior" example.

In an essay plaintively titled "Why Doesn't This Feel Empowering? Working through the Repressive Myths of Critical Pedagogy," Elizabeth Ellsworth describes herself as caught in just such a crisis. She asserts that "key assumptions, goals and pedagogical practices fundamental to the literature on critical pedagogy—namely, 'empowerment,' 'student voice,' 'dialogue,' and even the term 'critical'—are repressive myths that perpetuate relations of domination."[19] In particular, Ellsworth expresses her dissatisfaction with the critical pedagogy movement's reliance on rational critique because she believes "the myths of the ideal rational person and the 'universality' of propositions have been oppressive" to all those diverging from the mainstream. So in her own teaching she seeks not to "enforce" rational debate but rather "to interrupt institutional limits" on the time her class could devote to discussion.[20] That is, her role is not to teach at all. What is irretrievably lost in such a turn is any sense that a teacher has something of partic-

---

17. Halpern, *Poetics*, p. 29.

18. Alice Miller, *For Your Own Good: Hidden Cruelty in Child-Rearing and the Roots of Violence*, trans. Hildegarde and Hunter Hannum (New York: Farrar, Straus and Giroux, 1983), first published as *Am Anfang war Erziehung* (Frankfurt am Main: Suhrkamp, 1980).

19. Elizabeth Ellsworth, "Why Doesn't This Feel Empowering? Working through the Repressive Myths of Critical Pedagogy," *Harvard Educational Review* 59 (1989): 298. For an example of pedagogical practice that might be open to Ellsworth's criticism, see Jane Tompkins's description of her "modest proposal for revolutionizing the classroom," where she puts the responsibility for presenting the class material in the students' hands, but *she* makes up the syllabus, and they explore the subject that interests *her*: the account of her pedagogy is about what she "wanted" and what she "did" ("Teaching Like It Matters: A Modest Proposal for Revolutionizing the Classroom," in *Lingua Franca*, August 1991: 24–27).

20. Ellsworth, "Why Doesn't This Feel Empowering?" pp. 304–5.

ular value to offer a student in a mutual giving of knowledge through dialogue. This value may inhere simply in the experience of broader reading, as Erasmus recognized when he demanded an encyclopedic reading for his model teacher, but allowed his students to choose more narrowly.[21]

Ellsworth also tells how she and her class participated in demonstrations, with her course culminating in taking "actions on campus by interrupting business-as-usual (that is, social relations of racism, sexism, classism, Eurocentrism as usual) in the public spaces of the library, mall and administrative offices" at the University of Wisconsin–Madison.[22] Ellsworth would thus respond to Stanley Fish's mocking of most postmodern academics' desire to be "political"[23] by pointing to her own breaking down of the classroom's boundaries—albeit staying within the campus limits. Such action implicitly violates the notion of the classroom as the "safe space," whose boundaries characteristically protect it from outside interference. And with this boundary's collapse must go "academic freedom" as it is traditionally defined. Thus Michael Ryan has cautioned radical teachers: "To accept academic freedom as a rallying cry is tantamount to accepting a definition of the academy as a separable realm from the social world. . . . Instead of emphasizing the fact that the social world is constructed and that therefore it could be constructed in a different form, the liberal philosophy of academic freedom would make that world appear natural."[24] For many teachers, breaking down the schoolroom walls would be a welcome gain, allowing them to become what Antonio Gramsci described as organic intellectuals, who are defined less by professionalism than by their active participation in practical life, "as a constructor, organiser, 'permanent persuader,' and not just a simple orator."[25] Yet for many other teachers

21. See Freire, *Pedagogy*, p. 67.

22. Ellsworth, "Why Doesn't This Feel Empowering?" p. 319.

23. Stanley Fish, "Commentary: The Young and the Restless," in H. Aram Veeser, ed., *The New Historicism* (New York: Routledge, 1989), pp. 303–16.

24. Ryan, "Deconstruction and Pedagogy," p. 58.

25. Antonio Gramsci, *Selections from the Prison Notebooks*, ed. and trans. Quintin Hoare and Geoffrey Nowell Smith (New York: International, 1971), intro., p. 10. For a full discussion of the issues surrounding the intellectual's—and critic's—political role and a rejection of the "unworldliness of the classroom" (p. 1), see Jim Merod, *The Political Responsibility of the Critic* (Ithaca: Cornell University Press, 1987).

it would also be a loss. Abandoning a liberal notion or "fiction" of academic freedom as institutionally framed means losing its protection, under which teachers and students may advocate and exchange ideas without fear of outside intervention.

STUDENTS

Authoritarian pedagogies tend to foreground the teacher, characterizing the student as a vessel, or at best a disciple. In a postmodern pedagogy, in contrast, the teacher recedes and the class focuses on the students' needs, rights, and experience. Certainly, teachers' classroom behavior reflects what they think of their students. The early modern humanists saw students at once as empty vessels and forces of nature, both restrained and free, all alike yet all different in some way. This contradictory image of students was not only inseparable from the teachers' awareness of their relative social positions, but it also reflected their differing political and social ideologies. Humanist educational theory has always aimed to shape people to serve society and the state, but such theorists have not always agreed about what that society and polity should be, and their conceptions of their students have differed accordingly.

In our own quarrels over humanist education, the "freedom" that education grants has become tied to a student's race, gender, and class. For those we call "liberal humanists," education should be the great leveler in a democratic society: education should free one from the limitations otherwise imposed by economic status, gender, or racial identity. For such liberal theorists, education fosters integration, giving different social groups a common language in which they can communicate. As E. D. Hirsch, Jr., portrays it: "As the universal second culture, literate culture has become the common currency for social and economic exchange in our democracy, and the only available ticket to full citizenship. Getting one's membership card is not tied to class or race. Membership is automatic if one learns the background information and the linguistic conventions that are needed to read, write, and speak effectively."[26] Critics of Hirsch call such a notion "false egal-

26. E. D. Hirsch, Jr., *Cultural Literacy: What Every American Needs to Know* (Boston: Houghton Mifflin, 1987), p. 22.

itarianism" that ignores continuing oppression linked to race, class and gender.[27] Arguments such as Hirsch's also open themselves up to Bourdieu and Passeron's critique of state education: that while the "free" state system of education may represent its process and its actors as disinterested, they exist to reproduce existing class relations.[28] While appeals to literacy and "common culture" try to bring other cultures under the umbrella of literate culture, postmodern pedagogy insists that we pay attention to the "different voices, languages, histories and ways of viewing and experience in the world" rather than trying to erase them.[29]

However, a Foucauldian reader would detect that such recognition of "differences" has had a mixed history. In *Discipline and Punish*, Foucault argued that the attribution of individuality is a necessary function of disciplinary power. Thus interpreted, attention to differences would not undermine the primacy of "common" or universal culture but would ultimately support it. In Foucault's words, "the perpetual penalty that traverses all points and supervises every instant in the disciplinary institution compares, differentiates, hierarchizes, homogenizes, excludes."[30] For example, in *Sentimental Education*, his Foucauldian account of English education from the nineteenth century to the present, James Donald notes the scrupulous attention paid to the "individuality" of working-class children in the late nineteenth century. For Donald such regard for difference functioned as a covert means to know the Other intimately, with the end of that Other's maximum exploitation. According to Donald, such schooling "works by deploying an intimate knowledge of the individuals who make up its target population, and an expertise in monitoring and guiding their conduct."[31]

27. Stanley Aronowitz and Henry A. Giroux, *Postmodern Education: Politics, Culture, and Social Criticism* (Minneapolis: University of Minnesota Press, 1991), p. 48.

28. See Pierre Bourdieu and Jean-Claude Passeron, *La reproduction: elements pour une theorie du systeme d'enseignement* (Paris: Minuit, 1970), trans. Richard Nice, *Reproduction in Education, Society and Culture* (London: Sage, 1977).

29. Ibid., p. 51. Cf. Fish's critique of the notion of the "common," in *There's No Such Thing as Free Speech*, chap. 2.

30. Michel Foucault, *Discipline and Punish: The Birth of the Prison*, trans. Alan Sheridan (New York: Pantheon, 1977), p. 183.

31. James Donald, *Sentimental Education: Schooling, Popular Culture and the Regulation of Liberty* (London: Verso, 1992), p. 12.

Even in the case of Piagetian pedagogy, he argues, " 'allowing the child to develop' has instituted an emphasis on surveillance and monitoring; 'liberating the child' has involved stratagems as lovingly manipulative as any of those devised by Emile's tutor" in Rousseau's account of a "natural" education in *Emile*.[32] Like Halpern, who criticizes the loving "tyranny" of the early humanist master, Donald sees that (like the gardener who studies his plant's properties in order to maximize his own profit) humanist pedagogy will always be contaminated by its ends of serving a conformist, class-ridden society.

In a "postmodern" pedagogy that values difference above all, opposing the "humanist" imposition of a universal, white, middle-class culture, the sense that everyone is different may lead to Elizabeth Ellsworth's decision not to seek a common ground among her students. To ask them to find that ground or even to share a rational language, she insists, undermines the purposes of a radical pedagogy by imposing an identity on them.[33] Aronowitz and Giroux have responded to such frustration by arguing that teaching differences allows "a vision of community in which student voices define themselves in terms of their distinct social formations and their broader collective hopes"; that is, they should try to find what they share, as well as how they may be different, even if what they share is only "the experience of being oppressed."[34] All these teachers thus struggle to deal with the practical consequences of their own undermining of the comfortable associations of "difference" with individuality, the "common" with the rational.

The anxiety in these pedagogic circles about difference and sameness reflects the effort of leftist intellectuals to redefine the grounds for political action in a theoretical field stripped of familiar forms of political agency. Some members of "marginalized" groups have complained that postmodern theory has left them no self for which or with which to fight for freedom. As Nancy Hartsock has asked, "Why is it, exactly at the moment when so many of us who have been silenced begin to demand the right to name ourselves, to act as subjects rather than

32. Ibid., pp. 12–13.
33. Ellsworth, "Why Doesn't This," p. 318.
34. Aronowitz and Giroux, *Postmodern Education*, pp. 132–33.

objects of history, that just then the concept of subjecthood becomes 'problematic'?"[35] One reply has been that a person need not be a "subject" or an "individual" in order to act politically. Alan Sinfield would say to critics such as Hartsock that he "believes that feminist anxiety about derogation of the individual in cultural materialism is misplaced, since personal subjectivity and agency are, anyway, unlikely sources of dissident identity and action. Political awareness does not arise out of an essential, individual self-consciousness of class, race, nation, gender or sexual orientation; but from involvement in a milieu, a subculture."[36] That is, what empowers one to act is not one's separate identity but a group identity that underwrites collective resistance.

Another recourse has been to return to descriptions of the relationship between the citizen and the *polis* in civic humanism. For example, Terry Eagleton has recently drawn on J. G. A. Pocock's distinction between "civic humanism," which respects the "virtue" of each citizen committed to working for his or her community, and "commercial humanism," under which "the universe became pervaded by law, the locus of whose sovereignty was extra-civic, and the citizen came to be defined not by his actions and virtues, but by his rights to and in things."[37] To put it in terms of the early modern language of "property," political virtue in civic humanism is a citizen's "property" or nature, in contrast to a liberal or "commercial" humanism that values people's "property" in things, or rights to them. The civic humanist notion of virtue is not incompatible with the ideal of "natural virtues" central to the humanist pedagogues' comparison of teaching and gardening. At its best, such a comparison recognizes the potential (the seeds) for knowledge and virtuous action in each person who could serve the community. Although different people had different prop-

35. Nancy Hartsock, "Rethinking Modernism: Minority vs. Majority Theories," *Cultural Critique* 7 (1987): 196.

36. Alan Sinfield, *Faultlines: Cultural Materialism and the Politics of Dissident Reading* (Berkeley: University of California Press, 1992), p. 37.

37. J. G. A. Pocock, *Virtue, Commerce and History* (Cambridge: Cambridge University Press, 1985), p. 43; see Terry Eagleton, "Deconstruction and Human Rights" in Barbara Johnson, ed., *Freedom and Interpretation: The Oxford Amnesty Lectures, 1992* (New York: Basic Books, 1993), p. 132. Eagleton deals with the importance of property ownership in civic humanism by cheerfully acknowledging this humanism's quasi-Marxist materialism.

erties, just as plants did, each might flourish if cultivated with care and attention. The properties or virtues commanded the teacher's respect and recognition, withstanding the pressures of the institutional time-tables and curricular demands.[38] Inevitably, however, in the common-wealths of people and plants alike, difference asserted itself for many teacher/gardeners along the ladder of degree, race and gender, where "properties" meant the curse of determinism rather than the blessings of a virtue that cannot be kept from coming to fruition. Once the pedagogic relationship, with its give and take, is institutionally frozen, it becomes too hard to hold such a delicate balance.

BOOKS

All these issues—including the role of tradition; the freedom of teacher and student; and racial, social, and gender difference—meet in the debate over which books should be taught in American classrooms. Who should choose the books: the state, the institution, the parent, the teacher, or the student? What kind of books should they be: the masterworks of the Western European tradition, which some call the common currency of modern American culture, or the books that in-stead embody or speak to the diverse traditions that have coalesced here? Why should these books be read: to instill a common culture in a new generation, or to develop in each student a critical eye on the past and present?

Everyone seems to agree that *someone* must choose what books are to be read in school, if only because the institutional structure of ed-ucation demands it. In Chapter 4, I told how the early humanist teach-ers and educational theorists were vexed by choosing books to teach when their authors, like ours, elbowed one another for a space in a limited curriculum. Barbara Herrnstein Smith offers a view of our own situation that echoes the thoughts of those early humanist educational theorists: "It is commonly said that, with only a limited amount of time available, only the best writings should be studied. That, in our view, is correct. The question is: given the enormous store of literature,

---

38. For Foucault's discussion of the function of "time-table" in the discipline of "docile bodies," see *Discipline and Punish*, pp. 149–51.

the traditional and otherwise desirable educational objectives indicated above, and any set of specific students, conditions, and institutional constraints, which writings *are* 'the best'?"[39]

It often seems that no one can escape such conflict over the canon, in which a set curriculum has become the object of a struggle between those who defend the "classics" and those who claim the centrality of writers and traditions formerly marginalized. For one side to gain, it appears that the other must lose status and territory (most often, economic language is used to describe the conflict: Mary Louise Pratt writes of curricular "horse-trading,"[40] and Gerald Graff disparages the new "cafeteria-counter curriculum," which "has come about by a process of accretion, trade-offs, and 'Let's Make a Deal' games"[41]). Insofar as this war is waged over funds for programs and faculty in a time of reduced budgets, the battlefield's boundaries are indeed fixed. But the field of reading remains theoretically unbounded; that is, that field is composed not of any institutional list of books, "great" or otherwise, but of the contents of our public libraries and bookstores, which are vast, ever-changing, and accessible to anyone who can read with understanding.[42] Indeed, such breadth of learning was a basic principle of the early humanist educational program, which summoned the students (in Sir Thomas Elyot's words) to read "very much and in diverse authors of diverse learnings,"[43] as much as it counseled them to be selective.

I argued in Chapter 4 that the early modern humanists' compromise solution to the problem of choice lay precisely in what many have seen to be an intellectual weakness: attention to the parts of texts rather than the whole and a taste for anthologies, *florilegia,* and collections in which a wide range of authors could be read without any distinctly marked as dominant. Such anthologies and collections of common-

39. Barbara Herrnstein Smith, introduction to Gless and Smith, eds., *The Politics of Liberal Education*, p. 8.

40. Mary Louise Pratt, "Humanities for the Future: Reflections on the Western Culture Debate at Stanford," in Gless and Smith, eds., *Politics*, p. 18.

41. Graff, in Gless and Smith, eds., *Politics*, p. 59.

42. See Katha Pollitt, "Canon to the right of me . . . ," *The Nation*, September 23, 1991, pp. 328–30, on the restriction of assuming that one's reading is done only in school.

43. Sir Thomas Elyot, *The Boke named The Governour* (London, 1531; reprint, ed. H. H. S. Croft, New York: Burt Franklin, 1967), p. 131.

places were geared to the needs of the individual reader, whether the young town grammar scholar or the Christian prince. However, as we have seen, this habit of reading, while it never gave way completely, came into conflict with the estimation of a text as a whole. Combined with the early humanist practice of reading closely such emphasis on the text's body inevitably created a strain: how could you read carefully, cover the whole book, and still achieve the aim of universal knowledge? One of the results of this tension appears to have been the gradual decline of the commonplace book. After the sixteenth century, the tradition of collecting excerpts or commonplaces for the purposes of rhetorical embellishment continued, but the encyclopedia, which collected and presented facts rather than pieces of text, eventually took over the commonplace book's function as a repository of general knowledge.[44]

In the twentieth century, the New Critical approach to "close reading" intensified the conflict between the desire for coverage associated with the early humanists and the later neoclassical concern with details of literary structure and form. Such tension is especially acute today, given the pressure institutions feel to increase the number of writers taught in schools. For one example, witness the carefully balanced preface of volume one of the fifth edition of the *Norton Anthology of English Literature*, where the editors express their concern that "these works be so far as feasible complete, and also abundant enough to allow instructors to choose from the total those that each one prefers to teach" (while they also have taken care that "each volume, in size and weight, be comfortably portable").[45] The editors boast of how in this edition they have been able to "supplement or to complete works hitherto represented by more limited excerpts"—a result of their struggle to avoid fragmentation while seeking to augment representation of a variety of authors. Teachers trained in formalist close reading have the hardest time in trying to accommodate their scholarly habits to new curricular demands, but even historicist and materialist critics suffer the same fate insofar as

44. See Walter J. Ong, "Commonplace Rhapsody: Ravisius Textor, Zwinger and Shakespeare," in R. R. Bolgar, ed., *Classical Influences on European Culture, A.D. 1500–1700* (Cambridge: Cambridge University Press, 1976), p. 125.

45. M. H. Abrams et al., eds., *The Norton Anthology of English Literature*, 5th ed. (New York: W. W. Norton, 1986), vol. 1, pp. xxx–xxxi.

their teaching is meant to culminate in the classroom "reading" of a literary text. In 1981, during the florescence of psychoanalytic and poststructuralist criticism, Jonathan Culler commented that "whatever critical affiliations we may proclaim, we are all New Critics, in that it requires strenuous effort to escape notions of the autonomy of the literary work, the importance of demonstrating its unity, and the requirement of 'close reading.' "[46] As late as 1992, amid the proliferation of politically oriented criticism, Peter J. Rabinowitz still complained that "commitment to close reading may be the *cantus firmus* in the multivoiced canon of contemporary criticism."[47]

All sides still construct the canon debate as a matter of substitution or exchanges within a set number of texts, a number determined by classroom practice. George Kennedy has echoed Vives in his lament that "even in the surviving literature of Greece and Rome, not to say in Renaissance and modern literature, there is too much for any student to read." As his next sentence suggests, however, what any student can read is set by our habit of classroom discussion of texts: for "in the extreme case that every student read a totally different set of books, discussion of literature would be impossible."[48] While trying to change radically *what* we read we thus remain bound by our expectation of what the "discussion of literature" entails: the public, shared, close reading of a common text.

In recent years, medieval scholastic pedagogy has been praised as an alternative to humanist education, because scholastics taught ideas and modes of argument rather than texts themselves, and, some believe, it promoted disputes and independence of mind rather than the slavish copying of textual models. For some teachers, scholastic pedagogy might offer a tempting alternative to humanist practice by circumventing the canon problem entirely (like substituting the teaching of

46. Jonathan Culler, *The Pursuit of Signs: Semiotics, Literature, Deconstruction* (Ithaca: Cornell University Press, 1981), p. 3.

47. For a critique of close reading, see Peter J. Rabinowitz, "Against Close Reading," in Kecht, ed., *Pedagogy Is Politics*, pp. 230–44. While making a much broader argument, Rabinowitz also makes my point that "because close reading means, among other things, slow reading, it reduces the *number* of texts with which a reader is liable to be familiar" (pp. 237–38).

48. George Kennedy, "Classics and Canons," in Gless and Smith, eds., *Politics of Liberal Education*, p. 226.

theory for the study of literary texts).[49] The medieval schools had their own canons, of course, but when scholasticism dominated the schools the study of authors for their own sake declined. How many books or which books students read mattered less than how the students thought and argued. While textual commentary was always practiced at some level, in the medieval schools students mostly used books to extract from them an idea to serve as the subject of disputation. If we think of scholasticism as having taught logic as "language theory," while remembering that the humanists taught the interpretation of texts, it is not surprising that, along with other aspects of pre- or counter-humanist culture, scholasticism once again appears attractive to those who distrust humanism in all its forms.

Yet while the scholastics developed a language theory out of logic, the humanists elaborated a theory of language engaged in social and political life: language as rhetoric.[50] Turning from language understood as reason to language seen as action, humanism produced what scholasticism lacked most acutely: a consciousness of the text or discourse as an historical artifact. In scholastic teaching and commentary the ideas generated by applying logic to a text were important, but not the past embedded in its words. Although medieval literature does demonstrate a "historical consciousness,"[51] scholasticism itself was little concerned with the historicity of language. In contrast, the Renaissance

49. Emile Durkheim, in *The Evolution of Educational Thought: Lectures on the Formation and Development of Secondary Education in France*, trans. Peter Collins, (London: Routledge and Kegan Paul, 1977), and Anthony Grafton and Lisa Jardine, in *From Humanism to the Humanities*, for example, have praised the schoolmen's high theoretical sophistication and "independent" attitude, whereas they blame the humanists for fostering "obedience and docility" by means of their inculcation of good Latin (see Grafton and Jardine, pp. xiv, 24). For other forms of praise for scholasticism and education in the thirteenth-century universities, see R. W. Southern, *Medieval Humanism* (New York: Harper and Row, 1970), and the preface to A. J. Minnis and A. B. Scott, *Medieval Literary Theory and Criticism* (Oxford: Clarendon Press, 1988).

50. See Victoria Kahn, *Rhetoric, Prudence, and Skepticism in the Renaissance* (Ithaca: Cornell University Press, 1985), and her essay on "Humanism and the Resistance to Theory," in Patricia Parker and David Quint, eds., *Literary Theory/Renaissance Texts* (Baltimore: Johns Hopkins University Press, 1986), pp. 373–96. In general, I am indebted to her for pointing out the status of rhetoric as theory in the Renaissance.

51. See Lee Patterson, "On the Margin: Postmodernism, Ironic History, and Medieval Studies," *Speculum* 65 (1990), pp. 94–95.

humanists were obsessed with linguistic and cultural history. They sought to establish incorrupt versions of classical texts, ridding them of later emendations, because they believed that the integrity and the distinctiveness of ancient culture were traceable in its textual remains. Whereas scholastics elaborated logic as a form of language theory, the early humanists insisted on the importance of a detailed knowledge of language in practice.

A respect for the often productive tension in sixteenth-century scholarly discourse between rhetoric and logic, history and philosophy, interpretation and disputation, suggests that in our own literary pedagogy we might reexamine the relationship between the scholastic emphasis on the "forms" of thought articulated in language (rather than the forms of whole books) and the humanists' awareness of language's historicity and social function.[52] But it would be a mistake, I believe, to abandon humanist reading completely because of its now apparently unshakable association with "close reading." Rather, we might choose to draw on the strength of early humanist reading practices. In particular, as I have found in writing this book, we may come to respect again how, at their best, the humanists taught readers to see the power of words to make things happen, not just to represent the world. They may also teach us today to understand better how all texts are tied fast to both the past and the present, ever evolving and yet always rooted in their social uses and transformations.

52. In the sixteenth century humanism and scholasticism were not in fact the radically divided intellectual schools that both sides made them out to be; after the initial controversy in the English universities scholasticism and humanism often drew on the same sources and coexisted, if uneasily, for many years. On the complex relationship of humanism and scholasticism, see Paul Oskar Kristeller, *Renaissance Thought and Its Sources* (New York: Columbia University Press, 1979); C. C. Greenfield, *Humanist and Scholastic Poetics, 1250–1500* (Lewisburg, Pa.: Bucknell University Press, 1981); Mark Curtis, *Oxford and Cambridge in Transition, 1558–1642: An Essay on the Changing Relations between English Universities and English Society* (Oxford: Clarendon, 1959); also the preface to Minnis and Scott, *Medieval Literary Theory*. For a fuller description of what such a pedagogy might entail, see Rebecca Bushnell, "From Books to Languages," *Common Knowledge* 3.1 (1994) pp. 35–38 (from which part of this argument was borrowed).

Index

Index

Vives, Juan Luis, 96n, 101–2, 128n, 135n, 139n
  on comprehensive reading ideal, 122, 123–24, 126
  on corporal punishment, 31–32, 33
  on female education, 112, 113–14
  and fragmentation of texts, 130n, 133, 139
  on pedagogic authority, 41–42, 46–47
  on proliferation of books, 118, 200

Wall, Wendy, 139n
Wayne, Don, 181
Webbe, William, 119
Webber, Ronald, 87n

When you see me, you know me (Rowley), 55–56
Will, George, 11
Williamson, Arthur H., 160, 172–73
Wilson, Thomas, 80
Winter's Tale, The (Shakespeare), 104–6, 107–8
Wolsey, Thomas, 48
Women, 28–29, 40–41, 64
  education of, 110–14
Worlidge, John, 141

Xenophon, 51–53

Zavarzadeh, Mas'ud, 4, 5